LINGUISTIC DIVERSITY AND EUROPEAN DEMOCRACY

Linguistic Diversity and European Democracy

Edited by
ANNE LISE KJÆR
University of Copenhagen, Denmark
and
SILVIA ADAMO
University of Copenhagen, Denmark

Routledge
Taylor & Francis Group
LONDON AND NEW YORK

First published 2011 by Ashgate Publishing

Published 2016 by Routledge
2 Park Square, Milton Park, Abingdon, Oxfordshire OX14 4RN
711 Third Avenue, New York, NY 10017, USA

First issued in paperback 2016

Routledge is an imprint of the Taylor & Francis Group, an informa business

British Library Cataloguing in Publication Data
Linguistic diversity and European democracy.
1. Law--European Union countries--Language. 2. Language policy--European Union countries. 3. European Union countries--Languages--Law and legislation. 4. European Union countries--Languages--Political aspects.
5. Multilingualism--Political aspects--European Union countries.
I. Kjær, Anne Lise. II. Adamo, Silvia.
341.2'422-dc22

Library of Congress Catalouging-in-Publication Data
Linguistic diversity and European democracy / by Anne Lise Kjær and Silvia Adamo.
p. cm.
Includes bibliographical references and index.
ISBN 978-1-4094-0860-4 (hbk)
1. European Union countries--Languages--Law and legislation. 2. Law--European Union countries--Language. 3. Representative government and representation--European Union countries--Language. 4. Mul-tilingualism--European Union countries. 5. Judicial process --Language. I. Kjær, Anne Lise. II. Adamo, Silvia.
KJE5306.L56 2010
344.24'09--dc22

2010040096

ISBN 13: 978-1-138-27124-1 (pbk)
ISBN 13: 978-1-4094-0860-4 (hbk)

Contents

List of Figures and Tables

Figures

Tables

Notes on Contributors

Silvia Adamo is Assistant Professor at the Centre for Studies in Legal Culture, Faculty of Law, University of Copenhagen. Her research interests and publications revolve around migration law and citizenship law, including language requirements for migrants applying for citizenship, European Union law and the interaction between law and political philosophy on multiculturalism.

Joxerramon Bengoetxea is Professor Titular at the Law Faculty, University of the Basque Country, and specializes in the field of legal reasoning and European legal culture. Current research concerns cross-disciplinary studies of European integration and combines socio-legal studies, jurisprudence and political philosophy.

Michal Bobek is a PhD researcher at the European University Institute, Department of Law. He has qualified as a Czech judge, worked as legal assistant for the Chief Justice and served also as the head of the Research and Documentation Department at the Supreme Administrative Court of the Czech Republic. His areas of interest include various aspects of European Union law, comparative (public) law and legal theory.

Mattias Derlén is Senior Lecturer in the Department of Law, University of Umeå. His 2007 doctoral dissertation, as well as later publications, mainly concern the attitudes, *vis-à-vis* multilingual interpretation of EU law, displayed by the European Court of Justice as well as national courts in Denmark, England and Germany.

Bruno de Witte was Professor of European Union Law at the European University Institute in Florence from 2000 to 2010 and is now Professor of European Union Law at Maastricht University. He has published on many questions of EU institutional law and also on minority protection, language regulation and cultural diversity in a European perspective.

Magali Gravier is Associate Professor at the International Center for Business and Politics at the Copenhagen Business School. She is a political scientist. Her current research topics are in the field of EU studies, in particular, the staffing policies of the European Commission, the EU's language policy and the integration process.

J. Normann Jørgensen is Professor, Department of Scandinavian Studies and Linguistics, University of Copenhagen, specializing in studies in socio-linguistics, particularly youth language and multilingualism. He is currently involved in the Lanchart Centre study of language change in real time and is leader of the Center for the Study of Danish as a Second Language and editor of *Copenhagen Studies in Bilingualism.* He is a former Danish and Scandinavian sabre fencing champion.

Anne Lise Kjær is Associate Professor at the Centre for European Constitutionalization, Faculty of Law, University of Copenhagen and Director of the international research network Reline for interdisciplinary studies in Language and Law. More recent and current research concerns cross-disciplinary studies of legal integration in Europe and combines theories of language, discourse, culture and law.

Peter A. Kraus is Professor at the Faculty of Social Sciences and Director of the Centre for Research on Ethnic Relations and Nationalism at the University of Helsinki. He has published widely and in several languages on problems of democratization and democratic theory, politics in Southern Europe, ethnicity, nationalism and identity politics, and the present dilemmas of European integration. He is the author of *A Union of Diversity: Language, Identity and Polity-Building in Europe* (Cambridge University Press, 2008).

Lita Lundquist is Professor at the International Center for Business and Politics at the Copenhagen Business School. She combines comparative text linguistic studies of political, legal and EU texts with socio-political approaches, maintaining a focus on cognitive, pragmatic and cross-cultural aspects.

Robert Phillipson is a Professor emeritus at Copenhagen Business School. He worked in four countries before immigrating to Denmark from the UK. He has master's degrees from Cambridge and Leeds universities and a PhD from the University of Amsterdam. His books on language policy, linguistic imperialism and language rights have been published in 10 countries. For details, see www.cbs.dk/staff/phillipson.

Dagmar Richter is a Professorial Member of the Law Faculty of the University of Heidelberg (Germany), teaching constitutional and administrative law, European Union law and international law. She has published books and articles on German and Swiss public law, comparative constitutional law and international law with a special focus on human rights law and minority rights.

Sue Wright is Professor of Language and Politics and Director of the Centre for European and International Studies Research, University of Portsmouth. Her research interest is language practice at the macro-level and through time; she is author of a number of works on this aspect of language policy, including *Language Policy and Language Planning* (Palgrave, 2004). She is series editor for Palgrave's Language and Globalization book series and co-editor of *Sociolinguistica.* Current and recent research projects concern language in the European Parliament, language and citizenship and Francophonie.

Acknowledgements

The collection of chapters in this book were originally presented at a conference on Language, Rights and European Democracy held in Copenhagen, Denmark, in June 2009. First of all, we would like to thank the authors for their contributions and for showing us new ways to think about linguistic diversity in Europe. We are grateful for the support given by the Centre for European Constitutionalization and the Centre for Studies in Legal Culture at the Faculty of Law at the University of Copenhagen, under whose auspices the conference was held. Thanks are also due to European Research at the University of Copenhagen (EURECO) for its financial support for this publication, and to Alison Kirk and Adam Guppy, at Ashgate Publishing, for their kind assistance during the preparation phase of the book.

Anne Lise Kjær and Silvia Adamo
Copenhagen
Denmark

Chapter 1

Linguistic Diversity and European Democracy: Introduction and Overview

Anne Lise Kjær and Silvia Adamo

Introduction

Theorists of political science and sociology do not often ask themselves how deliberative democracy should function in polities that are made up of many linguistic groups and seem to forget the impact that linguistic diversity may have on political communication and mutual understanding across languages. If language is considered at all in studies of democracy, it is treated as a companion to culture, as the essential core of national or minority group identity. Likewise, although lawyers spend a great deal of time carefully studying the language of statutes and court decisions, they do not seem to be sensitive to the issue of language when reflecting on norms of deliberative democracy,[1] or they tend to address the issue only from the point of view of human rights and constitutional guarantees of the right to speak one's own language. Similarly, lawyers interpreting European Union law think of "the language" of EU legislation and speak of "the wording of the text" without taking into account that language and wording within the framework of the EU always imply a multiplicity of 23 official languages. In other words, multilingualism and linguistic diversity are matters that are not commonly analysed or even thought of as matters of relevance in mainstream political, sociological and legal theories of EU law and democracy.

At the same time, much relevant knowledge about language, cognition and communication remains within the confines of the academic disciplines of linguistics and communication studies and is seldom utilized in the related disciplines of law, sociology and political science. What language is, how it functions in real-life interactions, how people understand languages, and how they communicate across linguistic barriers are underexplored questions that ought to attract more attention in legal, sociological and political studies of EU constitutionalism and European democracy.

The ambition of this book is to fill the gap that exists among the disciplines of linguistics, law, political and social science in the study of polity-building in Europe. The goal is to explore, from a cross-disciplinary perspective, the

1 Addis (2007: 101–2).

role that linguistic diversity plays in European democracy at both the European and national levels and to shed new light on the issue by employing legal and political theories of law and democracy along with linguistic theories of language use and cognition. Linguistic diversity can be examined from many different perspectives that are usually mutually exclusive or competing. As such, multilingualism can be considered as: a democratic value to be protected, a fundamental right of minority groups, an obstacle to deliberative democracy and a hindrance to legal certainty and the possibility of uniform law, a cultural asset of Europe to be promoted and protected, a competitive advantage of businesses on the market and a prerequisite for the free movement of EU citizens. The aim of this book is to combine these and other perspectives, thereby addressing what we see as the fundamental characteristic of European language laws and language policy, namely the inherent tensions and contradictions. In order to achieve our goal, we have invited researchers representing a variety of disciplines that do not usually collaborate to contribute to the book, viz. EU law and legal theory, political science, sociology, sociolinguistics and cognitive linguistics.

Democracy, Language and Deliberative Communication

The conference from which the chapters of this book are derived was held just before the 2009 elections to the European Parliament. The research themes of the book are particularly interesting when seen against the backdrop of this European event, as the elections clearly illustrated the inherent paradoxes of European language policy and the language regime of the EU institutions,[2] as also evidenced in the official EU motto "united in diversity".[3]

At that time, 736 members of the European Parliament were to be elected by 375 million potential voters in the 27 Member States. There were no common campaigns across borders, no transnational political communication among citizens of different Member States and no common European parties addressing themselves to voters by means of common European media. When the Parliament facilitated Internet-based communication with and among the electorate, 10,000 voters responded to an online poll conducted at the end of May, and the majority view was that "politicians and media weren't giving the June European elections the attention they deserve". However, in spite of the common European democratic ambition thus pursued by the Parliament, the language paradox became apparent in statements like the following on the Parliament's website:[4]

2 As regards other paradoxes of European law and language, see Kjær (2008).

3 Available at: http://europa.eu/abc/symbols/motto/index_en.htm.

4 Available at: http://www.europarl.europa.eu/sides/getDoc.do?pubRef=-//EP//TEXT+IM-PRESS+20090511STO55546+0+DOC+XML+V0//EN [accessed: August 2010].

> The Parliament is running an intense campaign on the web, talking about the elections and why it matters that people vote for the Europe they want. There is our special interactive website on the elections in 22 languages.

On the one hand, communication in 22 languages (the 23 official languages minus Irish) is respectful of Europe's linguistic diversity and the language rights of EU citizens. On the other hand, the statement illustrates the top-down communication of the Parliament with EU citizens, who for their part are divided by their different languages and therefore dependent on the Parliament, their national politicians and the press to inform them about the elections and to debate on their behalf.

But the language problem is also evidenced in a new democratic tool introduced by the Lisbon Treaty, namely the European Citizens' Initiative (ECI), which invites EU citizens to participate more directly in the democratic processes of the EU. If a minimum of one million citizens across at least one-third of the Member States (currently nine out of 27) support such an initiative, they have the right to bring forward legislative proposals that the European Commission has to examine within a time limit of four months. In the Commission's "Proposal for a regulation of the European Parliament and of the Council on the citizens' initiative",[5] the objective and rationale of this democratic innovation is described as follows:

> This new provision is a significant step forward in the democratic life of the Union. It provides a singular opportunity to bring the Union closer to the citizens and to foster greater cross-border debate about EU policy issues, by bringing citizens from a range of countries together in supporting one specific issue.

The ambition to foster a greater cross-border debate about EU policy lies at the very heart of the attempt to create a European participatory democracy. At the same time, however, it exhibits the weakness of a democracy consisting of different peoples that do not share a language. According to the latest statistical report on Europeans and their languages,[6] only about half of Europeans are able to speak a language other than their own. This implies that in all probability the ECI will be utilized primarily by European elites who speak English and other widely used European languages with such fluency that they can engage in a cross-border debate with other citizens or by NGOs that have sufficient financial and human resources at their disposal to work across Member State borders.

However, the ECI also exposes the above mentioned inherent contradictions of the European democratic vision of creating unity in diversity: Linguistic diversity is supported and protected at the EU level, yet in real-life interactions

5 COM (2010) 119 final, published on 31 March 2010.

6 European Commission. 2006. "Europeans and their Languages", Special Eurobarometer 243, February.

among Europeans, linguistic diversity soon meets its limits.[7] In this respect, it is interesting to note that Article 4(1) of the proposal for a regulation on the citizens' initiative stipulates that the organizer of an ECI must register the initiative with the Commission, providing information on the subject, objectives and background of the initiative "in one of the official languages of the Union".

In other words, the goal of "bringing Europeans from a range of countries together", as the Commission proposal has it, tends to put the citizens' right to speak their own language at risk. They have to agree on one common registration language, which will in all probability be English.

Linguistic Diversity as a Fundamental European Value

At the time of writing (August 2010), the EU has 27 Member States and 23 official and working languages. Moreover, depending on how languages are defined and what inclusion criteria are used, more than 100 regional and minority languages are spoken in Europe.[8]

So, the obvious questions are why the EU – in the interests of European democracy – does not agree on one common language[9] and why it does not recommend and support foreign-language teaching that would prepare Europeans to be highly competent in that common language in addition to their mother tongues? Why not use a "mother tongue plus one common European language" strategy instead of the "mother tongue plus two foreign languages" that is currently stated to be the aim in Commission policy instruments?[10]

The answer to these questions is probably multifaceted. One simple reason is that the language spoken by approximately 38 per cent of EU citizens, besides their mother tongues, is so-called global English,[11] and speakers of the other European "majority" languages – especially French, German and Spanish – object to the anglicization of Europe.[12] Another reason is that the protection of linguistic diversity and the protection of language rights are regarded as

7 See, similarly, Kraus in this volume.

8 In 1992, the Commission initiated a study on minority language groups in the European Union. While the so-called *Euromosaic I* study listed 48 linguistic minority groups living in the 12 Member States at that time, a survey conducted after the 2004 enlargement counted approximately 90 minority groups in the new Member States, differentiated on the basis of language.

9 For a more in-depth discussion of this question, see Wright in this volume.

10 See Gravier and Lundquist in this volume.

11 European Commission. 2006. "Europeans and their Languages", February 2006.

12 Consider, e.g., "Die Mannheim-Florentiner Empfehlungen zur Förderung der europäischen Hochsprachen" (The Mannheim-Florence Recommendations for Promoting European Standard (or National) Languages) formulated by the language institutions of some EU Member States, notably Germany and Italy. See also Phillipson in this volume.

fundamental European values and are thus essential to the very concept of a European substantive democracy.[13]

The idea of linguistic diversity as a specific European value that distinguishes Europe from other parts of the world is evidenced in several talks given by the former European Commissioner for Multilingualism, Leonard Orban, who was commissioner from 1 January 2007, when Romania became a member of the Union, until the new Commission was set up after the entry into force of the Lisbon Treaty on 1 December 2009. At a conference on multilingualism in Romania on 15 May 2009, he rather grandiosely summed up the underlying principles of European language policy as follows:

> Today we live in a globalized world and Europe is building an ever closer Union. While, on a global level, some "big" languages tend to dominate the scene, Europe is not a melting pot where differences are blotted out. Europe is a common home where diversity is celebrated, and where our many mother tongues are or should be a source of wealth and a bridge to greater solidarity and mutual understanding.[14]

The paradox of the commissioner's speech is, of course, that the "many mother tongues" may be seen as a source of greater cultural wealth and a catalyst for greater solidarity, but at the same time they impede mutual understanding and almost invite being bridged – by a common language. On the one hand, linguistic diversity is a symbol of European democracy, but on the other hand, linguistic diversity complicates political dialogue and the exchange of ideas in "a community that cannot communicate".[15] Thus, linguistic diversity runs counter to the ideals of the "four freedoms" of the internal market, but it is a fundamental European value protected by the EU treaties and the Charter of Fundamental Rights of the European Union and promoted by several Community initiatives. In a market where goods, capital, services and persons are encouraged and expected to move freely, the diversity of languages is, in fact, a hindrance to such movement. However, it is politically and legally impossible to acknowledge this point. The pragmatic solution is to make linguistic diversity a commodity, a valuable cultural good and a political instrument in the hands of Europe's minorities, by means of which they can circumvent the national level and strive for more European integration. This is the policy that is actually pursued by the Commission. In the latest policy initiatives in the field

---

13 Article 22 of the EU's Charter of Fundamental Rights requires the EU to respect linguistic diversity and Article 21 prohibits discrimination based on language. Article 2 of the Treaty on European Union lists the common values of the EU Member States, including pluralism, non-discrimination and equality.

14 Available at: http://ec.europa.eu/commission_barroso/orban/news/docs/speeches/090515_discurs_Cluj/Discurs_Cluj_EN.pdf [accessed: May 2010].

15 Terminology borrowed from Sue Wright (2000).

of language and multilingualism, the Commission stresses the importance of multilingualism and learning languages, not only for European culture, but also for European business and creativity.[16]

Linguistic Diversity and EU Law

The inherent paradox expressed in the motto "united in diversity" also affects the legal regime of the EU.[17] EU legislation with general application throughout the Community must be published in all 23 official languages. On the face of it, this rule seems reasonable as the EU passes laws that are directly binding on individuals and companies in the Member States. But the publication in all 23 languages is not primarily for information purposes, enabling EU citizens and their legal advisors to read EU legislation in their own languages. It is first and foremost a matter of equal treatment of small and large Member States; consequently all 23 language versions have equal authenticity, even if this makes the interpretation of EU law extremely complicated.

As stated by Greece in the case *Kik v OHIM*:[18] "Multilingualism is an indispensable component of the effective operation of the rule of law in the Community legal order, since many rules of primary and secondary law have direct application in the national legal systems of the Member States". In a similar vein, in its judgment in the famous *CILFIT* case,[19] the court held:

> It must be borne in mind that Community legislation is drafted in several languages and that the different language versions are all equally authentic. An interpretation of a provision of Community law thus involves a comparison of the different language versions.[20]

---

16 Leonard Orban, Commissioner responsible for multilingualism until December 2009, set up a Business Forum on Multilingualism in November 2007. The aim of the group was to identify ways to increase the multilingual capacities of companies to help them enter new markets, and to strengthen language skills of individuals so as to improve their employment prospects. The Business Forum presented its report, "Languages Mean Business", to the Commission in July 2008. See also the ELAN report: "Effects on the European Union Economy of Shortages of Foreign Language Skills in Enterprise" of December 2006. Similarly, the Commission recently commissioned a study on multilingualism and creativity; the research group published their report, "Study on the Contribution of Multilingualism to Creativity", in July 2009.

17 The legal consequences of multilingualism are subject to thorough discussions in the contributions of Bengoetxea, Bobek and Derlén in this volume.

18 Judgment of the Court in Case C-361/01 P, *Christina Kik v Office for Harmonisation in the Internal Market* [2003] ECR I-8283. The Hellenic Republic, intervened at first instance in support of the appellant.

19 Judgment of the Court in Case 283/81, *Srl CILFIT and Lanificio di Gavardo SpA v Ministry of Health* [1982] ECR 3415.

20 Paragraph 18 in the *CILFIT* case.

Paradoxically, it follows that the meaning of EU provisions cannot be derived from any one of the official languages. Thus, in legal terms, the equality of the languages goes so far as to make the language versions of Community laws interdependent.[21] Hence, EU citizens cannot purely rely on their own languages when they want to know what EU law says on a particular issue. In principle, EU citizens must know the law in each and every official language because the meaning of the law is anchored not in one single language version, but in all the language versions taken together.

Despite the 23 official languages being of ostensibly equal standing, the wording of Community law will invariably differ from one language text to another as natural languages cannot by their nature be absolute copies of each other. Hence, European multilingualism can in some cases be a source of legal miscommunication, misinterpretation, incoherent and divergent texts and, ultimately, an obstacle to achieving what lies at the very core of the rule of law, namely legal certainty.

Moreover, as regards the inherent contradiction between the concepts of unity and diversity, the European Court of Justice long ago ruled that unity, that is, the uniform interpretation and application of EU law in the Member States, is so important that the diversity of interpretation that would arise if EU citizens were allowed to apply their own language versions should be avoided:

> The different language versions of a Community text must be given a uniform interpretation and hence in the case of divergence between the versions, the provision in question must be interpreted with reference to the purpose and general scheme of the rules of which it forms a part.[22]

Moreover, even if multilingualism is an "indispensable component of the effective operation of the rule of law in the Community legal order", the European Court of Justice ruled in the *Kik* case that the references in the Treaty to the use of languages in the European Union:

> cannot be regarded as evidencing a general principle of Community law that confers a right on every citizen to have a version of anything that might affect his interests drawn up in his language in all circumstances.[23]

What is it about language that seems to make things so complicated?

Linguistic Diversity and Language Rights

To most researchers other than linguists, "language", in the singular at least, is a trivial subject, which is not worth studying when one wants to discuss matters

21 Van Calster (1998).

22 Judgment of the Court in Case 30/77, *Régina v Pierre Bouchereau* [1977] ECR 1999.

23 Paragraph 82 in the *Kik* case.

relating to law, society and politics. Language as a discipline probably reminds people of language teachers and lessons at school: Put the comma in the proper place, spell correctly and beware of dangling participles and split infinitives!

At the same time there seems to be widespread agreement across the various research communities that language in the plural ("languages") and multilingualism are not trivial matters. On the contrary, the protection of linguistic diversity and the struggle for language rights are acknowledged as battlefields for a variety of interests: political, legal and cultural. In other words, languages in the plural are much more fascinating than the school teacher's narrow interest in the nitty-gritty details of "language".

But what can possibly be the connection between the "boring" language lessons at school and the much more inspiring subjects of language rights and language diversity in European law and politics?

To answer the question, a comparison between language and music is instructive. Some time ago, the well-known and respected Danish cellist Morten Zeuthen was interviewed on Danish national radio. He described his love for music and his fascination with his own instrument, the cello. He also touched on his teaching at the Royal Danish Academy of Music: position fingers precisely, hold the bow correctly and read the notes! These are some of the technical instructions he gives his students. The point is that such tasks have nothing to do with the music that is made once the students have learned to place their fingers correctly, hold the bow and read the notes. Furthermore, they have nothing to do with the students' love of music and their instruments.

Now imagine that a cello player was forced to shift to another instrument. The following instructions might be given: "In this orchestra we all play the violin, and it is not possible for you to play the cello. You are free to do so at home, but when you are with us, you have to play the violin". Imagine that all musicians other than violin players were told the same thing, regardless of whether their expertise was in playing the flute, the viola, the horn, the piano or another instrument. How would the musicians react? They would probably fight for their right to play their own instruments.

The love of one's own first language may be compared with the love of one's instrument – and is probably felt most strongly when one's right to speak that language is prohibited. A particular language is not just an arbitrary instrument of communication as far as native speakers are concerned. It is the reservoir of their memories, the reflection of their identity and the language that they speak when they want to be precise, intimate or poetic. Therefore, being forced to speak another language, by others or by circumstances, is not a trivial matter easily dealt with and accepted.[24]

24 In her contribution to this book, Dagmar Richter presents the Swiss solutions to the conflicting and contradictory problems caused by multilingualism at local, regional and national levels.

The comparison between language and music has its limits, however. It is, of course, possible for musicians to meet and play different instruments – in fact, it is not only possible, it is desirable; that is how orchestral pieces are played. When it comes to languages, however, they are like the secret codes invented in the schoolyard: codes that are only understood by those who know the rules and the specific vocabulary.

Thus, the contradiction of being "united in diversity" emerges once again. Languages are exclusive, and they exclude. Even if the possibility for speakers of a minority language to speak their own language should be protected, representing a fundamental constitutional right in democratic societies, supported at both national and European level,[25] minorities would be culturally, socially and politically isolated if they were unable to speak the language of the majority. Therefore, one might conclude that language rights should be concerned not only with the protection of linguistic diversity and the right to speak one's own language, but also with the right to learn the language that enables one to be among those who exercise power, or, less ambitiously, to understand the linguistic code of those in power.[26]

The Language of European Democracy

The diversity of languages means richness, but it also means difference, divergence and even mutual isolation. If one wants to communicate despite the diversity, one either has to insert mediators – translators and interpreters – who can bridge the language gap or communicate in a common language, that is, learn the handful of languages necessary to communicate with other Europeans.

What is the language of democracy? This question is one posed by the political philosopher Will Kymlicka, who answers the question by maintaining that the language of democracy is the vernacular: the mother tongue.[27] But what is then the language of European democracy? Jürgen Habermas has suggested that English should be the common language of Europe.[28] Clearly, language diversity seems to represent a major hindrance to Europe-wide democracy – at least if we endorse a conception of democracy under which the political participation of the general population is required.

The linguistic paradox of European democracy is, however, that if the EU were to enact a one-language policy, which might be sensible in terms of developing a European public sphere, it would at the same time contravene what lies at the very heart of that democracy, namely non-discrimination and respect for difference and diversity.

---

25 This is the subject matter of de Witte's contribution in this volume.

26 For a discussion of the very notion of "language", see Normann Jørgensen in this volume.

27 Kymlicka (2001).

28 Habermas (1998).

Most EU Member States seem to endorse the view that diversity is valuable only if they are in charge of that diversity, defining its meaning and limits. Thus, minority language rights are protected and diversity celebrated only with respect to languages with a long historical presence in Europe. The increasing and widespread presence of non-European immigrant languages is not protected by language laws. On the contrary, immigrants are generally obliged to learn the national languages of their new countries, and in several European countries, language tests requiring high-level linguistic competence have been introduced during the past few decades.[29] Paradoxically, a command of the national language is not a requirement that high-skilled workers and academics have to meet. They are generally free to use the global common language, namely English.

It does seem as if "united in diversity" is a normative vision of Europe with limited descriptive value. In real life, diversity is supported and upheld only if it is practicable and compatible with values and goals that are considered more important: the efficient working of the EU institutions, the functioning of the free market, continued legal and political integration and European participatory democracy.

Overview of the Book

The book is opened by *Peter A. Kraus*, who gives us the first indications of how to explore the connections between the issues of European democracy and linguistic diversity. Language has played a prominent role in the construction of modern nation states but also in the consolidation of an understanding of democracy based on "integrated communicative spaces", where the creation of a public sphere communicated by means of a common language makes possible the monitoring and thus the legitimation of political decision-making. This model of political integration via linguistic standardization encounters clear difficulties when translated to EU level. Kraus challenges the understanding of democracy as "democracy in one language", which in a certain way obstructs the development of multilingual democratic practices. At the same time, he indicates the contradictions pervading cultural and linguistic diversity in the EU. One of the dilemmas is that communication in a multilingual supranational setting involves the use of either a common language or interpretation, while another obstacle is the nation state-based conception of "minority" when linguistic rights are defined. The process of EU integration aims to preserve European citizens' cultural and linguistic diversity, but the initiatives and legal instruments adopted so far in this field have lacked normative impact. Thus Kraus makes us reflect on the necessity,

29 See, for example, the special issue of the *International Journal on Multicultural Societies* "Citizenship Tests in a Post-National Era" (guest editor: Sue Wright, 2008), and in the same issue the analysis of the Danish legal setup as regards linguistic requirements for applicants for citizenship presented in Adamo (2008).

in order actively to defend the EU's cultural and linguistic diversity, to develop other types of enforcement mechanisms (including social and cultural); these may have to be adapted from those that fostered the "dynamics of democratization" in EU Member States.

Sue Wright opens the discussion on European democracy, asking the fundamental question: What does democracy mean to Europeans? As the European polity has not yet fully evolved, the elements which characterize democracy in a nation state cannot yet apply to the EU, where the concept of democracy does not refer to any single overarching concept. Wright considers in particular the element of debate as an essential democratic practice and investigates whether there are any lessons we can draw from the democratic experiences of the past, from the elite democracy of ancient Greece to the adoption of the French and American Constitutions in the eighteenth century. From this perspective, Wright notes that the current debate in the European public sphere is clearly still underdeveloped as citizens try to form opinions often based only on information gathered from national news. She reminds us that public participation and a common language can foster the conditions for a truly democratic debate on a common European constitution, although, at the end of the day, it is the powerful and symbolic value of their national constitution that is the key to democracy in the eyes of most of the electorate.

Robert Phillipson's contribution focuses on the more problematic aspects of multilingualism in Europe. He suggests that the primary role acquired by English in a variety of administrative and working contexts in the EU institutions can result in asymmetrical communication and uneven dissemination of information and documents. Phillipson reviews the obstacles that lie ahead when establishing equity of treatment of languages in the EU, and stresses the need to clarify what "functions, contexts, and users of particular languages" are at stake as the different uses can entail different requirements under a policy of multilingualism. Phillipson's view on legal and political initiatives so far taken at EU and Member State level is that they have not succeeded in directing language policy in a focused way. A shift to a true multilingual infrastructure would mean the need to address and cope with the issue of the predominance of one language. As the issue of language is an integral part of European political integration, Phillipson argues that true multilingualism can only be achieved if it is actively discussed and formulated on an informed basis, not left to market forces, and if professional expertise and scholarly research on linguistic matters assume a more prominent role in the decision-making process than they have done hitherto.

The chapter by *Magali Gravier* and *Lita Lundquist* provides an overview of laws and policies governing multilingualism in the EU. They discuss how the issue of multilingualism is closely associated with issues of (passive and active) representative democracy and also with a cognitive-cultural dimension. The value *per se* of supporting citizens learning multiple languages is complemented by the cultural value of encouraging mutual understanding among EU citizens. Multilingualism is promoted via the recruitment rules for EU civil servants to ensure that EU institutions are multilingual at staff level. Moreover, translation and interpretation services have the practical task of making the great flow of documents intelligible for all parties involved and for making communication in meetings possible. In line with the latest initiative by the EU Commission to promote trilingualism among EU citizens, Gravier and Lundquist propose an alternative approach. As studies in linguistics have highlighted, it is possible intuitively to comprehend a foreign language belonging to the same language family; exploiting the mutual structures and common features of languages would consequently promote foreign language teaching and learning. Gravier and Lundquist argue in favour of introducing a system of foreign language teaching that supports the acquisition of a plurality of languages, which should in their view be endorsed not only at the EU institutional level, but ideally also by via Member States' initiatives.

The chapter by *Joxerramon Bengoetxea* takes a special look at the multilingual challenges posed by the work of the European Court of Justice. Drawing parallels to the stunning new architecture of the Court, Bengoetxea argues that its legal reasoning does not always live up to its own, case law-based commitment to multilingualism and to the duty to compare the equally authentic official language versions of EU legislation. Bengoetxea's review of how multilingual judicial reasoning is carried out in practice makes clear the importance of linguistic matters in the functioning of the Court. EU law is inherently multilingual, reflecting the reality of linguistic diversity in Europe, and the product of legal practices carried out in a number of languages, assisted by the vital work of the translation services. The Court is forced to work in a common language, as it is unrealistic to expect the judges and advocates general to master all 23 official languages. Also, the authenticity of the final judgment is in practice often tied up with the language of the case, while the judgments are published in all official languages. Although the differences in legal cultures affect how the Court functions, Bengoetxea argues that the legal reasoning is in practice usually monolingual and that the cases in which a comparison of language versions is used as a means of interpretation are relatively few.

Michal Bobek offers an analysis of the practical and legal consequences of the multilingual regime of EU law at the national level, when national authorities (courts and administrative authorities) apply EU law. The chapter focuses first on the duty to publish EU legislation in all official languages and, in the light of the landmark decision in the *Skoma-Lux* case,[30] discusses the problem of national enforcement of unpublished EU legislation in the new Member States. Second, he examines the use of corrigenda that rectify mistakes in particular language versions. Bobek shows that such corrections are not always of a purely formal nature: in some cases they change the legal meaning, thus giving rise to doubts concerning the interpretation of the legislative act and the legal status of the corrigendum. Finally, Bobek presents the jurisprudence of the European Court

30 Case C-161/06, *Skoma-Lux sro v Celní ředitelství Olomouc* [2007] ECR I-10841.

of Justice in relation to divergent language versions and the duty to compare the texts in all official languages. As the burden of comparing the language versions falls on the national authorities, the author sees as a likely outcome the emergence of "language clusters". In other words, the comparison of versions in similar languages can provide a viable solution to prevent linguistic disunity caused by divergent national interpretations and at the same time allows interpreters at national levels to rely on the wording in their own text version, read in the light of related languages.

The chapter by *Mattias Derlén* reflects on how multilingualism *per se* is not the problem many assume it to be when initially approaching the subject; rather it is that "the conflicting and unclear directions concerning the relationship between multilingualism and the interpretation of Union law emanating from the European Court of Justice" mean that multilingualism tends to become problematic when it is tied up with the interpretation of EU law. The Court has gone so far as to require that all language versions have to be consulted, thereby underlining the fundamental importance of multilingual interpretation. Derlén notes that this practice has not paved the way for genuine multilingual interpretation on the part of the national courts, nor has any single method been employed by the Court to decide in cases of a divergence of meanings between language versions. He concludes that multilingualism is, in fact, an asset of EU law, as multilingual interpretation may help interpreters establish the correct meaning of EU legislation. However, the obligation to compare all 23 language versions makes genuine multilingual interpretation impossible for practical reasons. Therefore, the author suggests what he calls "limited multilingualism". As he puts it:

> By using English and French side by side with the national language version, we would encourage more multilingual interpretation and aid national courts in the difficult task of applying EU law.

Bruno de Witte explores the topic of language rights. Language rights are defined as the fundamental right to speak the language of one's choice: a right expressed in some national constitutions and increasingly in EU law as well. In the opinion of de Witte, language rights gain depth and substance through the link with other rights such as freedom of expression, equality and non-discrimination and the right to education. In this vein, de Witte argues that the protection of linguistic rights is improved when such rights are seen through the prism of general fundamental rights, especially because, when conceived as such, they compel governments to justify any denial of a language-related claim. De Witte explores these points by looking at the development of language rights in national law during the last two decades and also analyses the emergence of an EU-wide supranational standard of protection. He discusses the respective roles of domestic and EU developments and their interaction, in the evolution of language law, in a selected number of Western European countries: the United Kingdom, Italy and Belgium. In his concluding remarks, de Witte argues that the protection of minority language rights in Europe has evolved with limited recourse to litigation before the courts: mostly it has been put forward and promoted by way of political mobilization.

Dagmar Richter introduces us to the legal setup for the protection of linguistic diversity in Switzerland. With the help of a "linguistic map", Richter takes us on a journey through a country where German, French, Italian and Romansh are recognized as national languages and where federal and cantonal institutions are obliged to protect the country's linguistic diversity. Richter presents the principles of territoriality and linguistic freedom, as expressed in the Swiss Federal Constitution, which are the core principles of the legal regime in relation to languages in Switzerland. Factual and normative criteria establish the official language(s) of a region's institutions (the territorial principle), taking account of what the author describes as regional "linguistic imprinting". When the regional linguistic imprinting collides with the constitutionally guaranteed individual linguistic freedom, the particular circumstances and the interests at stake are taken into consideration for each individual. Richter suggests that Switzerland's linguistic model could serve as an inspiration for linguistic protection in other countries too. She argues that the linguistic territoriality principle provides a basic structure, counterbalanced by the principle of linguistic freedom, in a case-by-case approach.

Finally, the chapter by *J. Normann Jørgensen* challenges our preconceived notions of language and introduces us to a (late modern) sociolinguistic approach to language studies. On the basis of empirical analyses of language as it is actually used by people in real-life communication, Normann Jørgensen rejects a conception of language as a static phenomenon linked to a specific culture and nation and claims that languages in this essentialist sense of the word are sociocultural or even ideological constructions. He demonstrates how the common definition of language, which also underlies language laws, does not reflect the everyday use of language. The chapter gives examples of how features from different languages are combined in linguistic interactions among contemporary urban youth in the EU. Such language use is what he calls the polylingualism norm:

> Language users employ whatever linguistic features are at their disposal to achieve their communicative aims as best they can, regardless of how well they know the involved languages.

A sociolinguistic perspective on language may help Europeans to rethink how they structure language policies and language laws, and what is actually at stake when we talk about the right to use one's language. The polylingualism norm can be used in this view as a cornerstone in the building of an alternative system for the protection of linguistic rights, tentatively described by Normann Jørgensen as follows:

In private, as well as in business, people have the right to communicate through language of their choice. In their relationship with public institutions people have the right to expect that the communication be held in language they understand.

References

Adamo, S. 2008. "Northern Exposure: The New Danish Model of Citizenship Test". *International Journal on Multicultural Societies*, 10(1): 10–28.

Addis, A. 2007. "Constitutionalizing Deliberative Democracy in Multilingual Societies". *Berkeley Journal of International Law*, 25(2): 101–48.

Derlén, M. 2009. *Multilingual Interpretation of European Union Law*. Aalphen aan den Rijn: Kluwer Law International.

European Commission 2006. "Europeans and their Languages". *Eurobarometer 243* (February).

Habermas, J. 1998. "Does Europe Need a Constitution? Response to Dieter Grimm?". In *The Inclusion of the Other: Studies in Political Theory*, edited by C. Cronin and P. De Greiff. Cambridge, MA: MIT Press, 156–61.

Kjær, A.L. 2008. "Language as Barrier and Carrier of European Legal Integration". In *Paradoxes of European Legal Integration*, edited by H. Petersen, A.L. Kjær, H. Krunke and M.R. Madsen. Aldershot: Ashgate, 149–56.

Kraus, P.A. 2008. *A Union of Diversity: Language, Identity and Polity-Building in Europe*. New York: Cambridge University Press.

Kymlicka, W. 2001. *Politics in the Vernacular*. Oxford: Oxford University Press.

Phillipson, R. 2003. *English-only Europe? Challenging Language Policy*. London and New York: Routledge.

Van Calster, G. 1998. "The EU's Tower of Babel – The Interpretation by the European Court of Justice of Equally Authentic Text Drafted in More Than One Official Language". In *Yearbook of European Law*, Vol.17, edited by A. Barav and D. Wyatt. Oxford: Clarendon Press, 363–93.

Wright, S. (ed.). 2008. "Citizenship Tests in a Post-National Era". *International Journal on Multicultural Societies*, 10(1): 1–9.

Wright, S. 2000. *Community and Communication: The Role of Language in Nation Building and European Integration*. Clevedon: Multilingual Matters.

Chapter 2
Neither United nor Diverse? The Language Issue and Political Legitimation in the European Union

Peter A. Kraus

Introduction: The Challenge of Unity in Diversity

The last two decades have been a period of lively debates, involving both scholars and politicians, revolving around the democratic deficit of the European Union (EU). Obviously, the intensity of these debates can only be understood in relation with the Union's claim to be committed to democracy. Title II of the *Treaty of Lisbon* contains the "Provision on Democratic Principles" guiding EU politics and policies; Article 10.1 of the Title reads: "The functioning of the EU shall be founded on representative democracy". Notwithstanding such declarations, after the failure of the Treaty establishing a Constitution for Europe and the painful ratification of the Lisbon Treaty, the issue of European democracy seems far from being resolved, and one might even argue that the legitimation problems the Union confronts have kept increasing. At any rate, the questions concerning the requisites of political legitimation that are or should be available at the European level resurfaced forcefully as a key element of the crisis of the euro triggered by the developments in Greece. If the EU is not only about achieving ever higher rates of economic efficiency across state borders but is also to be conceived of as a union of solidarity between states and citizens, what are the bases of this solidarity supposed to be? Neither among the Member States nor within the citizenry of the euro zone does there seem to be an emerging agreement on the answer to such a critical concern. Twenty years after Maastricht, Europe continues to be to a considerable extent a "stateless market" (Kapteyn 1996). The lack of synchronicity between economic and political integration remains a striking feature of Europe's institutional architecture.

It is against this very background that those who advocate a stronger weight of the Europe of the citizens, both *vis-à-vis* the Common Market and the Europe of the states, insist on paying closer attention to the sociocultural embeddedness of integration for better grasping of its political dynamics. From such a perspective, the legitimation of European politics is ultimately contingent upon the emergence and consolidation of a European civil society. In the long run, "political Europe" would lack sustainability if it were not connected to "social Europe". However, as the French expert on European social policy Jean-Claude Barbier (2008) cogently claims, this connection cannot be established as long as there are no processes of collective communication which are supported by (and, at the same time, support) a shared political culture. Indeed, the current impasse of integration seems to corroborate the view that the "minimalist" approach to polity-building, nurtured by the belief that adopting common institutions such as the European Parliament would provide the EU with the necessary degree of legitimacy, has clearly underestimated the specific weight of the "social" factor in democratic politics. Reflecting on the current situation, we should therefore recall one of the key points made by Karl Deutsch (1976: 14), one of the pioneers of integration theory: Whatever sophisticated political templates for creating transnational institutions there may be, the success of integration will ultimately depend on its being grounded in the realm of the social and on its receiving and maintaining a sufficient level of social support from the citizenry.

It is no coincidence that Deutsch, as an integration theorist, paid substantial attention to language as a main indicator of the dynamics of political integration. In his classic study on the foundations of nationality, he brings into focus the Czech and Finnish cases to show how closely the processes of social mobilization initiated under the flag of nationalism and popular sovereignty in Europe in the nineteenth and twentieth centuries were connected with the spread of a language defining the very identity of the nation, with the spread of a "national" language (Deutsch 1966). Indeed, one can easily argue that the history of democracy in modern Europe is to a great extent a history that links the formation of nation-states to the development of discrete political cultures and their standardized vernaculars (Rokkan 1999). It must be emphasized that to point at this link does not entail taking for granted dominant narratives that suggest the existence of quasi-perennial bonds between nations and languages. What can be observed empirically should not be conflated with normative considerations: There is plenty of evidence that the standardization of cultural and linguistic identities entailed high costs for those groups – who we nowadays call minorities – who were forced to adopt a standard which was not their own. Nonetheless, looking at the past should make us aware of the high stakes involved with a political project that is supposed to have us "united in diversity", as the official motto of the EU puts it. It is not too exaggerated to see the explicit affirmation of the value of diversity as an element that sets the project of constructing Europe apart from the historical record of polity-building in modern Europe. In a nutshell: If the nation-states were about achieving unity through homogenization, the EU is about working out an approach to integration that cherishes cultural and linguistic diversity.

Accordingly, the challenge faced by those who want to deepen the Union politically and to bridge the legitimation gaps between European institutions and the "Europe of the citizens" certainly has major historical dimensions. In view of the self-assigned imperative of respecting and even promoting cultural diversity, the architects of a Union that should become more legitimate by being more democratic have to follow a path that has little in common with the legacy of European modernity, as this modernity is quintessentially embodied by the compact – and ultimately homogeneous – institutional framework of the nation-state. Rather than being prone to protecting diversity, European nation-states have been based upon the pillars of a normative monism which blended one people, one identity, one territory and one sovereign source of power into a uniform sociopolitical space.

This chapter will offer an assessment of how the challenge of becoming united in diversity has thus far been dealt with in the process of constructing the European Union. My main thesis is that the weight of intergovernmental decision-making (which is, by definition, decision-making by nation-states) and the primacy of market imperatives constitute obstacles that the EU has not been able to overcome on its alleged way to creating a polity that should combine shared political commitments with diverse cultural and linguistic attachments. I will develop my argument in three steps. First, a brief recapitulation of the role of language in the making of European nation-states is offered. The subsequent section concentrates on the relationship between legitimation and diversity in the EU and discusses why diversity became a central concept in the Union's normative discourse. The final part of this chapter is then devoted to highlighting the main elements of what might be called Europe's "linguistic constitution" and to assessing its contribution to achieving the goal of unity in diversity.

Language, Nation-Building and Democracy

One aspect that sets Europe clearly apart from other world regions is the salient role of the linguistic factor in the configuration of state boundaries. A quick glance at the political map of the continent makes this quite clear. With very few exceptions, European states' official denominations offer us a direct reference to a state's official language, be it Greek in Greece, Polish in Poland, Danish in Denmark or French in France. This is not the case in the Americas, for instance, where languages such as "Canadian", "Mexican", "Bolivian" or "Brazilian" simply do not exist. To a significant extent, the history of modern Europe can be interpreted as the history of the formation of a system of discrete nation-states. In this process, language clearly played a key role (Rokkan 1999: 170–90). The idea of the national language is a European idea, and the importance of linguistic factors in nationalist mobilizations has been a defining feature of Europe's modern history (Coulmas 1985: 29–31).

The convergence of nation-building and cultural standardization has been analyzed in detail by political sociology, with language being a key element in this context: European nation-states were constructed as integrated communicative spaces. Typically, the process was initiated in the period of state formation following a *top-down* logic, as can be seen in the cases of Spain and France. Here, linguistic standardization is best understood as part of the dynamics of rationalization underlying the formation of the modern state, as studied by Max

Weber (1980: 815–37) and by historical sociologists working in the Weberian tradition. From the perspective of modern state-making, the strife for establishing uniform linguistic standards at the institutional level corresponds to the interest of state elites in administering the territory over which they rule in one language for reasons of efficiency. The *Ordonnance de Villers-Cotterêts* (1539) is an example of the emergence of an absolutist language policy in France (Jacob and Gordon 1985: 111–12). The edict stipulated that French must be the language of all written legal communication in the domain of rule of the French monarch. It has to be noted that at that point in time, French – the *Langue d'Oïl* – was hardly used in substantial portions of the kingdom's territory. Breton was the language of the bulk of Brittany's population, Basque was spoken in the Southwest and Occitan dialects predominated all over the Southern half of the country. By and by, in France as in other parts of Europe, the criteria adopted by administrative elites began to intermingle with the "proto-nationalist" efforts of absolutist rulers to use language in a similar way as religion, namely as an asset for achieving political legitimation. The Scandinavian area offers a specific profile in this respect: The unchallenged triumph of Lutheranism entailed the establishment of state churches and a smooth transition to the use of vernaculars in religious settings and schools. The situation in the North stood in sharp contrast with the protracted use of Latin by Catholic institutions in Southern and Central Europe and made for comparatively strong "proto-nationalizing" effects already at an early stage.

After the French Revolution, with the rise of democracy, linguistic nationalism gained momentum as a consequence of *bottom-up* mobilizations. In the case of France, these remained basically committed to the homogenizing objectives of the central state powers, albeit under different ideological premises: French was now celebrated as the language of the Republic and, as such, allegedly embodied the principles of democratic reason against the "counterrevolutionary" vernaculars used in the rural peripheries. In other cases, the linguistic mobilizations from below resulted in heavy clashes with the established state structures and the inherited patterns of cultural hegemony. In Eastern Europe, during the course of the nineteenth century, this would become the dominant tendency (Hroch 1985): Taking up a message first formulated by Herder, who attributed equal value and dignity to all linguistic groups, regardless of the "higher" or "lower" status of their particular cultures, speakers of national vernaculars turned their languages into an icon of collective protest against imperial rule, which was rule in German, Russian or Turkish. Ultimately, almost everywhere in Europe, language politics and policies were characterized by some kind of interplay of top-down and bottom-up factors. On the one hand, the larger and older territorial states tended to adopt the strategy of "official" nationalism[1] and aimed at enhancing their democratic credentials by assimilating minorities into the majority language. On the other hand, particularly in Eastern Europe, resistance to assimilation led to the creation of new states. In such cases, the successful "populist" nationalisms were

1 The category is taken from Anderson (1991: 83–111).

sometimes less tolerant towards linguistic differences in their territory than the previous imperial administration had been.[2]

The dynamics of democratization in Europe cannot be properly understood if their study does not take into account linguistic integration as well. Representative democracy developed in close connection with the public sphere, which offered the broader citizenry the opportunity to participate in, and to impact on, the general political debate (Habermas 1990). However, the very constitution of the public sphere along national lines implied that it did not only provide the citizens options for political participation, it also implied attempts at assimilating layers of sociocultural diversity into one common – and thereby largely homogeneous – discursive frame.[3] Accordingly, since the emergence of democratic publics in different parts of Europe, the grand narratives of democracy and the nation clashed with counter-narratives that denounce the hegemonic character of national integration (Cederman and Kraus 2005: 293–7). After all, however, the story that is told or, rather, summarized, by the political map of contemporary Europe is less intricate; it is the story of those identities that prevailed in the protracted (and, in most cases, ongoing) conflicts about constructing and defining the nation and thereby attained an official status. Thus, in our collective imagery, which is to a great extent an imagery based on how we learned things at school, and on how we see them continually reproduced in our institutional environment and in the mass media, we rarely conceive of an Italian citizen as somebody speaking German, of a Romanian citizen as somebody speaking Hungarian, of a British citizen as somebody speaking Welsh or of a Swedish citizen as somebody speaking Sámi: The language of *the* nation and *its* citizens is the language of the majority.

In our view of how political integration works, this dominant model, which links linguistic standardization to nation-building and democracy, attained an all-pervasive character. A combination of the approaches put forward by Weber and Habermas has become a general template for our understanding of democratic politics: In the historical sequence that is synthesized in a compact way by the template, the processes of bureaucratic rationalization creating and sustaining modern government are followed by the making of a public sphere where informed citizens play an active role in monitoring political decision-making and thus contribute substantially to its legitimation. When we apply the template, we generally take for granted that the question of the language to be used in a given democratic setting has been settled – *de jure* and *de facto* – by the results of the historical process of nation-state construction. Accordingly, the assumption that there is one standard language which serves as the main vehicle of political communication underlies the bulk of literature on democratic politics. The assumption is not always made explicit, although an influential line in political

2 For the developments in East Central Europe after World War I, see Galántai (1992).

3 The connection between public sphere formation and nationalism is emphasized in several contributions to the volume edited by Calhoun (1992).

theory, which spans from John Stuart Mill (1972: 391–8) to Jürgen Habermas (2001: 116–24) holds that a democratic public will not be able to realize its deliberative potential unless those who participate in the tasks of self-government from different social and political angles address each other in a common language. From the corresponding view, a shared political culture requires a shared linguistic medium; without such a medium, the spaces of communication in a polity remain segmented, and the encompassing public sphere needed for proper democratic control cannot emerge.

Few democratic theorists would disagree with the view that the democratic process has to be supported by "enlightened understanding" (Dahl 1989: 111–12) on the side of the citizens. But it is rarely made explicit what the material bases of this understanding ultimately are. The question of language is no exception here. When we reflect on how democracy works, we tend to assume that democracy is democracy in one language. The observation does not only apply to "the people" as the ultimate source of democratic sovereignty but also to distinct institutional areas of democratic representation and deliberation. The interest of political scientists in analyzing the specific features of political discourse in multilingual parliaments, for instance, has thus far remained rather limited. It is true that parliaments in which more than one language is used in political debates are the exception in Western democracies. Still, parliamentary chambers of this kind do exist in Belgium, Switzerland and Canada; several subnational and regional parliaments (in the Basque Country, in Wales or in South Tyrol, to mention just three European examples) could be added to the list. It also has to be said, however, that the languages used in such cases rarely exceed the number of two. Accordingly, we confront a very peculiar situation in the European Parliament, where there are currently 23 languages enjoying an official status, and the art of political rhetoric is dramatically affected by the imperatives of interpretation. Accordingly, the little evidence we have regarding the praxis of a democratic multilingualism cannot easily be extrapolated to better grasp the dynamics of political communication at the European level.

Diversity and Legitimation in the EU

Since the 1950s, when France, Germany, Italy and the Benelux countries started the project of unification, diversity has played a prominent role in the official discourse of European polity-building. At a stage at which integration was still largely defined in terms of establishing a common market, key figures of the process, such as Walter Hallstein (1973: 112), were already highlighting the central importance that the protection of cultural diversity should be given in the construction of Europe. Since Hallstein's days, the normative emphasis that European authorities put on diversity has only kept growing. In the early 1990s, in the aftermath of the establishment of the European Union, the often quoted statement by Jacques Delors that "you don't fall in love with a common market:

you need something else"[4] indicated the concern at the level of the Commission for giving the European project a compelling normative frame beyond the expectation of sheer economic prosperity. In effect, the concern became clearly visible in many key documents produced after Maastricht. In a nutshell, the normative formula underpinning these documents combined the support for market freedoms with the promotion of human rights, democracy and diversity. The highlighting of diversity may well be considered as the genuinely new element of the European Union's incipient "constitutional" discourse, an element that set the EU apart from the historical precedents of nation-state construction. At the turn of the millennium, emphasizing the importance of deepening integration on this basis became the rationale of institutional politics in the EU. To use Delors' expression: the search for "something else" culminated in the decision to elaborate a constitution for Europe.

From the early stages of unification, the approach to building Europe adopted at the institutional level connected the objective of fostering market integration with the imperative of respecting the cultural features considered to be constitutive of the identities of the Member States. Thus, the formal adoption of the principle of "integral multilingualism" by institutions such as the European Parliament or the European Council ultimately indicated the Union's commitment to the diversity embodied by the "national languages" (that is, the official languages of the nation-states). In this regard, Europe's multilingual consensus reflects, in the first place, the continuing significance of nation-state identities in an institutional setting that is supposed to transcend the legacy of exacerbated nationalist conflict. By granting all state languages equal official status, the architects of Europe aimed at immunizing the European institutions against the nationalist setbacks they anticipated in case some Member States felt symbolically discriminated against because of the preferential treatment given to the languages of others (Coulmas 1991). Ever since the ratification of the Treaty of Rome in 1957, the political elites devoted to the European cause refrained from activating the conflict potential inherent to tackling the language issue in ways that would be conducive to defining a common – and, thereby, unavoidably limited – linguistic repertoire for European citizens. Although such a repertoire could well be conceived of in terms that pay tribute to diversity, moving towards its elaboration would require a political debate that EU institutions have thus far preferred to evade. Rather, during the last decades, the Union has been sharpening its profile as a prolific producer of declarations of good will that emphasize the value of cultural and linguistic diversity in the process of building Europe. These statements, however, do not add up to a consistent programme that would clarify on which grounds and in which particular societal and cultural domains diversity has to be protected from the impact of market standardization or institutional integration.

The EC (European Community) began to engage in what with hindsight might be called transnational identity politics at the Copenhagen summit in December

4 Cited in Bideleux (2001: 25).

1973, where the then nine Member States agreed upon drafting a "Declaration on European Identity". Since Copenhagen, two main features appear recurrently in Europe's institutional identity discourse (Stråth 2000). The first one relates to a set of common political values shared by all parties that participate in the undertaking of uniting Europe. The second one stresses the central role of cultural diversity in articulating a trans-European political framework. In this respect, the EC/EU's approach to the issue of European identity has been clear-cut from the beginning: The attempt at getting citizens committed to the European cause must not involve any measures that could be interpreted as homogenizing. After the Copenhagen Declaration, the pledge to respect and to protect cultural diversity became an almost obligatory component of the programmatic statements prepared by European authorities. Obviously, most Member States are reluctant to accept that core areas supposed to represent and reproduce their national identity become subject to supranational control. Debates on cultural issues easily lead to conflict in European politics, as they are often symbolically connected to contrasting national imageries. In this regard, it seems no coincidence that the proposal to add a specific mention of the Christian roots of Europe to the Treaty establishing a Constitution for Europe triggered an exceptionally intense and controversial debate among the members of the Convention in charge of drafting the text (Olsen 2004: 80–89). The success of the diversity formula as a normative template for the integration discourse seems to lie in its aptitude for satisfying different interests: While it may serve as a substantive value to be displayed at the European level, diversity can also be viewed by the Member States as a guarantee of the persistence of their identities in the Union. Thus, the career of diversity as a key element officially used for defining what Europe stands for is hardly surprising. In the decades after 1973, the major treaties and declarations that document the successive construction of the European polity have generally included a section advocating cultural diversity. The tendency becomes especially graspable in the agitated period that led from the signing of the Maastricht Treaty in 1992, through the Eastern enlargement and the stalled constitutional process, to the arduous ratification of the Treaty of Lisbon, which could be concluded only after holding a second referendum in Ireland in 2009.

The Treaties of Maastricht and Amsterdam (1997) incorporated an amendment of the Treaty establishing the European Communities, also known as the Treaty of Rome, signed in 1957. A specific title on culture is part of this amendment. With a minor modification, the title finally also found its way into the Treaty of Lisbon.[5] In this document, the title's key sections read as follows:

1. The Union shall contribute to the flowering of the cultures of the Member States, while respecting their national and regional diversity and at the same time bringing the common cultural heritage to the fore.

5 Treaty of Lisbon, Title XIII, Article 167.

2. Action by the Union shall be aimed at encouraging cooperation between Member States and, if necessary, supporting and supplementing their action in the following areas:
   – improvement of the knowledge and dissemination of the culture and history of the European peoples;
   – conservation and safeguarding of cultural heritage of European significance;
   – non-commercial cultural exchanges;
   – artistic and literary creation, including in the audiovisual sector.
   (...)
4. The Union shall take cultural aspects into account in its action under other provisions of this Treaty, in particular in order to respect and to promote the diversity of its cultures.

All in all, the Maastricht and Amsterdam Treaties began displaying a tendency that was turned into a stable pattern in the course of the drafting of the Charter of Fundamental Rights and the Constitution for Europe, which finally became the basis for the Treaty of Lisbon: The goal of establishing a deeper Union based on common political values and the goal of preserving the diversity of cultures – a diversity which in the first place reflects the different identities of nation-states – are presented as closely connected objectives, so that no major institutional efforts seem to be required to mediate between two potentially conflicting rationales.

In December 2000, the European Parliament, the Council and the Commission solemnly proclaimed the "Charter of Fundamental Rights of the European Union" in Nice. The Charter was supposed to be ratified as Part Two of the Constitutional Treaty. After the failure of the constitutional project, the decision was made not to incorporate it in the Treaty of Lisbon. Although the Charter has thus remained a legally non-binding document, it puts forward in a condensed form the key elements of the Union's official approach to diversity. The Charter's Preamble includes the following paragraphs:

> The peoples of Europe, in creating an ever closer union among them, are resolved to share a peaceful future based on common values.
>
> Conscious of its spiritual and moral heritage, the Union is founded on the indivisible, universal values of human dignity, freedom, equality and solidarity; it is based on the principles of democracy and the rule of law. It places the individual at the heart of its activities, by establishing the citizenship of the Union and by creating an area of freedom, security and justice.
>
> The Union contributes to the preservation and to the development of these common values while respecting the diversity of the cultures and traditions of the peoples of Europe as well as the national identities of the Member States and the organisation of their public authorities at national, regional and local

> levels; it seeks to promote balanced and sustainable development and ensures free movement of persons, goods, services and capital, and the freedom of establishment.

In the last paragraph, an interesting distinction is made between the respect that is given to the cultural diversity of Europe's "peoples" and the respect due to the national identities of "Member States". Again, such a distinction barely conceals the moments of tension inherent to the attempt at simultaneously promoting the diversity of peoples and sustaining the identities of states in multicultural and multinational settings. In many cases, the very correspondence between these two levels of belonging and identification is far from being self-evident, but rather is politically contested. Whereas several European states comprise different peoples, some European peoples are spread among different states.

Article 22 of the Charter consists of just one compact sentence that places additional emphasis on the political relevance that the EU assigns to cultural diversity: "The Union shall respect cultural, religious and linguistic diversity". It has to be noted that the article on cultural diversity is one of the seven articles that the Charter chapter devotes to equality. This underlines that, from the normative perspective adopted by the Union, the respect of diversity is a substantial aspect of the task of promoting the principle of equality for all European citizens.

The preeminent normative status of diversity is also acknowledged in the text that became the substitute of the failed Constitution for Europe, that is, the Treaty of Lisbon, which to a great extent continues reflecting the results of the Convention's deliberations. The main objectives of the EU are summarized in Article I-3 of the treaty. Two paragraphs of this article can be interpreted as a succinct explication of the meaning of unity in diversity in the Union's political discourse:

> It [the Union] shall promote economic, social and territorial cohesion, and solidarity among Member States.

> The Union shall respect its rich cultural and linguistic diversity, and shall ensure that Europe's cultural heritage is safeguarded and enhanced.

The two sentences taken from the Treaty of Lisbon neatly capture the challenge pointed out in the introduction of this chapter: Promoting cohesion and solidarity at the European level appears to be an all but unreachable goal as long as there is no common political identity based on a context of transnational communication. The massive difficulties the Member States belonging to the euro zone experienced in early 2010, when they had to agree upon a frame of minimum solidarity in response to the Greek financial crisis, ultimately mirrored the fragmentation of Europe in different national publics that not only have different views on what the mutual obligations within the Union imply but are not even able to engage in a trans-European debate on what the reasons for these differences are and how they could possibly be overcome. Against such a background, the question of defining a frame for political communication that might allow for articulating a transnational political discourse without hampering cultural diversity in Europe obviously gains crucial significance.

Since Jacques Delors' period at the top of the Commission, the Union's political architects have made major efforts to substantiate the meaning of European identity beyond the formal level of treaties and official declarations. Such efforts materialized, in the first place, in the institution of European citizenship in 1992. In addition, European symbols have made their way into virtually all realms of social life, and there has been a steady proliferation of European programmes targeting the areas of education and culture. It does not seem exaggerated to say that the identity dimension nowadays figures prominently in many EU policies.[6] However, the attempts at identity-building from above have thus far not produced the desired outcomes. Two decades after the introduction of European citizenship, most Europeans keep identifying with their states or with their regions rather than with Europe. There is even evidence that the increased salience of the European factor in day-to-day politics has contributed to a growth of anti-EU attitudes in several Member States.[7] For a polity such as the EU, being united in diversity certainly is an appealing normative formula. However, political reality has shown that living up to the expectations conveyed by the motto is not just a question of good intentions but requires a great amount of institutional ambition and creativity. Let us now look into how the EU has proceeded with regard to the political articulation of linguistic diversity.

The Language Issue in the Politics of Integrating Europe

Multilingualism can be considered one of the key characteristics – if not *the* key manifestation – of cultural diversity in Europe today. Accordingly, how the EU deals with the language issue has great significance when it comes to assessing its record in the field of developing an innovative approach to diversity. Although the Union has thus far not produced a statute laying down the guidelines of its language policy, one may still speak of Europe's "linguistic constitution". In the sense the concept is used here, constitution does not refer to a specific legal document, but to the different regulations and practices that give the Union's language regime its actual form.

6 See Delanty (2005) and Shore (2000) for critical evaluations of the European approach to identity issues.

7 According to Eurobarometer data, Union citizens who conceive of themselves primarily as Europeans continue to be a small minority, and identification with Europe has neither increased after Maastricht nor after the Eastern enlargement. Moreover, the support for the European project has gone down even in key historical Member States, such as France and Germany. See Kraus (2008a: 50–57) for a longitudinal overview.

Much has been said in the previous pages on the value diversity has attained as a normative template for European polity-building. Nevertheless, from a historical perspective, it is also true that the initial impulses for integration did not stem from the will of a group of *avant-la-lettre* multiculturalists to institutionalize a trans-European political space based on diversity. As the official denomination of the entity established in 1957 by the Treaty of Rome clearly indicated, Europe was primarily about the European Economic Community (EEC): uniting Europe became virtually synonymous with establishing the Common Market. This Common Market has nowadays become a reality for most Europeans. It is sustained by four pillars, which stand for the free circulation of goods, capital, services and persons. Being at the heart of Europe's institutional development, the four market freedoms also play an obvious role in the context of regulating linguistic diversity. They must be seen as an important background condition in the development of Europe's linguistic constitution, as realizing market activities requires a linguistic medium. In a common economic space, respecting language diversity and safeguarding market freedoms may turn out not to be easily compatible. The potential tensions between the two goals can be easily made out if we consider the free circulation of services and persons. To what extent, and in which areas, is it legitimate to limit the professional mobility of people in Europe adducing linguistic criteria? In which cases must the provision of a service remain connected to the service being delivered in a particular – for example, national – language? How can we establish a proper balance between the two goals in different professional fields? Our common sense may tell us that the right to free mobility in the European labour market should not imply that a Polish nurse in Denmark is exempt from proving some competence in Danish, or that a Greek doctor in Berlin should not be required to be able to address his patients in German. However, what is the situation regarding car mechanics, barbers or plumbers? What should the regulations be in higher education, in research and in the media sector? Our daily experience shows that the implementation of the freedoms of the Common Market is not always neutral towards culture and language. In many cases, the logic of market integration only leaves little leeway for the logic of cultural particularity (Kraus 2008b: 90–93).

In fact, the emphasis the Union places on the protection of diversity corresponds to a great extent to the intention of insulating the realm of cultural identities against the spill-over effects of market integration, first and foremost with regard to the elements of these identities held to be distinctive attributes of nation-states, as the "national languages" are. Regarding linguistic diversity, the basic principles delineating Europe's language regime were set down in a Council directive in 1958. The directive reflects the agreement on giving the languages of the Member States equal status. Hence, all official state languages also become official at the European level. Although the directive introduced the terms *working languages* and *official languages*, it did not spell out criteria for distinguishing between the two modalities within Community organs (Kraus 2008a: 113–15). When it was adopted, the European Economic Community (EEC) had six members (Belgium,

France, Germany, Luxemburg, Italy and the Netherlands), who made four official European languages (Dutch, French, German and Italian). Since 1958, the Community and the Union have gone through several rounds of enlargement, but the successive entry of new members has not led to revisions of the principle of equality of state languages. Thus, at present, the EU counts 27 Member States which make up 23 languages with an equal official status. In view of the weight it places on making the diversity of languages institutionally graspable, the Union has been characterized as a polity committed to "integral multilingualism" (Haarmann 1991).

At the same time, the commitment to defending linguistic diversity has been extended to minority languages as well, albeit in a less generous way than with respect to state languages. Institutions such as the European Parliament gave active support to the European Charter of Regional or Minority Languages (1992) and the Convention for the Protection of National Minorities (1995). Although both the Charter and the Convention were drafted and ratified within the Council of Europe, and thereby not directly connected to EU activities, the Union did unambiguously share in the efforts to create a common basis for a European human rights regime offering satisfactory provisions for the protection of minorities. In this context, the linguistic dimension obviously plays a pivotal role. The basis was only developed for "autochthonous" minorities and hence does not include immigrant groups. Moreover, the Charter and the Convention leave the signatory states abundant leeway for a discretionary interpretation of the legal framework they introduce. Nevertheless, the documents convey the emergence of a consensus to limit the prerogatives of nation-states in their dealing with language minorities on their territory. This consensus attained particular relevance when the political criteria for the accession of countries from Central and Eastern Europe to the Union were defined. In Latvia, Estonia, Bulgaria, Romania and Slovakia, monitoring the situation of linguistic minorities became part of the external supervision initiated by the EU under the denominator of "conditionality" of accession.[8]

Conditionality, however, did not stretch beyond securing a minimum of linguistic rights in correspondence with a contemporary understanding of human rights. It did certainly not involve a substantial narrowing of the "entitlement gap" that is observable between state and minority languages at the European level. When it comes to assessing linguistic rights, the key point still is that the protection of diversity must largely be understood as the political tribute paid to the idea of the "national language", which continues to carry great weight in Europe's institutional framework. In this respect, the "integral" dimension of multilingualism is very much a state-centred one. The subjects of linguistic rights are, in the first place, not citizens as members of language communities, but citizens as members of nation-states. A simple example makes this evident: if the whole of Cyprus, and not only the island's Southern half, had joined the EU in 2004, the

8 For the European Union's approach to language minority issues in the context of enlargement, see Sasse (2006) and Nic Shuibhne (2008).

chances are that Turkish, spoken by about 250,000 people and being official in the North, would have become an official language of the Union too.[9] In contrast, the fact that several million people on the Union's territory – including a sizeable "autochthonous" minority in Bulgaria – have Turkish as their mother tongue bears no relevance for how the official multilingualism of EU institutions is articulated. It thereby becomes evident that the regime of integral multilingualism is not so much devoted to respecting diversity in terms of equal dignity as to reproducing a hierarchical relationship among language communities, a hierarchy that mirrors the unequal access of these communities to political power resources. From this angle, we may question whether the EU effectively applies what it normatively subscribes to, namely, the view that promoting the equality of European citizens requires the due respect of these citizens' diverse cultural backgrounds. In the Union's official discourse, the respect of linguistic diversity is framed as a means for guaranteeing equality; in reality, however, what we find is a regime that assigns different status levels to different linguistic communities.

The market-driven push towards more communicative efficiency and the differentiation of linguistic status end up impacting on the officially privileged national languages as well. Integral multilingualism is a *de jure* arrangement which has evident *de facto* limits in the Union's day-by-day functioning. Thus, in the internal proceedings of the Commission, for instance, the clearly prevailing working languages are French and English, with a small symbolic space still occupied by German. After the Northern and Eastern enlargements, there has been a constant growth of the use of English at the expense of French (and, *a fortiori*, of German). It is obvious that, with 23 official languages, living up to integral multilingualism must remain constricted to a few, politically sensitive areas of communication. Yet being pragmatic cannot offer an easy excuse for avoiding a thorough normative assessment of what linguistic justice in the EU should mean today, more than 50 years after the Treaty of Rome. Tackling the European language issue would require a straightforward and open debate on how multilingualism could institutionally be processed in a reflective way in European institutions, as well as in the communication between European institutions and European citizens. Notwithstanding the recurrent rhetorical invocation of the principle of unity in diversity, this very debate has been and remains absent from the Union's political agenda.[10]

All in all, the most characteristic feature of the EU approach to recognizing linguistic diversity may be its multiple contradictions. As we have seen, the recognition of cultural and linguistic diversity by and in EU institutions is normatively inconsistent, as it shows a pronounced bias towards the identities embodied by nation-states to the detriment of non-dominant and "minoritized"

9 The accession of the South did not alter the Union's official language regime as Greek already was part of it.

10 Critical evaluations of the institutional language policy of the European Union are presented in Kraus (2008a: 111–38) and Phillipson (2003: 105–38).

identities. Moreover, in the transnational citizenship regime established by EU legislation, there is a strong differentiation between "old" and "new" minorities, as well as between intra-European and extra-European migrants: The more migrant, and the more extra-European a person is, the more restricted that individual's cultural rights *vis-à-vis* European and national authorities will prove. The Turkish government recently tried to question this differentiation in its bilateral relations with Germany and claimed that the "German Turks" should be assigned similar rights as national minorities typically are, thereby being provided with their own school and university system.[11]

In the realm of language, the contradictions entail conveying a notion of diversity that has no proper political thrust. Diversity is used as a convenient token, supposedly exhibiting the Union's higher goals, yet its subordination to an identity politics controlled by intergovernmentalism makes it a remarkably vague principle. As a concept that is supposed to equally satisfy nation-states and stateless nations, majorities and minorities, dominant and dominated groups and, in addition, should not collide with the smooth functioning of the Common Market, diversity is at risk of becoming just permissive diversity, a formula successful to the extent that it does not involve any sacrifices or costs for those who claim to act on its behalf. In an all but ritualistic way, EU institutions pay lip service to the importance of multilingualism for representing and sustaining diversity. However, the lack of a debate on how to regulate multilingualism in European institutions, in European civil society and at the intersections of institutional and societal spaces implies that the recognition of diversity remains frequently constrained to symbolic politics. Moreover, it keeps prolonging the impasse at which we find ourselves with regard to finding an encompassing frame of communication for the Union. It is not too exaggerated to hold that the impasse reflects substantial normative and material deficits of the European project as it stands today. If we want to ponder the future of this project, we will have to tackle the key question raised by Deutsch some 50 years ago and look for the mechanisms which at the transnational level could serve as soft yet effective equivalents of the factors subjacent to the social and cultural mobilizations connected with nation-state formation at an earlier historical time. Only such mechanisms will eventually make for a unity that avoids normative monism and allows diversity to flourish.

References

Anderson, B. 1991. *Imagined Communities: Reflections on the Origin and Spread of Nationalism*, revised edition. London: Verso.

11 See the *Spiegel Online* feature "Erdogan fordert türkische Gymnasien und Universitäten in Deutschland" (8 February 2008). Available at: http://www.spiegel.de/politik/deutschland/0,1518,534052,00.html.

Barbier, J.-C. 2008. *La longue marche vers l'Europe sociale*. Paris: PUF.
Bideleux, R. 2001. "What Does it Mean to be 'European'? The Problems of Constructing Pan-European Identity". In *Uncertain Europe: Building a New European Security Order*, edited by M.A. Smith and G. Timmins. London: Routledge, 20–39.
Calhoun, C. (ed.). 1992. *Habermas and the Public Sphere*. Cambridge, MA: MIT Press.
Cederman, L.-E. and Kraus, P.A. 2005. "Transnational Communication and the European Demos". In *Digital Formations: Information Technology and New Architectures in the Global Realm*, edited by R. Latham and S. Sassen. Princeton, NJ: Princeton University Press, 283–311.
Coulmas, F. 1985. *Sprache und Staat: Studien zur Sprachplanung und Sprachpolitik*. Berlin: de Gruyter.
Coulmas, F. 1991. "European Integration and the Idea of the National Language: Ideological Roots and Economic Consequences". In *A Language Policy for the European Community: Prospects and Quandaries*, edited by F. Coulmas. Berlin: Mouton de Gruyter, 1–43.
Dahl, R.A. 1989. *Democracy and its Critics*. New Haven, CT: Yale University Press.
Delanty, G. 2005. "The Quest for European Identity". In *Making the European Polity: Reflexive Integration in the EU*, edited by E.O. Eriksen. London: Routledge, 127–42.
Deutsch, K.W. 1966. *Nationalism and Social Communication*. Cambridge, MA: MIT Press.
Deutsch, K.W. 1976. *Die Schweiz als ein paradigmatischer Fall politischer Integration*. Bern: Haupt.
Galántai, J. 1992. *Trianon and the Protection of Minorities*. Budapest: Corvina.
Haarmann, H. 1991. "Monolingualism versus Selective Multilingualism – On the Future Alternatives for Europe as it Integrates in the 1990s". *Sociolinguistica* 5: 7–23.
Habermas, J. [1962] 1990. *Strukturwandel der Öffentlichkeit: Untersuchungen zu einer Kategorie der bürgerlichen Gesellschaft*, new edition. Frankfurt am Main: Suhrkamp.
Habermas, J. 2001. *Zeit der Übergänge*. Frankfurt am Main: Suhrkamp.
Hallstein, W. 1973. *Die Europäische Gemeinschaft*. Düsseldorf: Econ.
Hroch, M. 1985. *Social Preconditions of National Revival in Europe: A Comparative Analysis of Patriotic Groups Among the Smaller European Nations*. Cambridge: Cambridge University Press.
Jacob, J.E. and Gordon, D.C. 1985. "Language Policy in France". In *Language Policy and National Unity*, edited by W.R. Beer and J.E. Jacob. Totowa, NJ: Rowman & Allanheld, 106–33.
Kapteyn, P. 1996. *The Stateless Market: The European Dilemma of Integration and Civilization*. London: Routledge.

Kraus, P.A. 2008a. *A Union of Diversity: Language, Identity and Polity-Building in Europe*. Cambridge: Cambridge University Press.
Kraus, P.A. 2008b. "A One-Dimensional Diversity? European Integration and the Challenge of Language Policy". In *Respecting Linguistic Diversity in the European Union*, edited by X. Arzoz. Amsterdam: John Benjamins, 85–103.
Mill, J.S. [1861] 1972. "Considerations on Representative Government". In *Utilitarianism, Liberty and Representative Government*, edited by H.C. Acton. London: Dent, 187–428.
Nic Shuibhne, N. 2008. "EC Law and Minority Language Policy: Some Recent Developments". In *Respecting Linguistic Diversity in the European Union*, edited by X. Arzoz. Amsterdam: John Benjamins, 123–43.
Olsen, T.V. 2004. "Europe: United Under God? Or Not?" In *Political Theory and the European Constitution*, edited by L. Dobson and A. Follesdal. London: Routledge, 75–90.
Phillipson, R. 2003. *English-Only Europe? Challenging Language Policy*. London: Routledge.
Rokkan, S. 1999. *State Formation, Nation-Building and Mass Politics in Europe*. Oxford: Oxford University Press.
Sasse, G. 2006. "The Political Rights of National Minorities: Lessons from Central and Eastern Europe". In *Political Rights Under Stress in 21st Century Europe*, edited by W. Sadurski. Oxford: Oxford University Press, 238–81.
Shore, C. 2000. *Building Europe: The Cultural Politics of European Integration*. London: Routledge.
Stråth, B. 2000. "Europe as a Discourse". In *Europe and the Other and Europe as the Other*, edited by B. Stråth. Brussels: P.I.E. Peter Lang, 13–44.
Weber, M. 1980. *Wirtschaft und Gesellschaft*, 5th edition. Tübingen: Mohr.

Chapter 3
Democracy, Communities of Communication and the European Union

Sue Wright

What is Democracy?

What does democracy mean to Europeans? We recognize that it is part of European heritage. Its genesis in Athens at the end of the sixth century BC is noted in every school curriculum; the British parliamentary tradition is acknowledged as the oldest model of a certain kind of representative democracy;[1] the French Declaration of the Rights of Man is recognized as a founding document for the concepts of sovereignty of the people and equality of citizens; the democratic innovations on the eastern seaboard of America in the late eighteenth century were instituted by a diaspora that was also part of this European heritage.

At the beginning of the twenty-first century, Europeans are generally agreed that democracy is a positive thing, inviting approval and bestowing legitimacy. They had witnessed an immense surge in the popularity of the idea as totalitarianism in its right wing form, in Spain, Portugal and Greece, and in its communist form, in Eastern Europe, disappeared from the continent.

What Europeans actually understand as democracy is not a single concept. It is and has always been an umbrella term for a variety of political arrangements and movements. The Athenian tradition of democracy is accepted as the origin of the idea, but its offspring are very different both from it and from each other. One historic split appears between the Anglo-American concept of democracy and the kind developed on the continent following the French model. Another dichotomy exists between capitalist and socialist democracy. Those committed to grassroots democracy in radical pressure groups or alternative movements would reject the very idea that the liberal representative version is democratic in any more than a token way. Interpretations are thus very diverse, traditions very disparate, and there is a confusing tendency to employ "democracy" as a "hurrah" word, "a propagandist device indicating approval of whatever is the practice or policy or institution to which it is applied" (Lively 1975: 1). However, despite the devaluation, the contradictions and imprecision, there is a common core agreed by

1 From 1688 onwards, British political power resided in Parliament rather than the monarchy (for example, Parliament decided taxation, there was freedom of the press and of association).

all. Democracy is the rule of the many, not the few, and the many can only participate in decision-making if there is a deliberative process in which alternative solutions are proposed and examined. In Lively's typology of democratic arrangements there is a cline. Deliberation may be minimal, occurring principally at elections. However, debate is always present at some point.

Since democracy can be categorized as a concept with a long European pedigree and as a form of political arrangement with almost universal acceptance in Europe, it is curious that the European Union is actually deficient in many of the defining variables of a democratic state. This seems particularly ironic since commitment to democratic procedures is a condition of membership.[2] The EU is accused of a "democratic deficit" both by those who wish to draw back from further integration and those who wish to progress towards a kind of federation. In the 1990s, the lack of legitimation of the polity by the citizens (Weale 1995, Bellamy, Bufacchi and Castiglione 1995, Bankowski and Scott 1996, Hix 1998, Merkel 1999) and a certain stalling of the political will to overcome the deficit (Castiglione 1995, Antola and Rosas 1995) were noted as problems. In the 2000s, varying aspects of the continuing democratic deficit concerned commentators (Bellamy and Castiglione 2003, Eriksen and Fossum 2000, Warleigh 2003, van Ham 2001, Weiler, Begg and Peterson 2003, Decker 2002, Rittberger 2004, Steed 2003), particularly in this period of expansion. The EU's departure from the general democratic trend occurs to some extent because it is a young polity, still to find its final shape, and to some extent because it is novel and without precedent. It is not a state in the old nation-state sense of the term, and the kind of state which it is becoming is not at all clear (Weiler 1997, Habermas 1999). So our first difficulty when enquiring whether the EU is democratic is caused by the question: a democratic "what"? We are attaching an adjective to an entity which is not a fully evolved polity and, indeed, may never be. Can we call the EU a state? At best, we can say that the EU is a supra-national polity in formation.

Because the EU is in the process of developing, it may yet become a more democratic polity. It has already taken seriously accusations of its own "democratic deficit" and has become more democratic in each phase of its existence. Direct elections, growth in the power of parliament, citizenship, subsidiarity and greater transparency have all been responses to calls for greater democracy. There is, however, another hurdle to be overcome before the EU can be fully democratic, and this might prove the most intractable. This is the issue of debate. The expectations of those who have experienced the nation-state model of representative democracy are that voters should be a reasonably homogenous group of citizens who can communicate with each other. The expectations of those who argue that we are moving into a post-national period also place deliberation at the core of the democratic process:

2 Greece, Spain and Portugal acceded after the end of dictatorship; countries from the former Soviet bloc acceded after the fall of communism and their adoption of democratic constitutions.

> Detaching democracy from the nation state, post-nationalists [thus] place their aspiration on the democratic process and put particular emphasis on "deliberative democracy". Proponents of deliberative democracy argue that democratic legitimacy is spurred by processes of deliberation and not by fixed conceptions of the common good … [or] from the aggregation of preferences of all (Eriksen and Neyer 2003: 8).

> Democracy is [thus] conceived of in a more abstract fashion, not as a principle that prescribes a particular organizational form (a representative democracy for instance) but as a legitimation principle which lays out the conditions necessary for finding out what constitutes the common interest and more generally a community or common identity (Rittberger 2004: 32–3).

How, when and where we make space for debate, how we remove the blocks to deliberation seem to me the key issues to resolve if we want to address the problems of democratic deficit for which the European Union is constantly attacked. In this chapter I want to look at democratic practices in the past and examine how debate was encouraged and managed. Are there lessons from the past that could help us build the community of communication that we need in the present?

The Mitylenian Debate: The Silent Majority that Decides

Fifth-century Athens saw the first major experiment in *kratos* (the rule) of the *demos* (people). Democratic governance[3] came into existence as aristocratic power was undermined by the actions of leaders such as Solon and Pisistratus. In 508 BC, Cleisthenes completed the process. He dissolved the traditional connection of tribes and clans completely and created a new system of *demes* (or parishes) into which the male citizens of Athens were grouped. All these male citizens were required to participate in the assemblies that became their method of governance. This form of democracy depended on the ability of the protagonists to persuade the voting public in the assembly of the justice of their argument. In Aristotle's studies of rhetoric and poetics, we can see how Athenians were schooled in rhetoric, how persuasion works and, perhaps most important for governance, how societal norms are communicatively co-constructed in domestic as well as foreign affairs (Gutmann and Thompson 2004).

We can illustrate this by studying the debate on the punishment of the Mitylenes, as it was recorded by Thucydides ([431BC]1997) in his *History of the Peloponnesian War.* The Mitylenes, allies of the Athenians, had just taken up

3 The democratic system of fifth-century Athens benefited from experimentation with rudimentary democratic institutions from the eighth or ninth century BC in a number of places in the Greek-speaking world, and there were others, for example, in Sparta (Watson and Barber 1988).

arms against them and had been defeated. Thucydides tells us that the Athenians debated the fate of the rebels and decided on harsh sentences: death for the Mitylenian men and slavery for the women and children. Then Thucydides explains how the Athenians reconsidered and wanted to review their decision. Two eminent Athenians, Cleon and Diodotus, present the two arguments. Cleon takes a hard line: He is against too much talk; he dismisses further deliberation as a waste of time and a signal of weakness. He argues that the Athenians should do what they had decided. The harsh punishment will send a message and the ends (respect for Athens) will justify the means (death and slavery of the captives). Diodotus opposes this. He argues that this decision will change the Athenian view of who they are and what they do. It would be a cruel and monstrous act that would not be good for the reputation of Athens. He appeals to Athenians to reconsider and act as they have in the past, with mercy. He also argues that the interests of the Athenians are best served by mercy, since harsh treatment will provoke those who oppose Athens to fight to the death rather than surrender. Thucydides does not supply information about those who listened and then voted. We only have the outcome, which shows that a small majority was convinced by Diodotus and did reconsider.

This silence of the *demos* is part of the democratic process. The mass of citizens might not have spoken in public debate, but they heard both sides of the argument without intermediaries and then made up their mind. In such a debate, the argument is not meant primarily to change the mind of the opponent. Its function is to present evidence to the silent, voting majority. In Book III of the *History*, Thucydides has given us an example of deliberative democratic process leading to collective responsibility. He records how the Athenians co-constructed political action in response to appeals to the moral and the pragmatic dimensions. The benefit of the process derives from the inherent possibility that minds can be changed with new evidence and new interpretation:

> Through deliberation, the city as many seeks unity in acting; but its inherent plurality, marked by the division between speakers and *demos*, persists in the openness of its actions to alternative interpretations (Zumbrunnen 2008: 85).

Democracy is, of course, dependent on the competence of the audience to evaluate evidence and draw conclusions from it. This has always been seen as the problematic aspect of democracy. Can the ordinary mass of people be trusted with decision-making? The Athenians were not at all sure about this; both Aristotle and Socrates expressed their doubts. However, we can argue that the very fact that a group is practising democracy goes some way to solving the problem. In *doing* democracy, a *demos* learns to do it. The silent mass listening to both sides of the argument will gain competence in evaluation over time.

In theory, the citizens of Europe could practise democracy in this tradition, be the silent majority that watches and then pronounces. The plenary sessions of the European Parliament are public and televised. We could follow debates in

Brussels and Strasbourg on the World Wide Web (WWW). In practice, the vast majority of us do not. And whereas national media monitor national parliaments and present key debates on national news, the European Parliament is not reported consistently and comprehensively. This is particularly true of Member States where the European project is still challenged (for example, the UK), but, surprisingly, it is also the case in Member States whose commitment to make the supranational experiment work is greater (for example, Germany). It may well be that the fact that most decisions are taken by the Council of Ministers meeting *in camera* convinces editors that the debates are of little interest, although this is also the case at national level, where decisions of government are made in cabinet.

It may also be the sheer size and complexity of the machine. When democracy moves from the local to the national, the tendency is to move to the kind of representative democracy where there is minimal involvement or understanding on the part of the citizen (Lively 1975). This dislocation of the citizen from the process results in the anomie that Walter Lippman ([1927] 1993: 3) evoked when he famously attacked twentieth-century American democracy for its failures:

> The private citizen today has come to feel rather like a deaf spectator in the back row, who ought to keep his mind on the mystery … but cannot quite manage to keep awake. He knows he is somehow affected by what is going on. Rules and regulations continually, taxes annually and wars occasionally remind him that he is being swept along by great drifts of circumstance. Yet these public affairs are in no convincing way his affairs. They are for the most part invisible. They are managed, if they are managed at all, at distant centers, from behind the scenes, by unnamed powers. As a private person he does not know for certain what is going on, or who is doing it, or where he is being carried.

The problems of size and dislocation are almost as large in the United States, with its 309 million citizens,[4] as in the European Union, with its 499 million.[5] However, in the latter the problems which come from size and complexity are compounded by problems of language. Even where the citizen wants to participate in the democratic process, that person finds that only a proportion of the information is readily available in languages he or she can understand, that some of the commentary is taking place within linguistic communities he or she cannot penetrate, but, most important, that the media focuses on the national. As long as national news systematically acts as a gatekeeper to European matters and interprets them narrowly through the lens of national interest, it is very difficult to see how the Europeans could move to the Mitylenian position and become the *demos* that listens to all constituencies and then decides.

---

4 A July 1, 2009 estimate by the Population Division of the United Nations Department of Economic and Social Affairs.

5 Eurostat 2009.

Here is the crux of the problem for democracy in the EU. In the democratic tradition, legitimation of policy comes through debate in the public sphere. As Habermas (1989: 25) shows, democracy developed as soon as there was a "forum in which the private people, come together to form a public, readied themselves to compel public authority to legitimate itself before public opinion". Rittberger (2004: 30) reminds us: "Government for the people proclaims that political choices – in order to command legitimacy – need to effectively solve the problems the citizens of a polity collectively care about". These cannot be known without debate. Without debate we move into the dangerous territory of Rousseau's "general will" and we cannot allow a situation where a technocracy *knows* what the people want. The Commission has been criticized for its tendency to *understand* what was needed and act in areas for which it had no remit. The political development of the EU was supposed to counter this. But, although in Europe we have the structures for democracy, we do not have the practice. On the other hand, although democracy in the United States may be attacked on many accounts, it cannot be condemned for lack of debate. The presidential election is a year-long conversation that the American people has with itself.[6]

The American Revolution and the Constitutional Moment

The issue of a constitution for Europe could have kickstarted a continent-wide conversation in the 2000s. This was the hope of pro-Europe project politicians like Valéry Giscard d'Estaing and pro-democracy theorists like Habermas. They had the model of the American constitutional moment to show that discussion about the nature of the society a group wants for itself can mobilize members. Although the American constitutional debate was elite-led, it penetrated deep into the population. Contemporary historians made very strong claims about the role that face-to-face and published debate played in the revolution. Benjamin Rush, in an essay published in 1798, contended that "we do not extol too highly when we attribute as much to the power of eloquence as to the sword, in bringing about the American Revolution" (cited in Looby 1996: 21). David Ramsey expressed the view that "in establishing American independence the pen and the press had merit equal to that of the sword" (Ramsey 1789, 2: 319). Present-day scholars concur. Dew (2010) has traced publication and dissemination of the events at Boston in 1773–4 and has shown how these were used to galvanize the proto-American people.

6 Critics have argued that this conversation is dominated by the agenda of press barons and TV magnates. However, new technologies have allowed citizens to overcome these constrictions on their debate. In the elections of 2008, communication on the Internet and via new telephony played a major role. Barack Obama's Democrats used these to great advantage.

Thus the period 1760 to 1780 saw an "explosion of the written word" (Howe 2004: 2). Moreover, it was not just that the leaders of the revolution were publishing; the mass of citizens was reading, as contemporary commentators noted. Samuel Miller wrote that the spectacle of the ordinary people informing themselves was something not seen before: "Never, it may be safely asserted, was the number of political journals so great in proportion to the population of a country as at present in ours" (Miller 1803, 2: 253). Warner records that there were 38 newspapers in the colonies in 1775. Networks of sympathetic readers constituted one of "the most important forms of political organization in the colonies" (Warner 1990: 68). In the press it is possible to follow the rise and spread of public anger. Public discourse moved from representation of elite to elite audience to a more impersonal communication aimed at a wider audience and intended to promote the public sphere and build civil society.

In his novel *Salmagundi*, Washington Irving[7] coined the new word *logocracy* or "government by words". His North African observer pronounces that the whole new American nation does everything *viva voce* or by word of mouth: "[T]he country is intirely defended *vi et lingua*, that is to say, by force of tongues" (Irving 1807–8: 144).

This process is particularly clear in the constitutional moment, that period when the form and substance of the new state was being negotiated. Benjamin Franklin argued the need to convince the people that they were the sovereign power. Print had to be central in the process; the key text was the Constitution. The written Constitution became the way of "literalizing the doctrine of popular sovereignty" (Warner 1990: 97). The debate leading up to the drafting gave those participating, or simply listening, a political education which prepared them for the new situation:

> [The] war of words and the fighting among political parties, branches of government and outspoken individuals over (the Constitution's) proper construction helped shape the age's understanding of the way words govern people and people govern meanings of words (Gustafson 1992: 9).

Once published, the text of the Constitution became a source of guidance. As Thomas Paine noted, almost every family he met had a copy of the Constitution. Any debate or any contestation, and men took the Constitution from their pocket and consulted it. He saw how the discursive process was at the heart of democracy and how, through familiarity with the text of the Constitution, the people came to feel they owned the ideas within it: "[The] constitution is the property of a nation and not of those who exercise the government" (Paine [1791] 1945: 147). Madison held the deliberative to be an essential stage in the move from legislation to implementation:

---

7 Or perhaps a trio of writers – Washington Irving together with his brother, William Irving, and James Kirke Paulding.

> All new laws, though penned with the greatest technical skill, and passed on the fullest and most mature deliberation, are considered as more or less obscure and equivocal, until their meaning be liquidated and ascertained by a series of particular discussions and adjudications (Madison 1788: 37).

The principle to take from the early years of the American Revolution is the virtuous circle of participation. The Constitution was, of course, a text for which the Americans had had to fight, but it was also a text for which they had had to debate. They saw themselves as owning it; they had striven to understand its precepts, and they used them. The experience, the outcome and the situation in the early republic allowed President Jefferson to believe in deliberative democracy. Writing to Richard Price from Paris in January 1789, he feels able to claim:

> Whenever the people are well-informed, they can be trusted with their own governance; that, whenever things gets so far wrong as to attract their notice, they may be relied on to set them to rights (cited in Looby 1996: 45).

This provided a possible model for Europeans who hoped to press forward towards a political Europe that would counterbalance economic Europe. Some expressed hope (Habermas 2005, Weiler 2002) that that the debate on the constitution would put in motion a virtuous circle: Participation in this debate would strengthen European civil society and the public sphere, which, in their turn, could legitimate democratic structures at the European level. Although Habermas claims Europeans have enough cultural common ground to do this, neither explain clearly the channels through which this could happen.

The group formed under Valéry Giscard d'Estaing's leadership to formulate ideas for a constitution for Europe was also hoping for a "Philadelphia moment". They thus tried to consult citizens and involve them in discussion. However, the EU project to contribute ideas on the constitution did not penetrate to the vast majority. Any study of media in the then 15 Member States shows the extremely patchy and overwhelmingly weak coverage of the issue.[8] And whenever the subject was reported and discussed, the treatment was almost always from a national interest perspective.

Members of the *Convention on the Future of the European Union*, aware of the need to show that they had tried to contact citizens (Article I 46–3 of the draft constitution laid down the requirement that EU institutions maintain an open, transparent and regular dialogue with civil society and carry out broad consultations) turned to the World Wide Web in the hope that a discussion board open to all citizens would bring in participants from all Member States. The numbers that responded to this offer were extremely small, and a 12-month project monitoring contributions concluded that the profile of contributors was

8 For an analysis of research of media coverage of the discussions, see Wright (2004a); for an analysis of why national media underreport EU affairs, see Wright (2009).

far from typical of European citizens (Wright 2004a). The contributors to the EU constitutional discussion board appeared from their names and opinions to come from all the states that were then members of the EU as well as from those countries applying for accession. Among these already tiny numbers, only a minute group originated from the British Isles. Nonetheless, most of the discussion was in English, the language most contributors appeared to share as a foreign language. Some comments in French, Spanish and Italian were posted, but, significantly, these did not always gain a response, indicating, perhaps, that most of the other contributors could not follow the argument in these languages.

It was, of course, widely optimistic to hope that debate about the European constitution would rouse Europeans as the debate on the eastern seaboard had galvanized Americans in the 1770s and 1780s. The low level of participation in the Internet debate may have had several different reasons apart from the inevitable linguistic barriers to communication. In the wake of the inadequate press coverage noted above, there was inevitably muted interest among the population in general. This may be because this constitution lacked the drama of its predecessors; constitutional moments had usually been revolutionary in a strong sense, cutting participants from the arrangements and allegiances previously in place. Fifth-century Athenians were separated from their clans; French revolutionaries rejected the *ancien régime*; American colonialists were freed from empire. In the new circumstances, the citizens recreated themselves as an imagined community, a *demos*, and this provided the momentum for a deliberative democratic tradition. Now, although the EU is also a revolutionary experiment that has dented national sovereignty in a great many spheres, it is unusual in that there is a continuing commitment to maintain the legacy of the previous regime(s). There is no question of breaking down the ties that link citizens to their nation states. Rather these have been explicitly recognized and are protected in the EU's commitment to unity in diversity. The EU constitutional debate was always going to suffer from this lack of revolutionary turn, from citizens' continued allegiance to the nation-state and from the consequent absence of imagined European community. Europeans were never going to be a *demos*, but they did not even constitute themselves as linked *demoi.*

The disinclination for debate could also stem from the novelty of the medium. It could be that citizens were not used to using the WWW in the early 2000s as the conduit to participate in such a process of political discursive co-construction. Social networking sites had an exponential explosion as the locus for exchange very soon after this date, and it could be that a political debate on the WWW would attract greater participation today. Certainly the 2008 Obama campaign demonstrates the possibility. But at the time of discussion of the European Constitution, the section of the population that would seek information and offer opinion on the Internet was perhaps more limited than today.

Out of these four reasons for lack of interest in the Internet debate on the constitution (a stronger allegiance to the nation-state than to the European Union, media coverage that stressed national interest rather than European

Union interest, the novelty of the medium and the block to debate among a group with no language in common), some are more intractable blocks to deliberative democracy than others. The physical space is beginning to exist. The new technologies of communication that allow the information flows of globalization and real-time exchange across vast space are spreading among populations. The media preoccupation with the national interest and, in certain sectors, a blatant hostility to the European project could be attenuated by a move to Internet-based news gathering and dissemination. The power of the press barons is under attack from this direction. Recalibrating the imagined community of the nation may be more difficult; the Constitution was signed by all Member States but not ratified. The Dutch and the French populations (two of the four populations to be allowed referenda on the matter) rejected it. Eventually a watered-down version of the Constitution, the Lisbon Treaty, came into force in 2009. Any study of the intranational debates of this process illustrates the continuing preoccupation of Member State populations with national advantage and disadvantage. However, the incremental convergence that results from free movement within Europe may in a much longer term dent the exclusively national imagined community and encourage layered identities. However, whether this can happen in the mosaic linguistic setting of the EU remains to be seen. The language question is by far the most insuperable hurdle to developing democracy in Europe. It is difficult to see how Europeans can come together in the discursive formation of a European public sphere if they cannot get past the language barriers that keep them in their national groups. The lack of a forum for debate is a major limitation to the development of a political Europe, in any of the traditional ways that we have experienced democracy so far.

The French Revolution and the Language Question

The language issue is not a novel problem. When the French revolutionaries set out to implement the idea that political power should be held by the many rather than the few, they too were faced by a multilingual group with no common linguistic currency and no space for debate. Indeed, the situation was even more challenging. Democracy had disappeared from Europe for nearly two millennia. Rule of the many had been replaced by rule of the few, and in Absolutism, rule of the *one*. Government had been underpinned by armed might rather than debate. Argument based on evidence had been eclipsed by belief grounded in faith. The Reformation and the English Civil War had seen some resurgence of debate as a tool for governance, but both religious and political dissent had been suppressed in seventeenth- and eighteenth-century France. Thus, as the revolutionaries set out to engage the population in the process of revolution, they had no tradition to call upon.

It is no coincidence that many of the major figures of the French Revolution were journalists and pamphleteers. In a complete transformation from a situation where the press had consisted of heavily censored papers little more than court circulars,[9] at least 11 newspapers representing all shades of opinion began to appear daily in 1789. Most of the key revolutionaries were involved in this war of words. Barère and Mirabeau reported the Assembly debates. Among others, Desmoulins edited *Révolutions de France et de Brabant and Le vieux Cordelier*, Brissot *Le Patriote français*, Marat *L'Ami du Peuple*, Fréron *L'Orateur du peuple*, Carra et Mercier *Les Annales patriotiques*, Collot d'Herbois *L'Almanach du père Gérard*, Loustalot *Les Révolutions de Paris*, Hébert *Le Père Duchesne*,[10] Robespierre *Le Défenseur de la Constitution*. For a while there was absolute press freedom. Debate in the press and in pamphlets was central in the political process and often extreme. Many of this group (for example, Marat and Hébert) called for change through violence and government by force. It was always likely that this period of free debate would be curtailed.

Until this happened, the new citizens were also addressed by orators in open meetings. Mass rallies and meetings brought the experience of debate to the masses in the early years of the Revolution. Contemporary commentators observed events and expressed the fear that the new political actor, the *demos*, would not be sufficiently prepared to play the role demanded of it. Abbé Maury, Condorcet, Daunou and Garat worried that the people would be swayed by rhetoric. For a period, of course, this did happen, and skilled orators manipulated the Paris mob. The revolutionary position was that education was the means to overcome the naivety that made the mob susceptible to manipulation (cf. Talleyrand 1791). At this point, there was greater fear of a return to the *ancien régime* than of the excesses which would lead to the *Terreur*:

> Faisant de la rhétorique l'instrument du mal, sinon la part du diable, les philosophes s'opposent à tous ceux qui voudraient voir la Révolution restaurer l'éloquence antique [Holding rhetoric to be the work of the devil, the *philosophes* opposed all those who thought the Revolution was returning to the oratory of the ancient world] (Sermain 1986: 147–65).

In 1791, the *Assemblée législative* set up the first *Comité d'Instruction Publique*. At this point, the French Revolution took a revolutionary decision on the issue of language. The committee determined that the population needed to be literate to take part in democracy and that this literacy would have to be in French. The committee felt it necessary to promote a single community of communication for the new patterns of political life and for the deliberative process that was central to

9 For example, *Gazette*, *Mercure* and *Journal de Paris*. There were also papers for a specialist readership such as *Le Journal des Savants*.

10 *Le Père Duchesne* was very popular, and 10,000 copies were printed of each issue, a huge circulation for the time. Like *L'Ami du Peuple*, *Le Père Duchesne* called for extreme measures against the aristocrats and the monarchy. Both papers can be seen as agents of the events of 1792–4.

it. Fraternity and equality could not be served by a linguistic regime that left many citizens outside the debate. In 1789, only a small minority of the French population spoke French (Grégoire 1793), and in the very early days of the Revolution, edicts and proclamations had been translated into the various languages of France before being sent to the non-French speaking majority. This now altered, and communication took place in French with a clear message to the people that they should shift to French, the language of the nation and the new philosophy. As the extremists took control of the Revolution and as the dynasties of Europe formed a coalition to oppose the Republic, the language question became more acute. Now use of a language other than French was construed as lack of loyalty, as treason. Barère famously said:

> Le fédéralisme et la superstition parlent bas-breton; l'émigration et la haine de la République parlent allemand; la contre-révolution parle italien, et le fanatisme parle le basque. Cassons ces instruments de dommage et d'erreur [Those who insist on speaking Breton support federalism and the old superstitions; those who speak German are full of hate for the Republic and help the émigrés; Italian speakers work against the Revolution; Basque speakers are fanatically opposed to it. Let us rid ourselves of these languages which lead to harm and error] (Barère 1794).

Through constraint and fear of punishment, through exhortation and appeals to patriotism, French spread. The Revolution had normalizing and standardizing effects on French and helped to bring about a congruence of national language and national space.

It also had consequences for the spread of literacy. The 24 members of the *Comité d'Instruction Publique* agreed there was a need for citizens to be able to write in order to be able to take part in the political process. Talleyrand (1791) proposed a French-speaking primary school teacher in each commune. Because of war and defeat, this policy was not enacted until the end of the nineteenth century when Jules Ferry's reforms made primary education free, secular and compulsory. French had, however, spread before that date among the classes that progressed to secondary school:

> L'enseignement public est partout dirigé de manière qu'un de ses premiers bienfaits soit que la langue française devienne en peu de temps la langue familière de toutes les parties de la République [Everywhere public schooling is managed in such a way that one of its main benefits is that French is quickly becoming the common language of the whole Republic] (1927 XI.1: 147–8).

The French Revolution promoted the idea that a state should comprise "un peuple, un territoire, une langue" [one people, one land, one language]. This trinity became a central tenet of French Republican ideology, and state policies homogenized the nation linguistically.[11] There was both corpus and acquisition language planning in pursuit of the linguistic aim. The grammarian Destutt de Tracy thought that the language could be moulded to be the necessary tool for participatory politics; linguists could strive for the clarity and precision that would make the new democratic practices accessible to those who would be part of them.[12]

Through their policies on language and education, French revolutionaries revealed that they believed there to be two preconditions for deliberative democracy. The first is the need for citizens to be educated to the level where they can assume their role as participants in deliberation. The second was that deliberation is most easily managed in a monolingual forum. They were able to implement their monolingual policy because persuasion was underpinned by threat. Moreover, the French people experienced a process similar to the Athenians under Cleisthenes in that all horizontal ties, both communitarian and associative, were abandoned. Territory was repartitioned and organized as departments that had new names and boundaries that cut across old allegiances and identities. The Preamble to the 1791 Constitution specifically stated that citizens were freed from the social classes that had placed them in social roles among which there was no mobility.[13] Citizens of the new republic were under the authority of the law, defined by Declaration of the Rights of Man and of the Citizen. In this new beginning, the imposition of a new linguistic regime echoed all the other ruptures.[14]

---

11 There is still much support within France for linguistic homogeneity.

12 The revolutionary government wanted a new dictionary to reflect the new lexis being coined. Like much of the wish-list of this period, this aim was not fully achieved. In 1799, Cabanis presented the *Conseil des Cinq Cents* with the new edition of the *Académie* dictionary, prepared by Smits and Marandon, the publishers. They had just added 12 pages of new coinings.

13 Il n'y a plus ni noblesse, ni pairie, ni distinctions héréditaires, ni distinctions d'ordres, ni régime féodal, ni justices patrimoniales, ni aucun des titres, dénominations et prérogatives qui en dérivaient, ni aucun ordre de chevalerie, ni aucune des corporations ou décorations, pour lesquelles on exigeait des preuves de noblesse, ou qui supposaient des distinctions de naissance, ni aucune autre supériorité, que celle des fonctionnaires publics dans l'exercice de leurs fonctions. Il n'y a plus ni vénalité, ni hérédité d'aucun office public. Il n'y a plus, pour aucune partie de la Nation, ni pour aucun individu, aucun privilège, ni exception au droit commun de tous les Français (available at: www.conseil-constitutionnel.fr [accessed November 2009]).

[There is no longer nobility, peerage, distinctions through birth or class; we no longer have the feudal order, the old patriarchal justice system and all the titles, distinctions and prerogatives which derive from them; we do not recognise orders of knights, seigneurial corporations and honours for which one had to prove one's nobility through lineage. Now there is no hierarchy apart from public servants carrying out their duties. There is no venality, no public office that can be inherited by the next generation. No longer is any member of the nation privileged, no one is exempt from the common law that applies to all French people].

14 The American revolutionaries had also debated the need for a community of communication, and it had been suggested that the newly united states should choose Greek as their official language to mark their break with Britain, their new direction and their

What conclusions are there to draw from the French experience? The democrats among the revolutionaries saw the need for a forum for debate. The language policy and planning needed to achieve this could be imposed in a period of upheaval, violence and relocation. French citizens were pressed to assimilate linguistically; language use became a mark of loyalty and patriotic duty. There is little here on which those concerned to promote democracy in the European Union can draw. There is no revolutionary moment, no dislocation. The European Union cannot engineer group cohesion on the old nation-building model. The constituent groups would not accept top-down directives in the way that the citizens of the first three French Republics did.

Moreover, the European Union has explicitly rejected any idea that a community of communication is one of its desiderata. The founding principle of the Union is unity in diversity and strict respect for national difference. Within the institutions, the founding treaties explicitly protect the multilingual heritage of Europe or at least that part of the heritage that is national standard language. Among the populations, EU policy[15] is also to safeguard and promote linguistic diversity. For the last 25 years, EU financial support for language acquisition and research on pedagogy has gone to preserve diversity in the foreign language curriculum. Now, although reconciliation of the unity in diversity principle and the community of communication that democratic governance clearly needs could be achieved by encouraging bilingualism (the maintenance of the national language as first language of home and literacy, and the acquisition of an agreed *lingua franca* learnt as a foreign/second language in school), the Commission has not countenanced this option. This policy position seems counter-intuitive. Whereas it is easy to understand the EU's need to respect the language regimes of the constituent nation states, it is less clear why it should reject the bilingual solution, which maintains that respect while building a community of communication. Whatever the logic of the case, the promotion of bilingualism that adds an agreed *lingua franca* to a national language has not proved politically acceptable. There has been no top-down policy to promote acquisition of a single *lingua franca* which would slowly build the competence for transnational contact and exchange.[16]

However, grass roots reaction has been completely at variance with EU policy. The education systems of the Member States have largely ignored Commission calls for diversification in foreign language provision, and English is on the curriculum for the vast majority (Eurydice 2005). However, even if there is a growing number of Europeans able to use English in their work or travel, this is far

---

adherence to democracy. Of course, the imposition top-down of a language that no group in the territory actually used was never likely to happen, and English, the language of the majority of the revolutionaries, prevailed.

15 While the EU has no remit for education, which remains the preserve of the Member States, the Commission does fund language-learning initiatives.

16 For an extensive treatment of this subject, see Wright (2000, 2004b, 2009).

from saying that they are willing and/or able to use it in the political process. What evidence do we have that this does happen? What proof is there of transnational grass roots movements bringing European citizens together to act transnationally, to campaign and to lobby?

First there is no indication that audio-visual media are providing a platform. At present, nine transnational TV stations dedicated to political news and debate have a significant audience in Europe: BBC World, CNN International, CNBC Europe, Sky News, Deutsche Welle, TV5, France 24, Al Jazeera English and Euronews. Of these only Euronews[17] can be seen as pan-regional, with a European focus. The others are a mix of national broadcasters targeting a global audience and commercial broadcasters seeking a global audience (Chalaby 2005). Euronews reached 3–6 million viewers daily in the 2000s (TV Viewing Figures 2009) and is often chosen as the channel in European public space, airport lounges, and so forth (Brüggemann and Schulz-Forberg 2009). Subsidized by the EU, Euronews' mission is to portray the European perspective to Europeans and promote European views to the wider world. It has, however, proved a rather colourless channel with little editorial steer, no discussion and no interaction with the public:

> Euronews merely filters images and newsreels from associated European and Mediterranean channels, as well as two global agencies, dubs them in seven languages and broadcasts them simultaneously in all European countries. Euronews does not produce any original material of its own (Brüggemann and Schulz-Forberg 2009: 703).

The language question has thus been solved by eschewing interaction; the programmes are comment over image, broadcast in parallel translations. It has, unsurprisingly, not proved itself to be the medium for pan-European debate.

The written press has not provided a forum either. *The European*, launched in 1991 with the slogan "Europe's first national paper", folded in 1999. Its circulation always fell far below the expectations of Robert Maxwell, its founder (Cusack 2008). *European Voice*, published by The Economist Group has a small distribution of 15,000, roughly, and is read mainly in the "Brussels village" "integrat[ing] the communicative microcosm of EU officials, lobbyists, Brussels correspondents and policy experts" (Brüggemann and Schulz-Forberg 2009: 703).

The titles which sell widely in Europe are *Le Monde diplomatique*, *The Economist* and the *Financial Times*.[18] These treat EU matters among a mass of other concerns. However, *The Economist* takes a largely Eurosceptic view; the *Financial Times* has a financial/business focus; *Le Monde diplomatique* is, like the other two titles but perhaps even more so, designed for an intellectual elite. They do not thus constitute a forum for European citizens except for an elite stratum.

17 Euronews was launched in 1993, triggered by the reaction to the reporting of the Iraq War in 1991, judged to have been dominated by American images and interpretation.

18 All regularly achieve higher sales outside their country of production than within.

To summarize, it is fair to claim that in 2010 we do not have traditional media that European citizens share. The transnational media that use English do not attract a majority audience in Europe. The debates on EU matters, both theoretical and practical, remain bounded by linguistic frontiers. We may hope that the channels of the Internet will come to provide a medium for transnational connection. But even if this new technology of communication allows wider participation in publication and permits individuals to bypass the national media, it does not solve the language problem.

Conclusions

Despite its imperfections, we have nothing better than the democratic process. The challenge in the EU is to see how these imperfections can be dealt with in a supranational, multilingual setting. History shows us the prerequisites of democracy. The lesson from Athenian participatory democracy is that the *demos* should hear both sides of the argument, and preferably directly from the protagonists. The message from the American Revolution is that debate creates a public sphere and as it percolates through the population, constitutes the collective learning experience which creates the *demos*. The French revolutionaries' decisions reflect the fact that both *demos* and forum are more easily achieved in a single community of communication.

The European Union elites (particularly the drafters of the recent Constitution and the subsequent Lisbon Treaty) are clearly aware of some of these lessons. The commitment to promote transparency was articulated throughout the 2000s. The provision of access to public documents in all the official languages of the EU is now unproblematic. Analysis of information, although often seen as public relations, is available on the EU website. Public debates in the European Parliament can be seen on the Internet. Legislative meetings of the Council of Ministers are, by the provisions of the Lisbon Treaty, to be held in public. These are, however, all top-down communications.

Where is the principle of *participatory democracy* to be found? The debate about the European Constitution was a damp squib; it failed to galvanize the public; it was not a learning process. Perhaps this was because the main aim of the jurists and constitutionalist was to provide a single institutional framework; it was not a wider debate about the way we want to live. There was neither remit nor space for discussion about, for example, new directions in economic, social, societal or environmental matters and the institutional changes necessary to manage them collectively. However, a new provision in the Lisbon Treaty, the *one million citizen initiative*, shows, perhaps, that the Europeanists have understood the need to engage citizens on concrete issues of concern if they are to mobilize Europeans as Europeans. The initiative allows one million citizens coming from a significant number of Member States to invite the Commission to submit an appropriate proposal on matters where citizens believe that a

Union act is required.[19] It is perhaps possible that present levels of anxiety about climate and market economics will lead to some pan-European cooperation and initiatives.

Some wish to go further. Schwok (2009) suggests the introduction of legislative referenda. He proposes that the populations should have a veto on major Community legislation adopted by the Council and the European Parliament. "If 50 per cent of voters turned down the new law it could not enter into force" (Schwok 2009: 4). This is potentially cumbersome, but the spread and penetration of the Internet makes e-voting a possibility. Schwok argues that the main advantage for his proposed legislative referendum is that it respects the *sui generis* nature of the EU. It does not artificially create a European *demos* but encourages the idea of European *demoi* acting in concert if not in contact. This proposal from a Swiss-based academic draws on the Swiss tradition of referenda and would need muscular support for acceptance Europe-wide. However, if we are concerned to promote democracy at the European level, debates on concrete issues followed by meaningful political participation are one way of proceeding. We have seen that in the linguistically fractured EU, it is difficult to launch transnational deliberation. However, an ongoing debate on questions of mutual European interest ending with the possibility of registering one's opinion might transpose some feelings of political belonging to the European level. Were the idea to gain ground it would reproduce at supranational level an aspect of Renan's "plebiscite de tous les jours" [constant reaffirmation that one is part of the political group].

There is little doubt that if such legislative referenda were ever to be adopted, debate would not stay within national linguistic spheres. Those who wanted to reach out to persuade other constituencies would do so with the means that they had in hand. This is at present English, and English in its second language international form. Any growth in transnational democratic deliberation is likely to confirm use of English in this domain and promote an organic, unplanned spread. Whether those opposed to this could halt it would remain to be seen. Whatever move to deliberation is suggested, the language issue may well turn out to be the make-or-break element.

In the 15 years in which I have been writing on these matters, the EU has continued to address the accusation of democratic deficit. Increased transparency, accountability and greater power for the European Parliament have been milestones along this road. However, while the institutions have moved, the populations have not kept pace. "Most citizens do not understand how the EU functions nor do they grasp the importance of the decisions adopted there" (Schwok 2009: 2). Turnout at elections is in decline, despite the transfer of much sovereignty to the EU level. I suggest that the lack of a community of communication plays a significant role in this apathy. Jefferson was optimistic about government in a democratic

19 Constitution (Article I- 46(4)), Lisbon Treaty.

relationship with the people. In *Notes on the State of Virginia*, he lays down the rules for freedom of information:

> The discourse of a wise government ... must abjure sophistry and submit "facts" to a reasonable mind or "candid world" which then is permitted to draw its own conclusions freely (Jefferson, 275, note 98, cited in Fliegelman 1993).

This can only work when the communication flows are open. How we, Europeans, get these flowing is our challenge.

References

Antola, E. and Rosas, A. (eds) 1995. *A Citizens' Europe: In Search of a New Order*. London: Sage.

Bankowski, Z. and Scott, A. 1996. The European Union?, in *Constitutionalism, Democracy and Sovereignty: American and European Perspectives*, edited by R. Bellamy and D. Castiglione. Aldershot: Avebury, 77–95.

Barère de Vieuzac, B. 1794. *Convention Nationale. Rapport et projet de décret, présentés au nom du Comité de salut public, sur les idiômes étrangers, et l'enseignement de la langue française, dans la séance du 8 pluviôse, l'an deuxième*. Paris.

Bellamy, R., Bufacchi, V. and Castiglione, D. (eds) 1995. *Democracy and Constitutional Culture*. London: Lothian Foundation Press.

Bellamy, R. and Castiglione, D. 2003. Legitimizing the Euro-"polity" and its "Regime": The Normative Turn in EU Studies. *European Journal of Political Theory*, 2(1), 7–34.

Brüggeman, M. and Schulz-Forberg, H. 2009. Becoming Pan-European. *International Communication Gazette*, 71(8), 693–712.

Brunot, F. 1927. *Histoire de la langue française des origines à nos jours*, Tome IX. *La Révolution et l'Empire*. Paris.

Castiglione, D. 1995. Contracts and Constitutions, in *Democracy and Constitutional Culture in the Union of Europe*, edited by R. Bellamy, V. Bufacchi and D. Castiglione. London: Lothian Foundation Press, 75–102.

Chalaby, J. 2005. Deconstructing the Transnational: A Typology of Transnational Television Channels in Europe. *New Media and Society*, 7(2), 155–75.

Cusack, A. 2008. The Life and Death of *The European* [Online]. Available at: http://norumbega.co.uk/2008/06/30/the-_european/ [accessed March 2010].

Decker, F. 2002. Governance Beyond the Nation-state: Reflections on the Democratic Deficit of the European Union. *Journal of European Public Policy*, 9(2), 256–72.

Dew, B. 2010. Introduction, in *Tea and the Tea-Table in Eighteenth-Century England, Volume 4*. London: Pickering and Chatto.

Eriksen, E. and Fossum, J. (eds) 2000. *Democracy in the European Union: Integration through Deliberation*. London: Taylor and Francis.

Eriksen, E. and Neyer, J. 2003. The Forging of Deliberative Supranationalism in the EU?, in *European Governance, Deliberation and the Quest for Democratisation*, edited by E. Eriksen, C. Joerges and J. Neyer. Oslo: ARENA, 1–23.

Eurydice 2005. *Foreign Language Learning: A European Priority* [Online]. Available at: http://eacea.ec.europa.eu/ressources/eurydice/pdf/0_integral/061EN.pdf [accessed: March 2010].

Fliegelman, J. 1993. *Declaring Independence*. Stanford, CA: Stanford University Press.

Fossum, J. and Schlesinger, P. 2008. *The European Union and the Public Sphere*. London: Taylor and Francis.

Grégoire, A. 1793. *Rapport sur la nécessité et les moyens d'anéantir les patois et d'universaliser la langue française*. Paris.

Gustafson, T. 1992. *Representative Words: Politics, Literature and the American Language 1776–1865*. Cambridge: Cambridge University Press.

Gutmann, A. and Thompson, D. 2004. *Why Deliberative Democracy?* Princeton, NJ: Princeton University Press.

Habermas, J. [1962] 1989. *The Structural Transformation of the Public Sphere*, translated by Thomas Burger. Cambridge: Polity Press.

Habermas, J. 1999. The European Nation State and the Pressures of Globalisation. *New Left Review*, 235, 46–59.

Habermas, J. 2003. Towards a Cosmopolitan Europe. *Journal of Democracy*, 14(4), 86–100.

Habermas, J. 2005. *Time of Transitions*. Cambridge: Polity Press.

Hix, S. 1998. Elections, Parties and Institutional Design: A Comparative Perspective on European Union Democracy. *West European Politics*, 21(3), 19–52.

Howe, J. 2004. *Language and Political Meaning in Revolutionary America*. Boston, MA: University of Massachusetts Press.

Irving, W. 1807–8. Salmagundi: Or, the Whim-Whams and Opinions of Launcelot Langstaff Esq. and Others, 5 and 6. New York: David Longworth.

Lippman, W. [1927] 1993. *The Phantom Public*. New Brunswick. NJ: Transaction.

Lively, J. 1975. *Democracy*. Oxford: Blackwell.

Looby, C. 1996. *Voicing America*. Chicago, IL: University of Chicago Press.

Madison, J. 1788. Concerning the Difficulties of the Convention in Devising a Proper Form of Government. *Federalist Papers* 37. New York: J. and A. McLean.

Merkel, W. 1999. Legitimacy and Democracy: Endogenous Limits of European Integration, in *Regional Integration and Democracy: Expanding on the European Experience*, edited by J. Anderson. Lanham, MD: Rowman and Littlefield, 45–67.

Miller, S. 1803. *Brief Retrospect of the Eighteenth Century* (two vols). New York: T. and J. Sword.

Paine, T. [1791] 1945. *Complete Writings of Thomas Paine*. New York: Citadel Press.

Ramsay, D. 1789. *The History of the American Revolution* (two vols). Philadelphia.

Rittberger, B. 2004. *Building Europe's Parliament: Democratic Representation Beyond the Nation State*. Oxford: Oxford University Press.

Schwok, R. 2009. Introduce a Legislative Referendum. *Jean Monnet Contributions to the Reflection on the Future of Europe* [Online]. Available at: http://ec.europa.eu/education/jean-monnet/doc/future/schwok_en.pdf.

Sermain, J.-P. 1986. Raison et Révolution: Le problème de l'éloquence politique, in *Les Idéologues: Sémiotique, Théories et Politiques Linguistiques Pendant la Révolution Française*, edited by W. Busse and J. Trabant. Amsterdam: John Benjamins, 147–65.

Steed, M. 2003. Choice, Representation and European Elections, in *Choice and Representation in the European Union*, Federal Trust Series, edited by R. Morgan and M. Steed. London: Kogan Page, 115–46.

Talleyrand C. de. 1791. Rapport sur l'instruction publique, reported in Hippeau, C. (1881) *L'instruction publique en France*. Paris: Didier, 149–50.

Thucydides [431BC] 1997. *The History of the Peloponnesian War*, translated by Richard Crawley. Ware: Wordsworth Classics.

TV Viewing Figures: Commercials and profiles. [Online]. Available at: http://www.viewingfigures.com [accessed: October 2009].

Van Ham, P. 2001. *European Integration and the Post-Modern Condition*. London: Routledge.

Warleigh, A. 2003. *Democracy in the European Union*. London: Sage.

Warner, M. 1990. *Letters of the Republic: Publication and the Public Sphere*. Cambridge, MA: Harvard University Press.

Watson, P. and Barber, B. 1988. *The Struggle for Democracy*. London: W.H. Allen.

Weale, A. 1995. Democratic Legitimacy and the Constitution of Europe, in *Democracy and Constitutional Culture in the Union of Europe*, edited by R. Bellamy, V. Bufacchi and D. Castiglione. London: Lothian Foundation Press.

Weiler, J. 1997. Legitimacy and Democracy of Union Governance, in *The Politics of European Treaty Reform*, edited by G. Edwards and A. Pijpers. London: Pinter, 249–87.

Weiler, J. 2002. A Constitution for Europe? Some Hard Choices. *Journal of Common Market Studies*, 40(4), 563–80.

Weiler, J., Begg, I. and Peterson J. (eds) 2003. *Integration in an Expanding European Union*. Oxford: Blackwell.

Weiler, J., Haltern, U. and Mayer, F. 1995. European Democracy and its Critique, in *The Crisis of Representation in Europe*, edited by J. Hayward. London: Frank Cass, 4–39.

Wessler, H. (ed.) 2008. *Public Deliberation and Public Culture: The Writings of Bernhard Peters, 1993–2005*. Basingstoke: Palgrave Macmillan.

Wright, S. 2000. *Community and Communication: From Nation State Building to Europeanisation*. Clevedon: Multilingual Matters.

Wright, S. 2004a. Debating the European Constitution: Traditional and New Media. *LSS Working Papers*, Aston University.

Wright, S. 2004b. *Language Policy and Language Planning: From Nationalism to Globalisation*. Basingstoke: Palgrave Macmillan.

Wright, S. 2009. The Elephant in the Room: Language Issues in the European Union. *European Journal of Language Policy*, 1(2), 93–120.

Zumbrunnen, J. 2008. *The Silence of Democracy*. University Park, PA: Pennsylvania State University Press.

Chapter 4
The EU and Languages: Diversity in What Unity?

Robert Phillipson

Introduction

This chapter analyses the constraints affecting the EU's management of multilingualism in its institutions, and its efforts to promote languages in Member States.[1] It assesses whether the increasing use of English in EU institutions and in Member States is compatible with the EU's commitment to maintaining linguistic diversity. It reports on a range of EU initiatives aimed at strengthening multilingualism and relates them to the political and commercial market forces that are strengthening English. There are different language policy issues at stake in supranational institutions and in Member States, but language issues at the supranational and national levels are interconnected as a result of increasing European and global integration.

Traditionally, matters of culture, education and language have been seen as an exclusively national prerogative. All Member States promote national languages. Some states promote foreign language learning vigorously and successfully, others less so. Some promote their language abroad strongly, a policy that particularly strengthened English, French, German and Spanish as "international" languages. Regional minority languages are promoted very unevenly in different countries.

Among the many factors that impede supranational language policy formation is the historical fact that European states have evolved different cosmologies in distinct national linguistic cultures (Blommaert 1999, Schiffman 2006). Some countries are based mainly on national ideologies that stress ethnolinguistic criteria, *the cultural nation*, as in Germany (Herder, Blut und Boden) and Denmark (Grundtvig); other countries build on a political, republican principle, as in France (*la langue de la république est le français* [French is the language of the republic] according to the French Constitution) or Finland (with two parallel official languages), rather than consanguinity. In addition, each European country has evolved legal systems along distinct national lines throughout centuries,

1 I am grateful to participants at the University of Copenhagen conference in June 2009 for useful discussion of many language policy issues, to Seán O'Riain for useful comments on a draft of the chapter, and to anonymous reviewers.

drawing variously on Roman and Napoleonic law, common law and imperialist, fascist or communist experience.

Basic concepts like *language*, *dialect* and *nation* therefore mean different things in each language and state. Concepts in EU language policy declarations, such as *mother tongue* and *linguistic diversity* are open to several interpretations. Even such an apparently straightforward concept as *working language* is used inconsistently in media and political discourse, by both senior EU insiders and journalists.[2] For historical reasons, countries that have seen themselves as "great powers" assume that their languages are more important than others: There is a widespread Orwellian assumption that some languages are more equal than others and ought to be so. Inequality is confirmed by the status of English, French and German as "procedural" languages internally in the Commission, and with a hierarchy among them (Ammon 2009: 32). The logical conclusion to draw is that when the rule of law and European legislation are supposed to have the "same meaning" in 23 languages and 27 states, European Union in the sense of uniformity is an illusion or perhaps an ideal that the EU is attempting to move towards.

The result of loose terminology is that the rights of speakers of languages in the EU system or in interacting with it are often obscured. The right to use specific languages in EU contexts exists on paper for a range of functions, both in speech (via interpretation) and writing (official communications, approaches by the citizen), but it is constrained in many ways; for instance, it may be strategically important for an EU citizen or an MEP to write or speak in English rather than any other EU language.[3] Language rights are often neither understood nor acted on.

A key reason for the EU holding back from the analysis of language policy issues until quite recently is that the issues are politically sensitive; they touch existential national nerves, as frankly conceded by the German Head of Mission at the EU: There is "no more emotional topic in the EU than the language issue".[4] Or in the words of a senior French member of the European Parliament: "The topic can be considered explosive in Europe".[5] At the intergovernmental level, therefore, language policy has tended to be politically untouchable, apart from

2 Journalistic coverage of EU language issues tends to be ill-informed, even in the quality press, often with an exclusive emphasis on the cost of multilingualism or the tired myth of Babel. For examples, see Phillipson (2003: 19–23).

3 *Le Monde* reported on 17 February 2004 that three French MEPs tabled a motion on a financial topic not in French but in English: "We had to shift to English in order to be heard". Specifically, the issue was the words *standard* (in French = normal) and *normal*. "The problem could only be solved by resorting to English".

4 "Es gibt in der EU kein emotionaleres Thema als Sprachen". Wilhelm Schönfelder, cited in *Süddeutsche Zeitung*, 1 April 2005.

5 "Un sujet qui peut être qualifié d'explosif en Europe". Pierre Lequiller, président, réunion ouverte à l'ensemble des membres français du Parlement Européen, le 11 juin 2003, pour debattre le *Rapport sur la diversité linguistique au sein de l'Union européenne*, préparé par Michel Herbillon, auprès de la Délégation pour l'Union Européenne.

the endorsement of bland proclamations in favour of multilingualism and foreign language learning.[6] The Maastricht Treaty authorized the EU to fund activities in the field of language and education, since which time many programmes have been initiated, directly in school education, higher education and research, and indirectly in countless other ways. However, the rhetoric of multilingualism as a defining European characteristic ignores the fact that for the past two centuries, most European states have aimed at making their citizens monolingual. Principles of linguistic equality and multilingual diversity have thus only fragile roots to build on in virtually all Member States (Wright 2000).

The gradual expansion of the number of EU languages, from four in 1958 to 23 currently, obviously makes the management of multilingualism in EU institutions more complex. In addition, increasing integration has augmented progressively and very considerably the number of fields of activity in which the EU operates. The translation and interpretation services are confident that they have been able to expand the repertoire of languages triggered by each enlargement effectively and without a loss of quality. This has entailed recourse to a variety of procedures and technologies that are presented on the relevant websites.[7] Some of the challenges of making these services efficient, cost-effective and just are reported below.

The EU is officially committed to managing linguistic diversity equitably.[8] However, this laudable aim is up against massive forces that counteract its achievement. Identifying these forces, their historical antecedents and present-day impact is a necessary step towards understanding the complexity of EU language policies. There is a need for creating greater understanding of the structural determinants of language policy in order to move towards a more just and sustainable linguistic order. The alternative is to leave language policy to market forces, which is a recipe for an increased dominance by English and its users. An expansion of the use and learning of English in Member States and in the EU system runs the risk of promoting homogenization at the expense of diversity. Whereas court cases that deal with language issues require pragmatic decisions and solutions, the focus of the present chapter is on clarifying the type of unity that is possible in a diverse union of more than two dozen states and even more languages. The issues will be approached by considering the EU system first, thereafter activities in Member States that the EU supports and finally more global and general issues.

---

6 See European Council conclusions, 1995 and the Resolution on the European Year of Languages 2001, both reproduced in appendices in Phillipson (2003: 193–8).

7 Available at: http://ec.europa.eu/dgs/translation/index_en.htm; http://ec.europa.eu/dgs/scic/.

8 This underlying principle can be seen in the EU's constitutional commitment to "respecting" linguistic diversity (Article 2, Treaty of Lisbon, in force since 1 December 2009), in Eurolaw having equal validity in all 23 EU languages and in each Member State being entitled to a national language being accorded EU official and working language status.

Managing Multilingualism in the EU System

Analysis of the EU's management of multilingualism is often blurred because generalizations tend to be made without clarifying whether what is being referred to relates to a specific institution, to speech or writing, to a citizen in contact with the EU or to an EU employee. It is imperative to distinguish between the language regime of Eurocrats who are employed permanently in an EU institution, who can be expected and required to function multilingually, and temporary, short-term participation by EU citizens, whether politicians or experts in EU activities, who are attending meetings, reading or drafting texts, and so forth, for whom the right to function in any official language should be respected.[9] Issues of efficiency, linguistic justice and cost will not be clarified validly unless functions, contexts and users of particular languages are specified. Any analysis of multilingualism in Europe needs to distinguish carefully between what happens in the EU system itself and in sectors in Member States that the EU seeks to influence, such as school, higher education and research in particular.

Language policy has not been an EU priority, over and above ensuring the machinery of institutional translation and interpretation services. The principle that EU law overrides national law requires that at least one language of each Member State functions as an official and working language of the EU.[10] This principle was established in 1958 by Council Regulation 1. The functions of EU translators and interpreters are essential. They represent international consolidation in the use of 23 languages for a wide range of written and spoken purposes. Minority languages that are part of the European heritage have no place in EU affairs, though this principle is being eroded since Spain and the UK have ensured that some use can be made of Basque, Catalan, Galician, Scottish Gaelic and Welsh: There are clear criteria for granting EU co-official status to regional official languages (O'Riain 2009).

Far-reaching language policy decisions have been taken without prior clarification of the principle underlying a decision, such as granting preferential status to one language or a set of three. The *de facto* status of French as *primus inter pares* in EU institutions in earlier years was an outcome of power politics. English has increasingly taken over this role, particularly in the Commission, not as a result of a decision by the Council of Ministers but because of the market forces and internal and external pressures behind the language. The privileged status of English is reinforced continually by key decisions, such as determining that in all negotiations with applicant Member States, English should be used exclusively,[11]

9 See Phillipson (2003: Chapter 4).

10 The exceptions are officially multilingual states like Belgium and Finland.

11 This requirement in agreements between the Commission and Poland and the Czech Republic in the accession process is cited in Phillipson (2003: 123), e.g. "Any communication between the Commission and the Czech Republic related to this Agreement shall be in English".

a decision that was taken by the Commission unilaterally. It exemplifies language policy in the EU being treated as merely a pragmatic, instrumental matter even though language policy is in fact a major political issue (Kraus 2008).

A number of language policy scholars have analysed the functioning of the EU's translation and interpretation systems: van Els (2005) favours granting a distinct status to English; Ammon (2006) calls for demographically major languages to be accorded the same status and prestige as English; Gazzola (2006) combines an analysis of the economics of translation and interpretation with elaboration of different understandings of equality in language use. Issues of cost that tend to be stressed in journalistic coverage of the EU's management of diversity need counterbalancing since "The perception of how expensive a service is depends on the subjective value that the observer or the society attributes to it" (Gazzola 2006: 400). The EU's own services and MEPs are regularly involved in assessing the quality and nature of language services. There are manifestly no quick fixes in making translation and interpretation function optimally and to the satisfaction of all those who depend on them. Much could be gained if administrative and scholarly discourses could be integrated more assiduously, but the EU has hitherto shown little interest in collaboration of this kind.

Language policy issues were ignored by the Convention on the Future of Europe (2002–3), in the draft Constitutional Treaty, its resurrection as the Reform Treaty and in force as the Lisbon Treaty, despite pleas from NGOs from several countries for language rights to be strengthened. There is a mismatch between the broad sweep of Article 22 of *The Charter of Fundamental Rights of the European Union* – "The Union shall respect cultural, religious and linguistic diversity" – and the realities of how this is interpreted. The most extreme form of declaring that the Charter's commitment is merely hot air was given voice by a senior French civil servant in a conference paper in the United States. Yves Marek, counsellor to Jacques Toubon[12] when Minister of Culture and Francophonie, claims blandly that "in the field of linguistic rights, like in other fields of human rights, there is no right but only ... politics". This shows a national civil servant following the precepts of Machiavelli (*The Prince*, 1514), whereas the EU system attempts to ensure equilibrium among the interests of all Member States and their languages and requires states to make compromises. Marek also claimed that it is the French understanding of national languages that underlies how the EU handles multilingualism. This is a disturbing claim, since Marek also falsely states that in France there are no linguistic minorities, hence "no discrimination between so-called minorities" (for analysis, see Phillipson 2003: 45–7). It is unusual for a government representative to be so openly cynical or to reveal that he thinks that he can ignore universal human rights principles and determine how the EU should operate. It also exemplifies why it is so difficult to form supranational language

12 Toubon later became Minister of Justice, so that the name given to the legislation in France aimed at stemming the tide of the invasion of English in France in 1994 is popularly known as the *Loi Toubon*.

policies on the basis of a mutual understanding of what is at stake and what criteria and principles should be in force.

EU institutions can be considered as in effect practising linguistic apartheid, even if Eurolaw is promulgated in all official languages. Minority languages have no place. Documents for consideration in Member States are often sent in English, and possibly French, rather than in the relevant national language.[13] Full interpretation between all EU languages is only provided for in certain contexts. In the management of EU affairs there is generally a hierarchy of languages, with English now unmistakably at the top and most languages excluded. This development led the *Délégation nationale à la langue française et aux langues de France*, in its Annual Report of 2006 to conclude: "Le français tend à devenir une langue de traduction et non plus de conception" [French is tending to become a language used in translations and no longer in conceptualizing]. In other words, a monolingual culture and mindset within EU institutions affects both content and form.

The Commission's website invariably has all documents in English, fewer in French and far fewer in other languages. The websites of EU presidencies have been criticized by the European ombudsman for using an excessively limited choice of languages.[14] The rotating presidency's websites have typically been only in English, French and the relevant country's language. When some German speakers complained to the ombudsman about this inequality of access, he determined that presidencies were at fault in using such a small set of languages and that the practice should be changed. A follow-up vote in the European Parliament on 20 November 2008 specifying that "the information on the Council Presidency website should ideally be available in all official Community languages" was endorsed by an overwhelming majority. However, the Swedish presidency website in the second half of 2009 was exclusively in English, French and Swedish; thus, the ombudsman's recommendations have been ignored. The EU system fails to live up to the ideals of "respecting" multilingualism that the EU is committed to in principle.

Another example of inequality: When there is communication, spoken or written, between proficient users of English and others with limited competence in English, the communication is asymmetrical, unequal. Often this injustice goes unchallenged, because of the expectation that people can "manage" in English. As a result of many EU texts being written in unclear or incorrect English, and similar problems with French, the translation service has established a service for improving such texts before they are translated.[15] Clearly this use of English, and

13 There is a shortage of empirical documentation of this reality. For relevant research in Sweden, see Melander (2001). The issue is currently being examined in relation to EU links with Germany in the EU-funded Dylan project. Available at: www.dylan-project.org.

14 See the European Ombudsman's press release No. 6/2006.

15 The DG for Translation describes this involvement as the production of "edited originals". Available at: http://ec.europa.eu/dgs/translation/faq/index_en.htm#6.

to a much lesser extent French, reflects inequality and inefficiency, and does not facilitate culturally diverse language use.

Promoting Multilingualism in Member States

So far as the management of multilingualism in Member States is concerned, the EU has produced a series of resolutions and recommendations since the 1990s. There is a covert code – or possibly deliberate obscurity – in such texts. Thus the European Council Resolution *Linguistic Diversity and Multilingualism in the EU* (1995), does not define terms, but "multilingualism" refers here to the acquisition by Europeans of facility in foreign languages. "Linguistic diversity" by contrast refers to regional minority languages with a long history: their importance was stressed in several earlier European Parliament (EP) resolutions and led to funding for the European Bureau of Lesser Used Languages.[16]

The EU Commission has progressively expanded its activities to strengthen multilingualism and linguistic diversity.[17] In *Promoting Language Learning and Linguistic Diversity: An Action Plan 2004–2006*, a range of activities is specified. Support for many languages is stressed, and there are warnings against an exclusive concentration on English in school language learning. There is also a concern about the impact on national languages of a greater use of English as a medium of instruction in higher education. The ambitious *Framework Strategy for Multilingualism* (2005) recommends that Member States undertake the following:

- the learning in education of mother tongue[18] plus two languages
- the formulation of national plans to give coherence and direction to actions to promote multilingualism, significantly including the teaching of migrant languages
- improved teacher training for foreign language learning
- early language learning
- Content and Language Integrated Learning (CLIL), that is, the merging of a foreign language with another school subject
- more study of multilingualism in higher education

16 This EU-funded body played a central role in facilitating links between regional linguistic minority communities, and in the formulation of the Council of Europe's *European Charter for Regional or Minority Languages*. The Bureau closed in 2010, but some of its offshoots are continuing activity, including the Mercator centres in Aberystwyth, Barcelona and Ljouwert/Leeuwarden. Available at: http://www.mercator-research.eu/news/newsletter, and www.eurolang.net.

17 Available at: http://ec.europa.eu/education/policies/lang/languages_en.html.

18 Whether this refers to minority mother tongues or the dominant national language is left unclear.

- introduction of a European Indicator of Language Competence, a Europe-wide language testing scheme
- greater use in language learning of Information Society technologies
- the harnessing of languages to "the multilingual economy".

The regional minority communities such as the Catalans, Friesians and Welsh, are well-represented in the EP. The Parliament's Committee on Culture and Education unanimously recommended a series of measures to strengthen work on language policies.[19] However, when the Framework Strategy was debated in plenary session of the EP, a majority refused to approve this. Essentially this meant that linguistic nationalists schooled in monolingualism did not wish to promote diversity nationally.

From 2007 to 2009 there was a commissioner with a portfolio to promote multilingualism, Leonard Orban from Romania. Most of the commissioner's speeches consisted of platitudinous generalities about support for diversity and language learning, and it is probably in the nature of his role that they have to be. Orban's many speeches all over Europe stressed three interlocking goals:

- promoting the cultural dimension of languages to build inclusive societies and develop intercultural dialogue. I intend to promote the learning of all languages present in the European Union, including the languages of migrants …
- work with business, to help them identify how to build up their language capacities to enter new markets, and to improve job-satisfaction …
- a European space for dialogue with the citizens, to make sure that everyone can communicate with the institutions in their language, that the Community legislation is available to everyone in their languages.[20]

It is, however, doubtful whether "everyone" can be expected to wish or need to read Community legislation, and few citizens are likely to contact an EU institution in any language. Likewise it is doubtful whether the corporate world and educationalists look to the Commission for guidance in these areas.

A report of a High-Level Group on Multilingualism, published on 26 September 2007,[21] analyses many aspects of language policy and makes suggestions for activities to strengthen language learning. The Group's many proposals relate to raising awareness and enhancing motivation for language learning; the potential of the media in evoking, enhancing and sustaining motivation for language learning;

19 EP Report on a new framework for multilingualism, A6-0372/2006, 23 October 2006.

20 From "*Languages are a bridge for intercultural dialogue*", speech, Brussels, 29 June 2007, to The Group of Intellectuals for Intercultural Dialogue.

21 IP/07/1396. Available at: http://ec.europa.eu/education/policies/lang/doc/multireport_en.pdf.

languages for business; interpretation and translation, new trends and needs; regional or minority languages; and research into multilingualism. The key issue is whether EU or government funds materialize for implementing such ideas.

The efforts of the Commission to give language policy a higher profile are consolidated in the "Communication" *Multilingualism: An Asset for Europe and a Shared Commitment* of 18 September 2008. It refers to a number of consultative studies and includes a lengthy rationale for a range of activities. It makes very specific recommendations in each of the three priority concerns identified by the Commission (as in Orban's speech cited earlier), states what it intends to do to strengthen languages in lifelong language learning, teacher education, the use of technology, translation and so forth. It also "invites" Member States to undertake a series of activities to achieve the stated goals. This "invitation" is one that Member States can choose to take up – or ignore. It is thus difficult to imagine that the British will ensure that schoolchildren in the UK develop competence in two foreign languages since most British schoolchildren study one foreign language only, and few continue with it beyond the age of 14. The report on the implementation of the EU's *Action Plan "Promoting language learning and linguistic diversity 2004–2006"* indicates very uneven take-up in Member States, and several countries, among them Denmark, failed to produce a national report.[22]

A feasibility study concerning the creation of a European Agency for Linguistic Diversity and Language Learning was requested by European Parliament, and commissioned by the Directorate General for Education and Culture. The task was given to Yellow Window Associates, a consultancy with wide experience of servicing EU institutions. Their mandate excluded attention to the internal workings of EU institutions and migrant languages. Their report of 18 May 2005 was made available on the DG's website. The detailed 118-page study, on the basis of extensive consultation with a wide range of people concerned with many aspects of language policy, articulates an analysis of needs, conditions and modalities. The report confirms that a wealth of professional expertise exists that decision-makers ought to draw on. It makes a strong case for either a Linguistic Agency, like other high-prestige EU agencies (dealing with the environment in Copenhagen and racism in Vienna), or alternatively a network of Language Diversity Centres to strengthen policy formation and implementation, particularly for regional minority languages. The feasibility study reveals a widespread perception that there is a serious need for policy advice and information for national and EU decision-makers. This was overwhelmingly the case in new Member States, whereas the established ones consider such functions "not useful". The same pattern holds for perceptions of the need for research into language policy issues. There was also near unanimity in responses in rejecting English as a sole *lingua franca*. The study concludes: "A no-action scenario would seriously undermine the credibility of the EU in this field".

---

22 Available at: http://ec.europa.eu/education/languages/archive/policy/report_en.html.

In fact, the Linguistic Agency proposal was rejected unilaterally by the Commission. What it has done is to decide to support the Network on Promoting Linguistic Diversity within the framework of the programme "Integrated Lifelong Learning (2007–13)". However, funding for "regional and minority languages" has been significantly reduced, from 1.2 million euros annually to 149,000 euros annually.[23] This represents a massive downgrading of funding for these languages. Whatever credibility the EU might have gained by creating a portfolio for multilingualism in its own right in 2007 was seriously undermined by no-action on an academy and by reduced action on minority languages.

The EU has supported two cross-national research projects on multilingualism under Framework Programme 6. Languages in a Network of European Excellence[24] has subprojects on Multilingualism and Education, Language Policy and Planning, Language, Identity and Culture, Language and Economy. A second project is DYLAN (Language dynamics and management of diversity),[25] which is analysing links among language policy in EU institutions, the corporate world and educational practices. Both projects have informative websites. Both involve researchers in a considerable number of countries. Both address most of the issues raised in this chapter but have not yet reached a point where conclusions have been finalized or where the implications for EU institutions or national governments are clear.

One example of how a hegemonic status for English is being established, strengthening its position within the Commission and in Member States, can be seen in the way the DG for Research operates. In the "Guide for Applicants" for funding from the Seventh Framework Programme,[26] there is the following advice: "Proposals may be prepared in any official language of the European Union. If your proposal is not in English, a translation of the full proposal would be of assistance to the experts", that is, to those assessing the quality of the proposal for funding. The rhetoric of all EU languages being valid is formally acknowledged,

---

23 *Mercatornews* 33, September 2007, reports: "This new network aims at the strengthening of Regional and Minority Languages throughout Europe has been established on the initiative of the Welsh Language Board in Wales. The Mercator Research Centre is one of the partners of the network alongside with organizations and regional authorities from Wales, Catalonia, Finland (Swedish speakers), Estonia and Ireland. Around half a million euros has been provisioned for the new network for three years – the project partners/regional languages will finance the necessary equity contribution. Until now, in the Action Programme 2004–2006, the Mercator Centres in Ljouwert, Aberysthwyth and Barcelona had received earmarked financial support from the European Commission together with the European Bureau for Lesser Used Languages (EBLUL). As a result of this mainstreaming operation of the European Commission the total sum of EU funding for Regional and Minority Languages has declined from 1.2 million euros annually to 149,000 euros annually".

24 Available at: http://linee.info/linee/home2.html.

25 Available at: www.dylan-project.org.

26 Available at: http://cordis.europa.eu.

but it is clear that applications have to be written in English. Applicants for whom English is not the primary professional language – many in Southern and Eastern Europe and elsewhere – are at a significant structural disadvantage when the application has to be in English. The expert evaluators are drawn from all EU countries, for many of whom English is not the primary working language, even if they are professional researchers. Even if they can "manage" in English, their facility in being able to express themselves optimally in English may be limited, particularly when it comes to formulating the written response in English that all applicants are entitled to, when every word counts. This example of how the EU conducts its affairs reveals clearly that efficiency and linguistic equality are seriously constrained. This discrimination on grounds of language is in conflict with the EU's commitment to "respecting" language diversity. To argue that this way of conducting affairs is necessary for pragmatic or practical reasons is to ignore the reality of those with high-level proficiency in English being favoured.

It is difficult, if not impossible, to assess the impact of all of this EU activity in the language policy field. Some individuals and institutions in Member States have definitely benefited, just as the training of interpreters and translators has also been stimulated by EU funding. However, it seems unlikely that EU policy documents are read by many of those concerned with language in education at all levels in Member States, or by many in the corporate world, whereas presumably they are read by a few civil servants and politicians. Few members of the public are likely to subscribe to the flood of electronic information pouring out of Brussels and EU offices in the capital cities of Member States. The Commission is aware that new communication strategies are needed, if popular perceptions of the utility of the EU are to be changed, but at present the "communication" on offer is fundamentally unidirectional, bureaucratic and unappetizing. The language that characterizes EU texts is banal, homogenized and culturally indistinct, which contributes to the EU's legitimation crisis (Roberts 2006). EU discourses are unable to trigger loyalty or identification that is comparable to the strength of nationalism (Outhwaite 2006). This is true both of the passionate nationalism that extreme right-wing parties draw on and of the banal nationalism that is more latent but equally deeply embedded (Billig 1995) and which the EU has attempted to promote through competitions, prizes, flags and grassroots activities. A fundamental underlying problem is that language policy tends not to have a high priority supranationally or nationally except when major injustices or existential crises force it higher up on political agendas (for examples, see Phillipson 2003: Chapters 1 and 3).

European or Global Integration?

Identification with "Europe" is limited because of widespread ignorance about the EU and uncertainty about whether the project of European integration is leading to a federal United States of Europe (as advocated by Churchill, Monnet, and the US corporate-political elite), or to a "Europe des patries" [Europe of countries] (championed by de Gaulle and British nationalists). The links between the pioneer European architects of what has become the EU and the US political elite, before and after World War II, are detailed in Pascaline Winand's *Eisenhower, Kennedy, and the United States of Europe* (1993). While Monnet and many of the key Europeans were quite open about their wish to create a federal Europe on the model of the United States, the Americans were shrewd enough to influence policies decisively but to remain discreetly in the background for many years. Now there are annual EU-USA summits that coordinate economic and foreign policy.

The EU can be seen as a European integration *project*, involving a range of *processes* and *products* (Morgan 2005), interlocking with the *project* of making English *the dominant language* of the EU, which entails identifiable *processes* and *products.* Any more detailed analysis of the current role of English in Europe would need to see it in terms of *the English language as project, as process and as product* (Phillipson 2009a). Nobody is questioning whether English ought to be optimally learned or not. There is no dispute about the fact that proficiency in English is massively useful in the modern world, and that English serves multiple purposes, some constructive, some benign and some evil. But while English opens doors for some, it closes them for others. This is the case in Europe, just as it is on other continents.

The 2008 *Communication on Multilingualism* refers to an EP Resolution which goes beyond European languages in Europe.[27] It acknowledges "the strategic importance of European World Languages as a communication vehicle and as a means of solidarity, cooperation, and economic investment". The EP recommended that this concept should be "one of the main political guidelines of European policy on multilingualism". The Commission therefore states in the Communication (page 14) that it will:

- develop partnerships and enhance cooperation on multilingualism with non-EU countries, taking account of the opportunities offered by those European languages which have a worldwide coverage
- promote the teaching and learning of all EU languages abroad.

The Member States are invited to:

- further enhance networking and cooperation among relevant institutes to better promote EU languages abroad.

The "institutes" referred to are presumably the bodies concerned with the promotion worldwide of English (British Council), French (Francophonie agencies), German (Goethe Institut), Spanish (Instituto Cervantes) and, to a lesser extent, other languages. Hitherto such promotional activities have been exclusively a national priority which, in the case of France and the UK, has been of major national

27 In footnote 38 of the Communication, the reference is to the EP 2006/2081(INI).

and economic importance. But it is false to state that cooperation between these national concerns can be "further enhanced" when there exists virtually no such cooperation.[28] Is the Commission now going to allocate funds for the dissemination of Bulgarian and Finnish worldwide – when it has done little hitherto to fund familiarization of the languages and cultures of Member States in other Member States? The dominant EU languages, with space on school timetables as foreign languages, and their backers are in competition with each other. Whether the first Foreign Minister of the EU, Baroness Ashton, will act on her right and obligation to strengthen the work of consolidating the power of European languages "abroad", to use these "products" in a project of increasing European influence worldwide, remains to be seen. This part of the Communication looks like yet another example of empty rhetoric that does little to strengthen either the EU's unity or its diversity.

Concluding Reflections

Since English is the *de facto* default in-house language of the Commission, it has become the dominant supranational language. It benefits by structural and ideological preferment. Its users identify with it, whether English is a mother tongue (the British and Irish) or a second language, one that tends to be used more effectively by northern Europeans than others. Its use is accepted as normal, as being "natural", in similar ways to how the dominance of a hegemonic national language is internalized, with speakers of a prestige dialect, the standard language, privileged nationally. European unity is at one level being created by 23 national languages all having some supranational use and legitimacy, though the written form of Eurotexts is of only national rather than supranational significance. At the supranational level, it is English that currently plays a decisive and central role in shaping EU discourses in speech and writing and in how the management and integration of the EU is being undertaken and projected. It is, of course, not the language itself that accounts for its privileged status but rather the users of the language and the interests, commercial and political, that propel the language forward.

In the 2010 Commission, multilingualism has been returned to the education, youth and culture portfolio, in effect downgrading the topic. Even when there was a commissioner with a specific portfolio for multilingualism, the Eurocrat support staff were not specialists in language policy.

An additional factor that limits the extent to which language policy is dealt with effectively in the Commission is that overall responsibility for language policy is fragmented, shared between separate Directorates for Education, Research,

---

28 The USA and the UK have collaborated since the 1950s, but on a small scale. They are also in competition with each other. Occasionally the French were involved; see Phillipson (1992: Chapter 6).

Translation and Interpretation. The EU translation and interpretation services are impressive in many respects, but they are detached from international research and subject to an economic rationale, seeing themselves essentially as a service function rather than policy-making (Phillipson 2003: Chapter 4). Ultimately, language policy is an intergovernmental responsibility that only occasionally rears its head in the Council of Ministers.

The weakness of the EU's language policy infrastructure dovetails with the fact that in the ministries of most Member States there is also limited competence. There are well-qualified civil servants in language policy in some countries, such as Finland, Ireland and the regional governments of the Basque country and Catalonia in Spain, but these are the exception.

There is a modest amount of coordination among national language bodies (for the Danish language, German, Spanish and so forth), but this international collaboration is in its infancy (Stickel 2009). Typically the institutions in question are concerned with the purity of the national language domestically (Dansk Sprognævn, Institut für Deutsche Sprache, and so forth) and not multilingualism or education. The processes for dialogue among scholars, interest groups and policy-makers, nationally and internationally, are therefore fragile. The research community is small and scattered, and while there are a few distinguished language policy specialists, most social scientists working on European integration ignore language issues. Analysis and recommendations in book form by scholars for taking EU language policy issues forward (Grin 2003, Phillipson 2003, Kraus 2008) – the complexity of the issues requires book-length treatment, whereas a short chapter can only take up a selection of issues – seem to be ignored by politicians and Eurocrats. Efforts to get language policy higher up on political agendas by governments (for instance, a well-prepared approach by Slovakia in 2007) come to nothing.

The upbeat nature of many of the recommendations from the Commission contrasts with many symptoms of crisis in language policy in Europe, such as foreign languages other than English being learned less, the strengthening of English in the Bologna process that is integrating higher education and research (essentially all key policy statements seem to equate "internationalization" with "English-medium higher education", Phillipson 2006, 2009b) and in the internal management of multilingualism in EU institutions. Translators and interpreters for demographically "small" languages like Danish and Swedish, as well as the Baltic and Central European languages, are convinced that their languages are being treated as second-class. Languages that were earlier suppressed by Soviet occupation have special needs but are at the mercy of market forces and not protected by international charters (Druviete 2009). There is a conflict between the EU rhetoric of supporting all languages and the realities of linguistic hierarchies and marginalization (Phillipson 2009c).

How could some of these problems be resolved? There is manifestly a need for the professional expertise in language policy to be drawn on, as was recognized in the Europe-wide Linguistic Agency consultation referred to earlier. However, criteria for guiding equitable supranational language policy are relatively underexplored. Alternatives to market forces (the comparative advantage of English in the European linguistic market) and to linguistic nationalism (such as the use of Esperanto for restricted bridging purposes internally in the EU, or in education) have not been subjected to analytical scrutiny except in the work of a few scholars (for example, Grin 2005). In my book (Phillipson 2003), one chapter is devoted to analysing how equitable communication could be ordered more effectively. It draws on the experience of countries that have taken language policy issues seriously (Australia, Canada, post-apartheid South Africa), which entailed identifying the goals and assumptions of language policy. The book also has brief coverage of economics and language, a subfield of language policy that has produced many relevant insights. It is also important to distinguish between language rights and linguistic human rights, which is an evolving multidisciplinary field, mainly drawing on sociolinguistics and human rights law (Skutnabb-Kangas and Phillipson 1994). International law tends not to create positive obligations on states in this area (de Varennes 1999), and provides weak protection for minorities (Thornberry 1997). The education that indigenous peoples have been subjected to worldwide, exclusively in a dominant state language, has been explored within the framework of the UN Permanent Forum on Indigenous Issues, including analysis of whether this education can be considered as linguistic genocide and a crime against humanity (Skutnabb-Kangas and Dunbar 2010). The EU's commitment to "respecting" all languages in the Union, which implies linguistic equality, can potentially serve to strengthen the language rights of minority groups and of speakers of EU languages who sense that their languages are not being fully respected.

The final chapter of Phillipson 2003 sketches out best- and worst-case scenarios and makes 45 specific recommendations for what could be done to improve matters. They are grouped in four sections: national and supranational language policy infrastructure; EU institutions; language teaching and learning; and research. Very few of these ideas have been implemented: The Directorate General for Education has funded some useful research on language learning and teacher training and operates a number of schemes that aim at strengthening language learning in schools. In 2009, the DG for Research, in Framework Programme 7, solicited projects on "Vehicular languages in Europe in an era of globalization: history, policy, practice", including *lingua franca*, and commissioned one cross-national study. Alas, the budget size for research in the social sciences and humanities is modest as compared with other fields, and the competition for funding is fierce.

Language policy will only acquire a higher profile if policies that ensure a healthy balance between English and other languages are elaborated and implemented. The governments of the Nordic countries are committed to maintaining the vitality of national languages while promoting competence in international languages, particularly English. A Declaration on a Nordic Language Policy was approved in 2006 by the Nordic Council of Ministers, and promulgated in Danish, Faeroese, Greenlandic, Finnish, Icelandic, Norwegian, Saami, Swedish and English.[29] The document specifies the language rights of all residents in a Nordic country and sets out goals for language policy. It encourages key institutions to develop long-range strategies for choice of language, the parallel use of languages and language instruction. Implementation of the many recommendations has yet to be undertaken. However, since this is the first time that government-level language policy in this area has been made explicit, it is positive that language policy is not merely being left to market forces. The underlying thinking is both/and rather than either/or: not a focus on a single medium of instruction (an English-medium or local language-medium school or university) but a combination.

Europe-wide language policy could draw inspiration from such policy initiatives. They have evolved in the Nordic countries as a result of addressing rather than ignoring the real tensions among a dominant national language, the rights of minority languages and an invasive international language. There are comparable tensions at the supranational level as well as within all Member States. A study of the way the tensions between English and French in Canada have been addressed and choreographed can be useful in seeking to come to grips with the tension in Europe between, on the one hand, linguistic nationalism, national interests and rights, and on the other, the patterns of supranational language use and hierarchy.

> In this complex and often contradictory set of relations, language policy plays a greater and greater role. Not only is this the terrain on which borders are constructed, it is also the terrain on which tensions are neutralized, ambiguities constructed, contradictions masked. It is through language that the ideologies of nation and state are produced and reproduced. The Canadian federal government seeks to legitimize itself as the representative of all Canadians by promoting linguistic pluralism, while at the same time it seeks to construct some unifying symbols. To do so requires addressing the real social inequalities that obtain among ethnolinguistic groups, although too often the state opts instead for the discursive construction of a fictive equality (Heller 1999: 167).

The alternative is *laissez faire*, and why should something as important as language policy be left to market forces? The human rights system and the articulation of the fundamental rights of the EU are intended to assure that this does not happen. But is there agreement and unity on how the EU's linguistic diversity can be maintained?

29 Available at: www.norden.org.

References

Ammon, U. 2006. Language Conflicts in the European Union: On Finding a Politically Acceptable and Practicable Solution for EU Institutions that Satisfies Diverging Interests. *International Journal of Applied Linguistics*, 16(3), 319–38.

Ammon, U. 2009. Über die Dilemmata jeglicher EU-Sprachenpolitik, in *National and European Language Policies: Contributions to the Annual Conference 2008 of EFNIL in Riga*, edited by G. Stickel. Bern: Peter Lang Verlag, 19–34.

Billig, M. 1995. *Banal Nationalism*. London: Sage.

Blommaert, J. (ed.) 1999. *Language Ideological Debates*. Berlin: Mouton de Gruyter.

Délégation générale à la langue française et aux langues de France. 2007. *Les politiques des langues en Europe*. Paris: Ministère des Affaires étrangères et européennes.

De Varennes, F. 1999. The Existing Rights of Minorities in International Law, in *Language: A Right and a Resource – Approaching Linguistic Human Rights*, edited by M. Kontra, R. Phillipson, T. Skutnabb-Kangas and T. Várady. Budapest: Central European University Press, 117–46.

Druviete, I. 2009. The Latvian Language: Official Language of the Republic of Latvia and Official Language of the European Union, in *National and European Language Policies. Contributions to the Annual Conference 2008 of EFNIL in Riga*, edited by G. Stickel. Bern: Peter Lang Verlag, 79–85.

Gazzola, M. 2006. Managing Multilingualism in the European Union: Language Policy Evaluation for the European Parliament. *Language Policy* 5, 393–417.

Grin, F. 2003. *Language Policy Evaluation and the European Charter for Regional or Minority Languages*. Basingstoke: Palgrave Macmillan.

Grin, F. 2005. *L'enseignement des langues étrangères comme politique publique*. Rapport au Haut Conseil de l'évaluation de l'école (n° 19), Ministère de l'éducation nationale, Paris. [Online]. Available at: http://cisad.adc.education.fr/hcee/documents/rapport_Grin.pdf.

Heller, M. 1999. Heated Language in a Cold Climate, in *Language Ideological Debates*, edited by J. Blommaert. Berlin: Mouton de Gruyter, 143–70.

Kraus, P.A. 2008. *A Union of Diversity: Language, Identity and Polity-Building in Europe*. Cambridge: Cambridge University Press.

Melander, B. 2001. Swedish, English and the European Union, in *Managing Multilingualism in a European Nation-State: Challenges for Sweden*, edited by S. Boyd and L. Huss. Clevedon: Multilingual Matters, 13–31.

Morgan, G. 2005. *The Idea of a European Super-State: Public Justification and European Integration*. Princeton, NJ: Princeton University Press.

Ó'Riain, S. 2009. Irish and Scottish Gaelic: A European Perspective. *Language Problems and Language Planning*, 33(1), 43–59.

Outhwaite, W. 2006. Is there a European Civil Society?, in *The Shape of the New Europe*, edited by R. Rogowski and C. Turner. Cambridge: Cambridge University Press, 87–103.

Phillipson, R. 1992. *Linguistic Imperialism*. Oxford: Oxford University Press.

Phillipson, R. 2003. *English-Only Europe? Challenging Language Policy*. London: Routledge.

Phillipson, R. 2006. English: A Cuckoo in the European Higher Education Nest of Languages? *European Journal of English Studies*, 10(1), 13–32.

Phillipson, R. 2009a. *Linguistic Imperialism Continued*. New York and London: Routledge.

Phillipson, R. 2009b. English in Higher Education, Panacea or Pandemic?, in *English in Denmark: Language Policy, Internationalization and University Teaching*, Vol. 9 of *Angles of the English-Speaking World*, edited by P. Harder. Copenhagen: Museum Tusculanum Press and the University of Copenhagen, 29–57.

Phillipson, R. 2009c. Is There Any *Unity in Diversity* in Language Policies National and Supranational? English as an EU *Lingua Franca* or *Lingua Frankensteinia?*, in *National and European Language Policies: Contributions to the Annual Conference 2008 of EFNIL in Riga*, edited by G. Stickel. Bern: Peter Lang, 145–54.

Roberts, R.H. 2006. Gaia and Europa: Religion and Legitimation Crisis in the "New Europe", in *The Shape of the New Europe*, edited by R. Rogowski and C. Turner. Cambridge: Cambridge University Press, 146–66.

Rogowski, R. and Turner, C. (eds) 2006. *The Shape of the New Europe*. Cambridge: Cambridge University Press.

Schiffman, H. 2006. Language policy and Linguistic Culture, in *An Introduction to Language Policy: Theory and Method*, edited by T. Ricento. Malden, MA and Oxford: Blackwell, 111–25.

Skutnabb-Kangas, T. and Dunbar, R. 2010. *Indigenous Children's Education as Linguistic Genocide and a Crime Against Humanity? A Global View*. Guovdageaidnu/Kautokeino: Galdu, Resource Centre for the Rights of Indigenous Peoples. [Online]. Available at: http://www.galdu.org.

Skutnabb-Kangas, T. and Phillipson, R. (eds) 1994. *Linguistic Human Rights: Overcoming Linguistic Discrimination*. Berlin: Mouton de Gruyter.

Stickel, G. (ed.) 2009. *National and European Language Policies. Contributions to the Annual Conference 2008 of EFNIL in Riga*. Bern: Peter Lang.

Thornberry, P. 1997. Minority Rights, in *Collected Courses of the Academy of European Law*, VI, 2, edited by Academy of European Law. The Netherlands: Kluwer Law International, 307–90.

Van Els, T. 2005. Multilingualism in the European Union. *International Journal of Applied Linguistics*, 15(3), 263–81.

Winand, P. 1993. *Eisenhower, Kennedy, and the United States of Europe*. The Franklin and Eleanor Roosevelt Institute Series on Diplomatic and Economic History, Vol. 6. New York: St. Martin's Press.

Wright, S. 2000. *Community and Communication: The Role of Language in Nation State Building and European Integration*. Clevedon: Multilingual Matters.

Chapter 5
Getting Ready for a New Tower of Babel

Magali Gravier and Lita Lundquist

Introduction

What if multilingualism were not a curse but a challenge? What if it were a potential asset and a stubborn reminder of the fact that pluralism is essential to the survival of democracies (Sartori 1976: 12–25) as well as what mankind, fundamentally, is about: a collection of groups of individuals who think, act and speak in different ways? Of course, if one focuses on the question of languages, one can argue that, five centuries after Columbus' discovery of the American continent, the linguistic diversity of this continent has been reduced to four state languages: two in North America – English and French – and two in South America – Spanish and Portuguese. But, opposite to this trend, Europeans have struggled through the centuries to keep their linguistic diversity. On the whole, the number of languages spoken on the European continent has certainly dropped. Many languages have disappeared, and some European states have even managed to impose an almost perfect linguistic unity on their territory: English in the UK, German in Germany, French in France or Italian in Italy. Some states even share the same official language.[1] But none of the imperial experiments has led to a reduction of the number of languages below a certain threshold, and many states have not been able or simply not willing to do so: Spain counts one national official language and four official regional languages,[2] Switzerland has four languages,[3] Belgium three,[4] Finland, Ireland and Norway two,[5] plus the so-called "minority languages" spoken throughout Europe. This historical reality reflects the fact that Europeans have always been and still are attached to their linguistic diversity. It is part of their collective identity. This is the reason why the European project,

1 For instance, English is spoken in the UK and Ireland; French in France, Belgium, Switzerland and Luxemburg; German in Germany, Austria, Switzerland, Belgium and Luxemburg, and Swedish in Sweden and Finland.

2 Castilian, which all Spanish citizens are expected to speak, and Catalan, Galician, Basque or Aranese, according to the "autonomous communities" (*comunidades autónomas*).

3 German, French, Italian and Romansh.

4 Dutch, French and German.

5 Finish and Swedish in Finland, English and Irish in Ireland and Norwegian Bokmål and Norwegian Nynorsk in Norway.

which initially ignored the linguistic dimension, rapidly decided to take it into account.[6] Later on, not only were the Treaties of Rome establishing the EEC and the Euratom written in the then four official languages (Dutch, French, German and Italian), but also the very first regulations voted by each of their Councils[7] were dedicated to the linguistic regime of these two Communities. Together with the Euratom's Regulation No.1, the EEC's Regulation No.1, sometimes referred to as the "Charter of languages of the EU" (De Cillia 2003: 237) introduced for the first time the notion of "official language" (and of "working language") and posed the principle of multilingualism in the European integration project. If the successive enlargements of the EC/EU have challenged this principle, it has been defended each time on the basis that it is a "founding principle of the European project" (Kinnock 2002: 2). Article 2 of this regulation granted citizens and residents of the then Member States[8] the possibility to write to the institutions of the Communities in the official language of their choice and to receive an answer in the same language. Whether the regulation granted a *right* in the legal sense of the word was debatable since the phrasing was not explicit.

In 1970, the court decided[9] that if the Commission had not followed Article 3 of this same regulation[10] when writing to a citizen of a Member State, it did constitute an irregularity, but since the person had understood the content of the document sent by the Commission, the infringement to the regulation had not caused a prejudice and therefore the validity of the document was not affected. In deciding that the regulation could be ignored if not respecting it didn't cause a prejudice, the court seemed to consider that the regulation did not establish "hard" language rights, but merely principles. The decision seems unsatisfactory from a legal point of view (Milian i Massana 2002) and probably reflects a low level of language consciousness at that time. With the incorporation of Article 2 of Regulation 1 in the Treaty of Maastricht in 1992, the discussion about the

6 The Treaty of Paris, founding the European Coal and Steel Community, was signed on 18 April 1951 and entered into force on 24 July 1952. Its very last Article, Article 100, specified that the Treaty was written in only one copy, which happened to be in French. However, the six Member States decided during a two-day conference starting on 23 July 1952 that the four national languages of the Member States of the first European Community would all be official languages (Monnet 1976: 432–4).

7 *Official Journal*, No. 17, 6 October 1958, 385–6 and 401–2.

8 Article 2 reads: "Documents which a Member State or a person subject to the jurisdiction of a Member State sends to institutions of the Community may be drafted in any one of the official languages selected by the sender. The reply shall be drafted in the same language".

9 ACF Chemiefarma vs. Commission, 15 July 1970, case 41–69, *European Court Reports*, 1970, 661.

10 Article 3 reads: "Documents which an institution of the Community sends to a Member State or to a person subject to the jurisdiction of a Member State shall be drafted in the language of such State".

legal nature of this disposition was closed. Today, Article 24 of the TFEU[11] guarantees European citizens the right to write to the European institutions in the official language of their choice and to receive an answer in this same language.[12] Concretely, this means that a Danish citizen has the right to write in Danish to, for instance, the Commission and to receive an answer in Danish. This is quite demanding for the EU given the fact that it now counts 23 official languages for 27 Member States. This is much more than any other international organization. The United Nations, for instance, counts 192 member countries but has only six official languages (Arabic, Mandarin-Chinese, English, French, Spanish and Russian).

In order to live up to its self-imposed challenge of multilingualism, the EU has progressively elaborated a language policy, referred to as "multilingualism policy", aimed at promoting and ensuring as much as possible the effectiveness of this principle, even if considerations of pragmatism and efficiency sometimes lead to a certain inequality of treatment among languages (Nic Shuibhne 2004). Today, the EU's multilingualism policy, based on the 2005 "New Framework Strategy for Multilingualism" follows three goals: "to encourage language learning and promote linguistic diversity in society; to promote a healthy multilingual economy; to give citizens access to EU legislation, procedures and information in their own languages" (Commission 2005). The measures contributing to their achievement can be grouped in three categories: the staffing policy ensuring multilingualism within the institutions, the "Barcelona objective" promoting trilingualism among the citizens and within the "European society" and the interface between citizens and institutions, one of the most ambitious policies of translation and interpretation known in the world.

As will be shown later, the principle of multilingualism implies a set of logistic and financial constraints. Given this, and in addition, the argument of legal security and equality of rights (Milian i Massana 1995: 2002), one may want to ask why this principle was maintained and even developed. The theory of representative bureaucracy (Kingsley 1944, Mosher 1982, Meier 1993) which underlies loosely this chapter, focuses on the idea that a bureaucracy that looks like the population it administers is more likely to foster acceptance from this very population than one which does not because citizens tend to trust the decisions taken by civil servants who are like them ethnically, religiously, linguistically and so on. This is called "passive representation". Further, when pluralistic public administrations have a sufficient degree of autonomy in decision-making, they are expected to be less unfair towards minority groups than public administrations recruited mainly among members of one same social group or gender. This is called "active representation". According to the theory, both passive and active bureaucratic

11 Treaty on the Functioning of the European Union.

12 The phrasing has remained almost identical and still concerns only written communication: "Every citizen of the Union may write to any of the institutions, bodies, offices or agencies referred to in this Article or in Article 13 of the Treaty on European Union in one of the languages mentioned in Article 55(1) of the Treaty on European Union and have an answer in the same language".

representativeness can contribute to increase the legitimacy of a given political system and improve the quality of its democracy. This theory has been used to develop strategic recruitment measures known as *positive discrimination*. In the United States, for instance, Afro-American police officers have been recruited in areas with strong Afro-American minorities. In other countries, public institutions have developed staffing policies aiming at increasing the number of women in their staff. From a certain point of view, the EU's language policy offers another example of strategic representation (Gravier 2008b).

The theory of representative bureaucracy has another cognitive-cultural dimension. Its principle of representing ethnic, cultural or social groups, which in the European context amounts to representing different Member States and their languages, goes hand in hand with the linguistic-cognitive idea that language is not just a means of communication but just as much a means of conceptualizing and forming the mentality of their speakers. Since each language – via its symbolic units of words, concepts, grammatical organization and so on – subdivides the world in a specific way, it contributes to structuring the world of its speakers. Growing up in different language communities, speakers of different languages do not conceptualize reality in the same way and hence do not think, react and interact in the same way. This idea was promoted in modern times by W. von Humboldt (1822/24), and later formed the backbone of the so-called Sapir-Whorf hypothesis (Sapir 1929, Whorf 1942), stating that thought is a function of language. In a broader perspective, language also defines our ways of reasoning and of conceiving the sociocultural universe in which we evolve, what in more modern terms is expressed by the word *cognition*.

The multilingualism policy of the EU gains new importance in this perspective. Mastering several languages has not only an instrumental goal, but just as much a cultural human goal of mutual understanding and acceptance, which in itself is of primordial importance for the legitimatizing of the European idea. The multilingualism policy adopted, however, raises questions as to how many languages one can – and should – learn, whether there are methods which help increase the efficiency of the language learning process and in the last instance, whether multilingual polities are utopian or can really work. In order to answer some of these questions, the chapter will progress from the description of the EU's policy framework and its implications in terms of legitimacy and democracy to a linguistic analysis of language learning, a presentation of some language programs of the EU and some examples and suggestions showing how the findings of linguistics can be used to increase the likelihood of the EU's multilingualism policy to become reality one day.

Multilingualism within the European Institutions

At the very origin of the European project lay the idea that the Member States of the Community had to learn to cooperate so as to achieve the common goal they had agreed upon: peace and prosperity on the European continent. This required a strict equality between the two former rivals – France and Germany – and a fair integration of the other Member States (Monnet 1976: 413–14). During this initial phase, multilingualism was meant to trigger acceptance from the Member States and was a necessary element of the working culture of a handful of pioneers. In the eyes of the Founding Fathers, recruiting staff according to the level of excellence regardless of nationality – which meant recruiting from *all* Member States, in order to increase the chances of getting the best staff – and giving the languages of the Member States an equal status – which meant working in *all* languages spoken by the staff – appeared self-evident. They even spoke in English when it was the only possible language, even though this was not an official language at the time, since the UK was not yet a Member State (Monnet 1976). Multilingualism, which immediately became a fundamental characteristic of the European institutions as a professional environment, was integrated later on in the Staff Regulation.

Today, two major sets of rules ensure multilingualism inside the institutions. First of all, recruiting according to merit and geographical balance leads to a multinational staff coming from each of the 27 Member States (Gravier 2008a). With each of the nationalities coming with its own language(s), this strategy results automatically in a multilingual staff. But this is not enough: If everybody can speak only his or her language, communication will not work. Therefore, a second set of rules for recruitment and promotion imposes three linguistic requirements on EU civil servants. The first requirement is that, in order to be recruited, applicants must speak two languages of the EU well enough to be able to work in these two languages. For this purpose, the recruitment procedure (the so-called *concours*) takes place in two languages. According to present rules, while the first language can be any of the 23 official languages, the second language must be one of the "working" languages of the EU, that is, English, French or German. Between 2003 and 2008, the five most frequent first languages were French (16.8 per cent), Italian (10.7 per cent), Polish (8.7 per cent), Rumanian (7.9 per cent) and English (7.6 per cent). All together, they represented 51.7 per cent of the first languages chosen for the *concours*. During that same period, more than two-thirds of the applicants chose English as second language. The second important linguistic requirement, introduced in 2004, conditions the very first promotion after recruitment by the proof of a sufficient level in a third language. While this language can be chosen freely among the 23 official languages, in 2008, the three working languages represented 63 per cent of the choices, and the five most chosen languages 81 per cent of the choices (French 32 per cent; English 19 per cent; German 12 per cent; Spanish, 10 per cent and Italian 8 per cent), reflecting a well-known inequality in practice among EU languages.[13]

13 In fact, for Milian i Massana (1995: 2002), the inequality among EU languages is not just the result of practice; it is also the result of the complex linguistic regime, which introduces a *de jure* hierarchy among languages. The inequality increases even more if one takes regional languages into account.

Indeed, the most chosen languages are those of the biggest Member States, but they are also – and maybe above all – languages spoken worldwide. This explains most probably the fact that Spanish is chosen more often than Italian and that German is much less frequently chosen than French or English, though it is the EU language counting the most native speakers. The third important linguistic requirement concerns the so-called "linguists" (that is, translators, interpreters and linguist-lawyers) who build an exception among the EU officials: They must prove their proficiency in three languages already at the stage of recruitment.[14]

The idea behind these rules is to mirror the linguistic diversity of the EU population within the European institutions. In some states composed of several linguistic groups, like Canada or Belgium, federal civil servants can be asked, for certain positions, to speak all official languages of the federal administration: English and French in Canada or Dutch and French in Belgium.[15] In these two examples, the central administration represents the diversity of the population by employing staff speaking all official administrative languages. This effort is possible because only two languages are at stake. Since it is impossible to ask one person to speak 23 languages, the EU had to develop a different strategy. Instead of mirroring the composition of the population at the level of the individual civil servants, an overall mirroring is reached at the level of the institutions by asking each civil servant to contribute a little bit to the multilingual effort. This "little bit" is nonetheless more ambitious than in the two cases mentioned since the EU requires three languages from each of its officials.

In practice, however, the use of languages varies from institution to institution and within a given institution, from unit to unit as well as from working context to working context. Some institutions, like the Court of Justice, or some policy areas, like the Common Foreign and Security Policy (CFSP), have their own linguistic regime.[16] At the Commission, some General Directorates (DG) have their own tradition: While English is spoken in an increasing number of DGs, French still is the dominant language in the DG Human Resources and Security. Further, in most institutions, during internal working sessions, the number of languages is often reduced to one, two or three languages. This strategy is chosen in order to enable direct communication among the officials without interpreters. The choice of the language(s) depends on the participants, but it is usually one of the working languages, predominantly English. Conversely, the use of all 23 official languages is reserved to contexts that are meant to be public. Even so, this can only work with the help of a particularly impressive capacity of translation and interpretation, which the European institutions have developed through the years.

14 The statistics mentioned in this paragraph are drawn from Gravier 2008b.

15 Though Belgium has three official languages, there are only two linguistic groups when it comes to administrative purposes.

16 For the Court of Justice: Article 342 of the TFEU and Articles 29–31 of the Rules of Procedure of the Court of Justice; for the CFSP: "Declaration on the use of languages in the field of the common foreign and security policy", *Official Journal*, C 191, 29.7.1992, 104.

Linking Institutions to Citizens: The EU, the World's Biggest Translation and Interpretation Agency

With their 23 official languages, the European institutions must be able to manage some 506 linguistic combinations both for translation and for interpretation: Each of the 23 languages must be transposed in the 22 other languages. Quite logically, this requires the recruitment of a sufficient number of translators and interpreters. In 2008, around 10 per cent of the permanent staff of the Commission were translators (about three-quarters of them) and interpreters (about one-quarter). They worked in two different DGs: the DG Translation and the DG Interpretation. In 2007, the DG Translation provided the translation of some 1.76 million pages. The DG Interpretation provides yearly interpreters for around 11,000 meetings. This represents a huge volume; however, the EU has managed to keep the cost of these activities at a somewhat reasonable level. Today, the total cost of translation and interpretation, for all institutions, is estimated around 1.1 billion euros. This represents less than 1 per cent of the budget of the EU, or 2.50 euros per citizen yearly. Keeping costs under control after the 2004 and 2007 enlargements was a big challenge since the number of languages increased from 11 official languages to 23.[17] This was only possible through the development of cost-saving techniques like the use of "relay languages", so-called "bipolar" or "tripolar" translations,[18] the use of specialized software, interfaces and data bases (Poetry, DGTVista, Eur-Lex, IATE, Euramis and others) and relying on an increased number of external translators. In 2007, about one-fourth of the translations were made by external staff.

One should also stress that not all documents are translated. The broad principles for deciding which texts should be translated into all languages, which ones only into a limited number of languages and which ones are not translated at all depend on the type of text and the addressees of the text. For instance, the so-called *acquis communautaire*, comprising some 90,000 pages of treaties, laws, resolutions, declarations and decisions of the Court of Justice, and international

17 Though Irish had always been a "treaty language", that is, a language in which all the treaties but only the treaties were translated, it only became an official language on 1 January 2007.

18 A translation using a *relay-language* is, for instance, a translation for which a first translator translates from one language – e.g., Hungarian – to another language – usually English or French – and a second translator translates this translation into the intended target language(s) – e.g., Irish and Italian. One speaks of *bipolar translation* when a translator translates in a language that is not her/his mother tongue, for instance, a Dane translating not only Czech in Danish but also Danish in Czech. A *tripolar translation* is when a translator translates one language in another, none of which are his or her mother tongues, for instance a German translating a text from Polish to Spanish. These techniques are certainly cost saving (they reduce both the number of linguistic combinations and of translators), but they are said to reduce the quality of translation and are therefore criticized by some officials.

agreements, must be translated into all official languages. In the case of a new Member State, they must be translated at the latest on the day of accession. The same goes for documents destined to inform the broader public (such as booklets on the EU, its institutions or its policies and the website EUROPA). According to the topics, some documents, like press releases, are either translated into all languages, into a reduced number of languages or into one, two or three of the three working languages. Internal documents tend to be translated only into the working languages – if at all.

The reason why the EU has steadily developed its translation and interpretation policy is clearly political. EU decision-makers are aware that languages matter, that they are stark vehicles of identity and that if they alone cannot provide the EU with all the legitimacy it needs, the EU cannot do without the legitimacy they bring. In fact, this policy fosters two models of democracy – representative and direct. The DG Interpretation stands on the side of representative democracy. As the DG says on its website: "The citizens of Europe should not have to be represented in Brussels by their best linguists: they can send their best experts".[19] This formulation is not just symbolically very strong, it also points out a very concrete challenge of multilingual polities. If one can expect a civil servant who is going to spend his or her entire career working for an EU institution to invest in learning two foreign languages, it is much more difficult to expect members of the European Parliament (MEPs) to learn two foreign languages. The time it takes to learn them well enough to be able to work in these languages would take longer than the period for which an MEP is elected.[20] The same goes for experts who take part in meetings, conferences and events because of their competence, whether they can speak foreign languages or not. But even if they speak (at least) three languages, EU officials may need now and then to communicate with interlocutors who do not speak one of the languages they speak. The mission of the DG Interpretation is to solve these problems of communication by providing interpretation services. This activity can be said to sustain representative democracy because it enables the work of MEPs, EU and national officials, experts and representatives of sectored interests, who might take part in the preparation of legislation and policies.

Much bigger than the DG Interpretation, the DG Translation can be considered sustaining direct and representative democracy since the addressees of its translations are both institutional actors (representative democracy) and EU citizens (direct democracy). The website of this DG also reveals an explicit

---

19 Available at: http://scic.ec.europa.eu/europa/jcms/c_6636/what-we-do.

20 According to the psycholinguist U. Ammon, it takes some 10,000 learning hours to acquire a sufficient level in English to be able to participate in scientific conferences and for publication purposes. One can certainly be operational in a language with a lower degree of command than that indicated by Ammon, and the learning time also depends on the learner's ability, the number of languages this learner already speaks, as well as the family of language (s)he already speaks and is trying to learn. But Ammon's estimation indicates clearly that a language cannot be learned in 20 lessons.

political strategy. Indeed, one can read the following justification of the DG's activities: "for reasons of public service, openness and democratic legitimacy, the EU must be able to interact with Europeans in any of these languages".[21] Of course, the very notion of "direct democracy" is not mentioned in this quotation, only that of "democratic legitimacy" and the idea of "interaction". In practice, the translations produced by the DG Translation provide European citizens with a *direct* access to information. In a multilingual polity, such a direct access does not just imply disclosing relevant information to the citizens who ask for it but doing so in a language they understand. This access is a key to enlightened analyses and decisions, which, in turn, are a precondition for a direct democracy. This is all the more important in the context of the Lisbon Treaty, which has introduced the right to citizen's initiatives.[22] However, these efforts to improve the quality of the EU's democracy and the EU's legitimacy cannot be limited to the internal life of the institutions and the vertical relation between them and the citizens. Communication and exchanges must be possible also horizontally, that is, between citizens without the intervention of the EU institutions, for instance, to increase transborder economic activities and foster the development of a civil society. This is where the third facet of the EU's multilingualism policy comes in play.

Between the Language Policies of the EU and of the Member States: The Slow Birth of a Trilingual European Society

In standard political theory and EU studies, the EU's legitimacy and quality of democracy is assessed through the lenses of political participation, and, as Scharpf (1999) coined it, of input democracy and output democracy.[23] However, the question of legitimacy, as well as the quality of a democracy, can also be affected by the possibility offered to citizens to interact with one another (which is a precondition to the existence of a *demos*), as well as the well-being of the people, which depends in part on successful economic exchanges and on the capacity of a polity to guarantee the conditions for such economic exchanges. A high linguistic diversity prevents people from communicating with one another, and is therefore an obstacle to these exchanges. The last facet of the EU's multilingualism policy – the Barcelona objective – aims precisely at finding a solution to this huge challenge.

21 The DG Translation translates in the 23 official languages of the EU and, occasionally, in a few others. Available at: http://ec.europa.eu/dgs/translation/whoweare/mission/index_en.htm.

22 Articles 11 of the TEU and 24 of the TFEU.

23 Input legitimacy refers to the principles of democratic participation, representation and accountability while output legitimacy refers to what the political system delivers and whether or not this meets the citizens' expectations.

During the European Council held in Barcelona in March 2002, the Member States decided that the EU citizens should be taught "at least two foreign languages from a very early age" (Council 2002). Together with other goals, trilingualism was meant to "improve the mastery of basic skills", which was itself considered a necessary step in order for the EU to become a competitive knowledge-based economy (Council 2002). In other words, trilingualism was to become part of the Lisbon strategy. The decision to promote trilingualism was also taken in order to avoid the development of a *lingua franca* within the EU, which would have inescapably been English (Commission 2003). This perspective was not acceptable for a wide number of Member States that shared the opinion that "English alone is not enough" (Commission 2003). As far as policy instruments are concerned, the Barcelona objective did not lead to a transfer of new competences to the Commission. In other words and "according to the subsidiarity principle, Member States are key decision-makers on these matters" (Commission 2008a). In the absence of formal competences, the main policy tools the Commission has recommended are, on the one hand, the use of recommendations and of the Open Method of Coordination as a means of coordination among the Member States and, on the other, "mainstreaming multilingualism in current EU programmes and initiatives" (Commission 2008a). Actually, these tools apply not just to the Barcelona objective but, more broadly, to the overall multilingualism policy. Concretely, they mean that if the Commission chooses to be proactive and even paves the way for the Member States, it has no choice but to rely on the good will of the Member States that do not always live up to the goals they have agreed upon themselves. But the EU also supports multilingualism by means of important and already existing financial programs within general and professional education and culture, for example, the Socrates and Leonardo da Vinci programs, which with an investment of more than 30 million euros yearly have financed a series of language projects, such as continuing vocational training, partnerships, the development of e-learning programs and specific inter-comprehension language courses (see below). These programs have helped several thousand people acquire new or enhancing existing language competences.

In 2006, the Commission established a High Level Group on Multilingualism in order to consider the links between languages and research, between languages and the media, languages for business, the use of new technologies for translation and interpretation and strategies to promote language learning. In 2007, it created a new portfolio for Multilingualism,[24] with the aim of improving the EU citizen's ability to communicate in several languages. In fact, the Commission considers that multilingualism "enhances creativity, breaks cultural stereotypes, encourages thinking "outside the box"", which is in nice concordance with the cognitive-cultural perspective of languages each creating its "box" whereas access to the others' language means access to and understanding the others' "boxes" and cultures,

24 In the new Commission appointed in 2010, it was integrated to a broader portfolio for Education, Culture, Multilingualism and Youth.

thus preventing cultural stereotypes. Multilingualism helps "develop innovative products and services" and is "good for individuals, business and competitiveness. By extension, it is crucial for achieving the over-arching policy aim for the European Union: the Lisbon strategy to create more jobs and growth".[25]

More recently (July 2008), the Commission, following the Council's first ministerial conference on multilingualism (February 2008), adopted a renewed Social Agenda, setting up a new approach to managing change in our globalizing world, stating, among other things, that "everybody should have access to appropriate language training or to other means of facilitating communication so that there is no undue linguistic obstacle to living, working or communicating in the EU" (Commission 2008b). It stresses that the answer should be the ability to communicate in one's mother tongue plus two languages, but it also "invites Member States and the other EU institutions to endorse the cross-cutting policy framework for multilingualism … and to implement it at the most appropriate level".

The principle of multilingualism raises several dilemmas and contradictions. Most often, in standard political theory, democracies and public spheres are implicitly conceived of as linguistically and culturally integrated. Because of this, multilingualism and cultural diversity constitute "a serious dilemma for liberal democratic theory" (Kraus 2004: 44).[26] In fact, "the demos can't be simply taken as given in the EU's constitutional setting" (Kraus 2004: 42) with its linguistic and cultural heterogeneity that runs counter to the "grand" political democratic theory of political units necessitating a high level of linguistic and cultural homogeneity. For Kraus, it is time to look for ways to skip the nation-state, which is still the basic political unit in the EU, and instead look for other actors who can make real the European project. Focus has been directed towards the Europe of the citizens, the Europe of the regions or the Europe of organized interests (Kraus 2004: 51). An innovative alternative is the creation of common life-worlds horizontally among actors in the EU, first and foremost exemplified in the European education programs such as Erasmus, Leonardo da Vinci, Comenius and Grundtvig. These programs have increased the geographical mobility among European students, so that today 12 per cent of them study in another country, a number which should go up to 20 per cent by 2020. Studying in a foreign country with a different linguistic-cultural context enhances a linguistic and cultural awareness and recognition that goes hand in hand with a "policy of recognition" (Kraus 2004: 52), considered to be a possible solution to the challenges that linguistic and cultural diversity puts to the creation of an

25 Available at: http://ec.europa.eu/commission_barroso/orban/policies/policies_en.htm.

26 Kraus refers to Stuart Mills ([1861] 1972: 392) and his view that "a high level of communicative integration, often associated with the use of a common language, is a requirement for the functioning of an integrative public sphere" (Kraus 2004: 43). Kraus also refers to Habermas (2001: 122) for endorsing the view that "the formation of a European public sphere" is dependant on "a common linguistic medium (which) will be English" (Kraus 2004: 44).

EU *demos*. In fact, Kraus, linking it to the principle of subsidiarity that "allows people to remain sovereign "within their own circle'" while still participating in culturally heterogeneous polities, sees recognition as an indispensable component in the breeding of a "democratic interculturalism" in EU politics (Kraus 2004: 54).[27]

Intercultural Competence, Linguistic Empathy and Recognition

The condition for intercultural empathy and recognition is linguistic empathy and recognition, including acceptance of and respect for the other's ways of expressing thoughts, ideas and emotions. In a polycentric and multinational polity with 23 official languages – in fact probably around 60 languages if you include minority languages – it is of course not possible to acquire all the languages of the others. This is exactly the key argument for the acquisition of only one foreign language, an auxiliary language, which – as English – functions as a *lingua franca*. Against this "English only" strategy, arguments are raised that the use of a *lingua franca* respects neither diversity, equality nor cultural identity, since narrowing the number of languages down to one single language means making some people more equal than others and reducing languages from being bearers of specific conceptualizations, ways of thinking and cultural identity to being a mere tool of communication. But there is a third alternative, which is to be found in language itself, in language as a structure and in the general language competence of human beings.

Psychological and psycholinguistic experiments show that human beings possess a basic and species-specific "cooperative communicative competence" that enables them to attract and focus the attention of other people and create a common intentionality with them called "shared intentionality" or "we" intentionality" by Tomasello (2008: 6). This ability makes it possible for them to decode the intentions of other people. Further, humans beings also have a so-called language instinct (Pinker 1995), in other words, a general language competence, that enables them to treat a linguistic input in structures, that is in meaningful units, and hence to decode sentences and create meaning. The communication and language abilities are innate mechanisms, which allow the small child to acquire his or her first language, but they can also be transferred to the acquisition of foreign languages, provided that the structure and specific features of the other language(s) are explicated and related to the mother tongue. Furthermore, the explanation of characteristic cultural features of communication in the foreign country can facilitate the decoding of communicative intentions.

The examples in Table 5.1 (Lundquist 2008) show the parallelism between five EU languages, when it comes to sentence structure (syntax), with "arguments"

---

27 Kraus advocates for a European "citizenization" based on a political ethos nurtured by intercultural empathy (Kraus 2004: 54).

Table 5.1 Parallelism Among Five EU Languages

Argument 1/subject	Predicate/verb	Argument 2/object
Life	deceived	him
La Fac	concurrence	les Grandes Écoles
Der Bundesstaat	drängt – zurück	den Sozialstaat
Venezuela	exporta	Petróleo
Metrostress	koster	Liv

(grammatical subject and object) ordered around a "predicate" (verb). They also show that many words (the lexicon) can be deciphered with some imagination and good guesses.

Knowledge about systematic differences and similarities among the languages considerably reduces the complexity of the EU's 23 official languages. Linguistic research – for example, within the Romance, Germanic and Slavonic languages – has shown logical and consistent similarities among languages within these language families, which could be of great use to language teaching. This goes, for instance, for German, Dutch, English, Danish and Swedish (and Norwegian and Frisian, a non-EU language and a minority language, respectively) within the Germanic languages; for French, Italian, Portuguese, Rumanian and Spanish within the Romance family and for Bulgarian, Polish, Slovenian and Czech (and Russian, a non-official minority language in the EU) within the Slavonic languages (to this should be added the Finnish-Ugrian family with Finnish, Estonian and Hungarian and the Baltic family with Latvian and Lithuanian). An exploitation of common features within the language families should be obvious for foreign language teaching in the Member States in order to expand the language competencies of the EU citizens. For instance, three common "spaces" – Germanic, Romance and Slavonic – could be formed within which one could understand the other's language without necessarily being able to speak or write it oneself. If all EU citizens were equipped with such receptive competences in their "neighbouring language(s)", they would be able to communicate with each other in their own language.

This is not an abstract idea but the very principle which lies behind the Nordic model of language community and cooperation and which the Nordic Council[28] suggests as a viable model also within the EU and in other regions of the world. The Nordic language policy[29] aims at "enabling all Nordic people to

28 The Nordic Council is an intergovernmental forum for cooperation among the Nordic countries: Denmark, Finland, Iceland, Norway and Sweden and their associated territories, which include the Faroe Islands, Greenland, Svaalbard and Åland. The Scandinavian languages comprise Danish, Faroese, Icelandic, Norwegian and Swedish, Finish belonging to another language family (the Finish-Ugrian).

29 Declaration on Nordic Language Policy, September 2006.

communicate with each other in a Scandinavian language and all Nordic people to have general knowledge about what language is and how it functions".[30] The ideal is that "the Nordic language community be marked by the citizens' desire and aspiration to understand and respect each others' mother tongue".[31] In order to achieve these goals, it is recommended to reinforce the teaching of neighbouring languages in schools. But saying is one thing; doing is another. Witness are the Danish Ministers of Education who have not prevented the Swedish and Norwegian languages from being heavily toned down in the Danish high school system, with the result that today instead of being able to communicate with 15 million extra inhabitants in Sweden and Norway without asking them to switch to English, Danes can communicate only with their 5 million fellow Danes.

A similar model could be imagined for the EU context. In an EU with 23 official languages, the probability that an EU citizen mastering two foreign languages can communicate with another EU citizen is 36 per cent. If the 23 languages are grouped in the five language families mentioned above (the Germanic, Romance, Slavonic, Finnish-Ugrian and Baltic families),[32] thus reducing the total amount of language combinations, the probability that an EU citizen with knowledge of and receptive skills in one other language *family* can communicate with another EU citizen will be 66 per cent, and with knowledge of two other language families the probability will rise to 100 per cent. These calculations, to be taken with a pinch of salt it is true,[33] hint at another possible organization of and approach to foreign language teaching in the Member States, which could considerably enhance multilingual and intercultural communication within the EU and hence contribute to the creation of a European *demos*.

The probabilities mentioned above point to the fact that the EU citizens hold an enormous unexploited foreign language potential. The Commission has recognized that systematic common features among languages belonging to the same language family can and should be utilized in actual teaching programs. This is what happens in the project *European Intercomprehension*, EUROCOM, which welcomes you with the following words: "The languages in the European house are not foreigners. Within the Romance, Germanic and Slavonic language families people can understand each other. European intercomprehension is the culture-respecting supplementation for English as the world's auxiliary language.

30 In Swedish in the Declaration: "alla nordbor kan kommunicera med varandra, i första hand på ett skandinaviskt språk (och att) alla norbor har allmänna kunskaber om vad språket är och hur det fungerar".

31 In its Swedish wording: "Nordisk språkgemenskap präglas av medborgarnas strävan att förstå och respektera varandras modersmål".

32 We leave out here, for simplicity's sake, languages not belonging to these specific families, such as Gaelic, Greek and Maltesian.

33 These figures do not take into account the fact that the 23 languages and five language families are not spoken by an equal number of people.

EuroCom is protecting the linguistic and cultural wealth in Europe. EuroCom is the gateway to European multilingualism".[34]

The EuroCom language-teaching programs take their point of departure in the principle of the human "spontaneous grammar", that is, the general language competence of human beings mentioned above, in order to develop a multilingual consciousness and interlingual knowledge, where interlingual rules of correspondence are transferred from language to language. The programs take advantage of humans' cognitive capacity to generalize, that is, to transfer regularities from one language to another, and their ability for optimizing inferences, that is, for deducing similarities with the aim of creating meaning. Such inferential learning processes yield considerable learning economic or cost-saving effects, not least because the language acquisition process can, to a certain extent, be self-monitored. In contrast to the norm of correctness, which is the general rule in traditional foreign language teaching and which often has a strongly demotivating effect, the EuroCom programs aspire to an "approximately correct" norm for the receptive (reading) competences.[35]

The three existing programs, *EuroComRom*, *EuroComGerm* and *EuroComSlav*, for the Romance, Germanic and Slavonic language families respectively, are founded on the principle of "the seven sieves" (*die sieben Siebe*, in German). As another type of gold-digger, the EU citizen shakes the chaotic linguistic input through seven sieves in order to wash out the linguistic gold in the form of systematic similarities and differences among the languages in question. The seven sieves comprise, among others, a *lexicon sieve* where recognizable (from Latin or Greek) vocabulary is washed out, a *syntax sieve* that helps identify common patterns in sentence structure and a *morphology sieve* where regularities in, for example, verb morphology and word derivation are exploited. We might add to the seven interlingual sieves proposed by EuroCom an eighth sieve, a *text linguistic sieve*, which makes it possible to identify and comprehend regularities at text and discourse level, across languages and cultures (Lundquist 2008 and 2009a).

Table 5.2 shows an example of the lexicon sieve from the EuroComRom textbook for German-speaking people (Stegmann and Klein 2000). The table demonstrates similarities among six Romance languages in the first six columns, with French as the transfer language, that is, the starting point; the corresponding German words follow in the seventh column and most important, in the last column, the learner sees the "associations" by means of which he or she can anchor the "Romance" words in his or her German vocabulary. It is this anchoring of something new in something known that contributes to the stabilization of the new vocabulary.

---

34 Available at: http://www.eurocomcenter.eu/index2.php?lang=uk.

35 EuroCom guarantees that you acquire the receptive (reading) skills in all the Romance languages in one semester, using French as the transfer language.

Table 5.2 EurComRom – Example of Similarities Between Romance Languages for German Speaking People

FRZ	ITL	KAT	PORT	RUM	SPAN	DEUTSCH	Assoziation
clef clé	chiave	clau	chave	cheie	llave	Schlüssel	Kla-vikel, -vier
cuire	cuocere	coure	cozer	a coace	cocer	kochen	[urverwandt]
connaître	conoscere	conèixer	conhecer	a cunoaşte	conocer	kennenlernen	Connaisseur
cour	corte	cort	corte	curte	corte	Hof	Courtoisie
cueillir	cogliere	collir	colher	a culege	coger	sammeln	Kollektion
contre	contra, -o	contra	contra	contra	contra	gegen	kontra
couvrir	coprire	cobrir	cobrir	a acoperi	cubrir	bedecken	Cover-[girl]
corne	corno	corn	corno	corn	cuerno	Horn	Kornett
corps	corpo	cos	corpo	corp	cuerpo	Körper	Corpus, Corps
côte	costa	costa	costa	coastã	costa	Rippe, Küste	Küste
cul	culo	cul	cu	cur	culo	Hintern	Sansculotte
courir	correre	córrer	correr	a curge	correr	rennen	Kurier
de	di	de	de	de	de	von	de-
dix	dieci	deu	dez	zece	diez	zehn	Dezi-

Source: H.G. Klein, T.D. Stegmann (2000), "*EurComRom – Die sieben Siebe: Romanische Sprachen sofort lesen können*".

Similar tables of vocabulary are presented for the languages of the other language families and the same systematic representations, rules and transfer principles are established for the other six sieves of the programs. The characteristic and distinguishing features of a given language are presented in "mini-portraits" of the language in question.

In addition to the linguistic similarities among languages, each language family also presents internal similarities in its way of talking about the world and in its way of conceptualizing it. This has been shown for the Romance and Germanic language families that display systematic differences with respect to *lexicalizing*, that is, to encoding semantic features differently in nouns and verbs, to *syntax* with a tendency to endocentric sentence structure (concentration in the centre, that is, in the verb) in Germanic languages as opposed to exocentric in Romance languages (concentration outside the centre, in the nominal arguments) and with respect to textual organization with a preference for paratactic, linear organization in Germanic languages as opposed to hypotactic hierarchical structure in Romance languages.[36] Furthermore, studies[37] have shown that such differences in cognitive structuring of language, texts and communication are also related to ways of reasoning and mentality. The understanding and knowledge of such differences would provide

36 See the TypoLex project at the Copenhagen Business School, Herslund and Baron (2003), Lundquist (2009b).

37 As, for instance, Herslund and Baron (2003), Lundquist (2009b).

an additional tool to strengthen the intercultural empathy, acceptance and respect necessary for the creation of a European *demos*.

The Engagement of the Member States

The EU has, as we have seen, initiated a series of active measures in order to give impetus to the principle of "united in (and despite) linguistic diversity". It has among other things made it possible to create common life-worlds among members of the civil society, it has financed European education programs in foreign languages, it has appointed a commissioner for multilingualism and it has developed foreign language programs in order to consolidate interlingual and intercultural recognition and understanding. But what about the Member States? Which measures have they taken in order to contribute to the interlingual ethos and intercultural empathy – in other words, to the capacity to understand and respect the others' languages?

In Denmark, for example, the language policy has taken the opposite turn. Instead of improving and enhancing multilingualism, the Danish education system bets on a one foreign language strategy, according to which English is expected to become the Danes' "second first language". Following this logic, which confers a special "first" status on English, two foreign languages besides English should be taught according to the recommendation from the High Level Group on Multilingualism mentioned above. However, recent studies (for example, Verstraete-Hansen 2008) have shown that "the (former) three-language combination is close to being non-existent in Denmark" since only 6 per cent of the students graduating in 2008 had been acquainted with three foreign languages[38] as compared to 41 per cent before the Danish high school reform (of 2003; implemented from 2005) (Verstraete-Hansen 2008: 46–7). The former Danish model with three foreign languages has thus been abandoned for a less ambitious one, which doesn't even reach the Barcelona objective, considering the special status of English. A former Danish Minister of Education is quoted for admitting in 2004 that a reduction in the choice of foreign languages in the Danish educational system was out of time at a moment when the European countries have agreed more than ever on a common project, that is, the European project. Nor does the Danish Globalization Council ("Globaliseringsrådet"), whose mission is to develop Denmark into the world's most competitive society by innovative measures, take multilingualism into account. On the contrary, it emphasizes again and again that the road leading to globalization is the *English only* strategy (Verstraete-Hansen 2008: 57).

Reducing the number of languages spoken is not a very innovative choice. In a sense, it is what many nation states have done (or tried to do) in the past. The real innovative educational choice would consist in teaching a greater selection of

38 It is to be noted that in the Danish context "trilingualism" means the mastering of three foreign languages (not including the mother tongue).

foreign languages, using, for instance, as a teaching method the one developed by the EuroCom programs, which exploit the fundamental principles of systematic similarities and differences among the languages. EuroCom has reduced the complexity in the EU language diversity by narrowing down and proposing teaching programs for three big language families, the Germanic, the Romance and the Slavonic. Adding to these the Finnish-Ugrian and Baltic families, we end up with five language families in the EU. If every Member State in the EU implemented a foreign-language policy based on and exploiting the EuroCom principles of learning receptive skills, the teaching of one foreign language from a language family other than the mother tongue would, as shown above, raise the probability to 66 per cent that the EU citizen could communicate with another EU citizen without using English. Teaching two foreign languages from two language families other than the mother tongue, the probability would amount to 100 per cent (compared to the probability of 36 per cent mastering two foreign languages in a context with 23 languages). With Denmark as an example again, and using language families rather than diverse languages, a curriculum with a language from the Romance language family and another from the Slavonic (or a Baltic or Finno-Ugrian language) as a supplement to English or German (or Dutch) from the Germanic language family, would make the Danish citizen a stronger and more powerful actor within the EU context. Such national language-teaching policies would necessitate the development of further EuroCom programs, for the Finnish-Ugrian and Baltic language families as well.

Conclusion

Over the years, the EU has developed one of the world's most ambitious language policies, which applies to the internal functioning of European institutions, the civil society as well as the relations between the institutions and the civil society. The reason why the EU has invested so much effort in its multilingualism policy is because it expects to increase its legitimacy in the eyes of the Member States as well as the European citizens and to improve the quality of its democracy. These two goals are in fact complementary. A democracy that would lack legitimacy would progressively lose the support of its citizens. A total absence of legitimacy would end up in a revolt asking for a deep change in the political system – and, *in a democratic setting*, this revolt would have to be heard. In a way, democratic legitimacy can be considered the result of two things. On the one hand, citizens will consider legitimate a system which allows them to benefit from the outputs of the system (for example, having a job, a satisfactory quality of life, sharing the common wealth produced by the economic system). On the other hand, citizens will consider a system legitimate to the extent that they can take part in the political process, either by means of elections or using tools of direct democracy (for example, referendum or citizens' initiative). They might also need to see that the ruling class is not made of a group socially closed (a ruling "cast"), but that it is open to new members coming from the civil society. In Europe, this issue has taken the form of class struggle, with the workers' class asking the aristocracy and the high bourgeoisie for a share of the power to rule. In multicultural societies, struggles are not only among social "classes" but also and sometimes primarily among cultural groups, with minority groups or "dominated communities" asking for the right to share the political power and positions in central institutions. All these elements illustrate the famous definition of democracy attributed to Abraham Lincoln: "the government of the people, by the people and for the people".[39] So do the three facets of the EU's multilingualism policy. Ensuring multilingualism within the EU institutions is a way of displaying that all Member States indeed share the institutional power of the EU. The translation and interpretation policy enables political participation by providing understandable information to citizens. Last but not least, the Barcelona objective promoting intercultural and language skills (Commission 2003) is a precondition for increased and successful transnational exchanges, be they cultural, political or economic. Since it contributes to the enhancement of political participation, to the creation of wealth, to an increased economic efficiency and to a better mutual understanding by way of getting access to other people's language, thought and culture, the Barcelona objective contributes to the legitimacy and the democracy of the EU. The objective of trilingualism might seem at first sight a high threshold and therefore, maybe, an unrealistic one, but studies in linguistics provide us with helpful tools in order to cope with it. Together with the example of the language policy of the Nordic Council, these studies show us how multilingualism can be transformed into an asset instead of being seen as a hindrance to transborder exchanges.

Yet, beyond the theoretical potential of this policy area, the fundamental role played by the Member States as well as the specificity of some aspects of this policy explain the two major difficulties that the EU faces and which prevent the goal of this policy to be fully reached. The first difficulty concerns the impact of the translation policy and the somewhat unfair paradox that the best translations are characterized by their total invisibility to their users. Therefore, EU politicians cannot capitalize on it to trigger political support. Normally, successful redistributive public policies (for instance public health policies) produce visible effects. These effects are then used by politicians in office to keep political support and for the purpose of their re-election. This fundamental rationale doesn't work for the EU's translation policy. Indeed, if it were visible that a given text was originally written in another language and that what the reader is confronted with is a translation, it would mean that the translation is of a poor quality, probably provoking counter-reactions as non-acceptance, distance and rejection (Lundquist and Gabrielsen 2004, Lundquist 2003). The better the translator, the less you are aware that the text you are reading is a translation. So how can EU citizens see that it has taken a great deal

39 The Gettysburg Address, 19 November 1863.

of professional competences and political will to translate the website or piece of EU legislation they happen to be reading, if the translation is so good that there is no difference between a text originally drafted in their mother tongue and a text translated into their mother tongue? The fact that EU citizens are not aware of this aspect of the EU's language policy may be a sign of quality, but it also means that this policy cannot be expected to foster the same degree of legitimacy as "normal" public policies.

The second difficulty which the multilingualism policy faces is not specific to this particular policy but rather a consequence of the essence of the EU's multilevel system of governance: Without a substantial collaboration of the Member States, the intended results of a policy can be seriously hindered – even if the policy was elaborated by the Member States themselves. Like other strategies and policies of the EU, the language policy suffers from the ambivalence of the Member States that may promote one policy while sitting in the European Council and a different one back in their respective domestic contexts, leaving the EU to deal alone with the political effects of broken promises and goals not met. The EU's language policy offers a good example of this political pattern. Indeed, while the Member States decided during the Barcelona Council that promoting trilingualism among the European citizens was an official common strategy, their respective domestic language strategies sometimes head in an opposite direction. So, though the EU's language policy is one of the world's most ambitious ones and though it contains most, if not all, the elements that are needed to increase the EU's legitimacy and the quality of its democracy, the cultural self-centredness of its own Member States still is the first obstacle to overcome.

References

De Cillia, R. 2003. Grundlagen und Tendenzen der europäischen Sprachenpolitik, in *Europas Identitäten. Mythen, Konflikte, Konstruktionen*, by M. Mokre, G. Weiss and R. Bauböck (dir.). Francfort/New York: Campus Verlag, 231–56.

European Commission 2003. *Communication from the Commission to the Council, the European Parliament, the Economic and Social Committee of the Regions. Promoting Language Learning and Linguistic Diversity: An Action Plan 2004–2006*, COM (2003), 449 final, 29.

European Commission 2005. *Communication from the Commission to the Council, the European Parliament, the European Economic and Social Committee and the Committee of the Regions: A New Framework Strategy for Multilingualism*, COM (2005), 596 final, 30.

European Commission 2008a. *Commission staff working document. Accompanying document to the Communication from the Commission to the European Parliament, the Council, the European Economic and Social Committee and the Committee of the Regions. Multilingualism: An Asset for*

Europe and a Shared Commitment – Summary of the Impact Assessment, SEC (2008), 2445 final, 6.

European Commission 2008b. *Communication from the Commission to the European Parliament, the Council, the European Economic and Social Committee and the Committee of the Regions. Multilingualism: An Asset for Europe and a Shared Commitment*, COM (2008), 566 final, 15.

European Council 2002. *Presidency Conclusions*, Barcelona European Council, 15 and 16 March 2002, SN 100/1/02 REV 1,72.

Gravier, M. 2008a. The 2004 Enlargement Staff Policy of the European Commission: The Case for Representative Bureaucracy. *Journal of Common Market Studies*, 46(5), 1025–47.

Gravier, M. 2008b. Fonction publique et multilinguisme: L'administration communautaire au miroir de sa population, in *La fonction publique de l'Union européenne*, edited by Centre des Études européennes de l'ENA. Strasbourg: Presses de l'ENA, 57–73.

Habermas, J. 2001. *Zeit der Übergänge*. Frankfurt: Suhrkamp.

Herslund, M. and Baron, I. 2003. Language as World View: Endocentric and Exocentric Representations of Reality, in *Language and Culture: Copenhagen Studies in Language 29*, I. Baron (red.). København: Samfundslitteratur, 29–42.

Humboldt, W. von. [1822/24] 2000. *Ueber den Nationalcharakter der Sprachen*. Edition bilingue. Paris: Seuil.

Kingsley, J.D. 1944. *Representative Bureaucracy: An Interpretation of the British Civil Service*. Yellow Springs, OH: The Antioch Press.

Kinnock, N. 2002. Conference Interpreting and Enlargement: A Strategy for the Joint Interpreting and Conference Service in the Lead-up to 2004, SEC (2002) 349(2), 24.

Kraus, P.A. 2004. A Union of Peoples? Diversity and the Predicaments of a Multinational Polity: Political Theory and the European Constitution, in *Political Theory and the European Constitution*, edited by L. Dobson and A. Follesdal. London: Routledge, 40–55.

Kraus, P.A. 2008. *A Union of Diversity: Language, Identity and Polity-Building in Europe*. Cambridge: Cambridge University Press.

Lundquist, L. 2003. "Be orderly!" Language Types and Interpretation of Texts in the European Union, in *Tipologia linguistica e società*, edited by I. Korzen, and P. D'Achille. Florence: Franco Cesati Editore, 111–33.

Lundquist, L. 2008. *Navigating in Foreign Language Texts*. København: Samfundslitteratur.

Lundquist, L. 2009a. From Contrastive Text Linguistics to Didactic Applications – and Back Again. *New Approaches in Text Linguistics – Belgian Journal of Linguistics*, 23(1), 73–91.

Lundquist, L. 2009b. Adverbes initiaux en danois et en français: Langue, texte, mentalité, in *Lingue, culture e testi istituzionali*, I. Korzen and C. Lavinio (red.). Florence: Franco Cesati, 141–62.

Lundquist, L. and Gabrielsen, G. 2004. EU – fortolkningsfællesskab eller fortolkningsfællesskaber?, in *Europæisk retskultur – på dansk*, edited by H. Koch and A.L. Kjær. København: Forlaget Thomson, 123–66.

Milian i Massana, A. 1995. Le régime linguistique de l'Union européenne: Le régime linguistique des institutions et l'incidence du droit communautaire sur la mosaïque linguistique européenne. *Rivista di diritto europeo*, 35(3), 485–512.

Milian i Massana, A. 2002. Le principe d'égalité des langues au sein des institutions européennes et dans le droit communautaire, mythe ou réalité? *Revista de Llengua i Dret*, 38, 47–94.

Mills, J.S. [1861] 1972. Considerations on Representative Government, in *Utilitarianism, Liberty and Representative Government*, edited by H.C. Acton. London: Dent.

Meier, K.J. 1993. Representative Bureaucracy: A Theoretical and Empirical Exposition. *Research in Public Administration*, 2, 1–35.

Monnet, J. 1976. *Mémoires*. Paris: Fayard.

Mosher, F.C. 1982. *Democracy and the Public Service*. New York/Oxford: Oxford University Press.

Nic Shuibhne, N. 2004. Case Comment, Case C-361/01P Kik vs. Office for Harmonization in the Internal Market. *Common Market Law Review*, 41, 1093–111.

Pinker, S. 1995. *The Language Instinct*. London: Penguin Books.

Sapir, E. 1929. The Status of Linguistics as a Science. *Language* 5, 160–66.

Sartori, G. 1976. *Parties and Party Systems*. Cambridge: Cambridge University Press.

Scharpf, F. 1999. *Governing in Europe: Effective and Democratic?* Oxford: Oxford University Press.

Stegmann, T.D. and Klein, H.G. 2000. *Die sieben Siebe*. Aachen: Shaker Verlag.

Tomasello, M. 2008. *Origins of Human Communication*. Cambridge, MA: MIT Press.

Verstraete-Hansen, L. 2008. *Hvad skal vi med sprog? Holdninger til fremmedsprog i danske virksomheder i et uddannelsespolitisk perspektiv*. Copenhagen Business School.

Whorf, B.L. [1942] 1959. Language, Mind and Reality, in *Language, Thought and Reality: Selected Writings by Benjamin Lee Whorf*, edited by J.B. Carroll. Cambridge, MA: MIT Press, 246–70.

Chapter 6

Multilingual and Multicultural Legal Reasoning: The European Court of Justice

Joxerramon Bengoetxea

Introduction[1]

This chapter will look at the status of EU co-officiality of languages as it relates to the Court of Justice: What does it mean from the point of view of the Court to have a system where all the official languages of the Member States are official languages of the Court? Is this system at all practical? Does it turn the Court into a multilingual court and if so, in what sense? What solution has been found by the Court to address the simple fact of a multilingual law? Has this solution of a single, common working language led to a genuinely different type of legal reasoning?

The analysis of the process of judicial reasoning as it obtains in the different stages of the application of EC law by the ECJ might show the epistemological moments where diversity of languages might have an impact on the type of reasoning and it might offer a heuristic model for research into multilingual judicial reasoning. The chapter will suggest that even though the Court is a multilingual institution, its legal reasoning is not multilingual. Contrary to its own directives as set out in the *CILFIT* jurisprudence, the Court does not systematically compare the official language versions of the law it applies. Only occasionally, and normally on the initiative of the parties, will the Court compare the language versions. The Court will usually work from legal instruments, texts and pleadings written in or translated into French.

Thus, the impact of the diversity of legal or judicial cultures converging at the Court is greater than the impact of the diversity of languages in which EC law is equally official. Beyond and above multilingual challenges, there is the further issue that terms in any given official language become concepts interpreted from within different legal cultures and from a new form of shared European legal culture, which poses a challenge and an opportunity for transnational judicial dialogue. In this sense, the legal reasoning of the ECJ is more multicultural than multilingual.

---

1 This work has been produced within the framework of the Consolidated Research Group (GIC07/86-IT-448-07) led by Professor Jauregi, with the financial assistance of the Education, Universities and Research Department of the Basque Autonomous Government.

EU Multilingualism

Europe is rich and diverse in languages, and it has an important tradition of different languages that at different points in time and space have operated as *lingua franca*,[2] allowing communication beyond the vernacular. The reality of language diversity and multilingualism across the European subcontinent and its history of language dominations, language subjugations, language impositions and "national" language-based nationalisms are important factors leading to an elaborate discourse on language rights – sometimes conceived as cultural rights or even as human rights – and to the equality status of all the languages which are official in the Member States of the EU. These factors also explain the cultural and normative value of language diversity and the claims made by so many so-called "minority" language[3] speakers to have their sub-state language, co-official or not, recognized as an official EU language, claims that go from language protection to promotion. This elaborate discourse is part of a European cultural heritage in which we can pride ourselves. The result is an impressive multilingual Europe "united in diversity", a diversity manifested in different multiple and often overlapping or multi-pronged cultural expressions and identities: above all language (as recognized in Article 165 TFEU) but also literature, folk culture, landscapes, politics, social and economic structures, audio-visual arts and media, research, science, philosophy and, of course, *law* or legal discourse.

Law is a highly institutionalized communicative order regulating and giving a special meaning to social action by means of norms expressed in natural language, sometimes using technical terms, as opposed to artificial language with formalized and logical syntax and technical terms and symbols. As regards law and the European Union, the complex, vast and disordered[4] legal conglomerate known as Community law, now EU law, has to be made accessible in the Member States. Effective communication among social actors and a minimum threshold of legal certainty are necessary conditions for the effective operation of the law and probably a prerequisite for its legitimacy. This requires a *lingua franca*, that is, linguistic commonality, shared linguistic understanding and competence. Legislation drafted in one base language *L* addressed to the officials and to the

2 Initially, the expression *lingua franca* referred to the language of the Francs and later to Latin. Likewise, the *lingua franca* of the original EC-6 and of the present EU-27+ is not the same.

3 It is odd to call, for example, Catalan a minority language and to call Maltese a majority language, but for many, the status of statehood and national language make all the difference. In this chapter, the term *national language* will not be used; instead we shall speak of State or sub-state language.

4 The law is disordered insofar as constituted by an agglomeration of instruments, with corrigenda, amending instruments, and so on. The task of legal science is to convert such congeries into a legal system, or at the very least, into a legal order, but the risk is that it might alter it through systematization.

population of a *G*-speaking community who do not understand language *L* would be self-defeating. Translation would be necessary from base-language *L* to target-language *G*. Equally self-defeating, by the way, would be legislation drawn in language *L* using a high density of lexical registers and syntactic sophistications understood only by a small elite group of the community. Translation would then be necessary within technical base language L^t to ordinary target language. L^p Plain Language Movements have made important contributions to the practical science of *legisprudence*.[5]

There is no single language in the EU understood by the law officials (let alone the population) of all its Member States, and even if there were to be such *lingua franca* spoken in addition to the official language of the land, it need not be accepted as an official language in those Member States. The European Free Trade Association (EFTA) has such a system in operation with a language, English, official neither in Liechtenstein, Norway nor Iceland. Incidentally, its law lacks direct effect.[6] Unlike other entities like the Council of Europe or EFTA, the EU as an organization and much more clearly EC or EU law, are multilingual. The language regime of the then EU-15 was, rather bluntly, expounded by the Court in *Kik*:[7]

> 82. The Treaty contains several references to the use of languages in the European Union. None the less, those references cannot be regarded as evidencing a general principle of Community law that confers a right on every citizen to have a version of anything that might affect his interests drawn up in his language in all circumstances.
>
> 83. With regard to relations between citizens and the Community institutions and bodies, Article 8d of the Treaty, as amended by the Treaty of Amsterdam, requires, inter alia, that the institutions and certain bodies correspond with the citizens of the Union in one of the languages mentioned in Article 248 of the Treaty. That provision ... is not in any event generally applicable to all bodies in the Union ... [e.g. the OHIM].
>
> 84. Moreover, Article 217 of the Treaty authorises the Council to determine the rules governing the languages of the institutions of the Community, acting unanimously. It was in application of that provision that it adopted Regulation No 1, Article 1 of which lays down the official languages and working languages of the Community institutions. Those official languages are not, it will be observed, exactly the same as those identified in Articles 8d and 248 of the Treaty.

---

5 There is even a specialized journal dedicated to this constitutional branch of the general theory of law.

6 Case E-4/01, *Karlsson*, Advisory Opinion paragraph 28: "EEA law does not require that individuals and economic operators can rely directly on non-implemented EEA rules before national courts".

7 *Kik v OHMI*, Judgment of 29 September 2003 in Case C-361/01P, [2003] ECR I-8283.

85. Further, Regulation No 1, in particular Article 4, requires that regulations and other documents of general application be drafted in the 11 official languages of the Union. It follows from that provision, and from Article 191 of the EC Treaty (now Article 254 EC) requiring publication in the Official Journal of the European Union of regulations, directives, and decisions adopted in accordance with the procedure referred to in Article 189b of the EC Treaty (now, after amendment, Article 251 EC), read in conjunction with Article 5 of Regulation No 1, which provides for the publication of the Official Journal in the official languages, that an individual decision need not necessarily be drawn up in all the official languages, even though it may affect the rights of a citizen of the Union other than the person to whom it is addressed, for example a competing economic operator.

86. For an institution to address a citizen in his language does not therefore resolve all the linguistic difficulties encountered by citizens in the context of the activities of the Union's institutions and bodies.

In spite of more limited language regimes of some agencies like the Office for the Harmonization of the Internal Market (OHIM), multilingualism is an indispensable component of the effective operation of the rule of law in the Community legal order. If this law is to be the same throughout the EU, if it is to be directly applicable and if the rights and duties following from it are to be invoked by all persons in all the jurisdictions within the EU, it has to be addressed to all those concerned in their official language. EC law is thus multilingual, regardless of how and in what language it is produced as a matter of fact. This does not mean that the way EC law comes about is not important, and to hold that the legislator has approved all versions simultaneously is indeed a counterfactual but legally correct presumption (or fiction), but it does mean that we cannot assume that EC law will have been produced monolingually, as domestic law normally is produced, even in some bilingual systems (Irish,[8] Basque, Welsh). This assumption would lead to a misunderstanding of the EU, its institutions and its law.

According to the "Community method" for elaborating law, the Commission proposes and the Council and Parliament dispose. It might be the case that the preparatory materials leading to and arising from negotiations carried out by the legislators at the Commission, the Committees of national experts, the Council (and the Committee of Permanent Representatives – COREPER) and the Parliament committees and Plenum, and even the input of the Committee of the Regions or the European Economic and Social Committee are themselves the result or the combination of translations going in different directions. By contrast with many policy and consultation documents (for example, Green and White Papers) available normally in English or French, perhaps also occasionally

8 In case of conflict among the texts of a law enrolled in both the official languages, the text in the national language, (Irish) shall prevail, Art. 25 (4)(6) of the Constitution, Bunreacht na h'Éireann.

in German, Spanish or Dutch, a draft regulation, directive and a decision of general application initiated in a German or French language draft might receive feedback from Polish or Portuguese delegations and is translated back with new languages additions. The proposal itself might be based on English language drafts elaborated by lobbies operating outside the Commission. Which, would we then ask, has been the language of the legislative initiative? In such cases, the draft is already a multilingual product of translation. At any rate, once approved, the formal instrument, which is the source of valid law, will be equally official in all the official languages, and none of these will prevail above the rest, and none of these will be any more authentic than the rest; indeed they might all be amalgams of translations. Individual decisions have a different regime and can exist in only one official language, that of the addressee, it being the authentic version in the event of translations (as the Court stated in its *Kik* judgment). Needless to say, many nuances will have been lost throughout the different translation processes, but the question remains whether and when these nuances will be noticed and acted upon and whether the nuances are so grave as to lead to inconsistencies.

Babel Towers

The Babel metaphor is rather frequent when addressing the question of multilingualism in the EU,[9] but insofar as the system works, we can ask ourselves whether the EU is doomed or blessed for its multilingualism. Let us examine this Babel vision, quoting from the Book of Genesis 11 (1–9, King James' version):

> And the whole earth was of one language, and of one speech. ... And they said, Go to, let us build us a city and a tower, whose top may reach unto heaven; and let us make us a name, lest we be scattered abroad upon the face of the whole earth. And the Lord came down to see the city and the tower, which the children built. And the Lord said, Behold, the people is one, and they have all one language; and this they begin to do; and now nothing will be restrained from them, which they have imagined to do. Go to, let us go down, and there confound their language, that they may not understand one another's speech. So the Lord scattered them abroad from thence upon the face of all the earth: and they left off to build the city. Therefore is the name of it called Babel; because the Lord did there confound the language of all the earth: and from thence did the Lord scatter them abroad upon the face of all the earth.

Many paradoxical conclusions can be drawn from the text: For example, God must have been multilingual in order to confound the one people with different languages, monolingual status is a source of *demos* and unrestrained power

9 Van Calster (1998: 363).

threatening God's sovereignty and so forth.[10] We cannot deal with this issue at greater length here since we wish to move to a comparison of the Babel tower with the architecture of the Court of Justice in the project submitted by architect Dominique Perrault. The Court comprises:

- a two-storey peristyle building called the *Anneau* ("Ring" in English) in spite of its rectangular form, because it encircles the original *Palais*. The *Anneau* is designed to be a non-public area reserved for the work of the Judges and Advocates General along with their staff, which can accommodate up to 40 Members and their chambers;
- the original *Palais*, preserved but remodelled. The entire available space is now given over to courtrooms, in other words, to the public face of justice. These rooms are equipped with appropriate technology to comply with the Court's multilingual requirements and are sufficiently large to cope with the increase in judicial proceedings;
- two Towers to be joined, eventually, by a third tower, the construction of which will not jar with the overall scheme of the architectural project; ... From the start, the architectural project envisaged the accommodation of the translation service in Towers, whose size – 24 storeys each – and visibility reflect the importance of multilingualism in the very functioning of the Community Court ... Each language unit has its own space in the Towers over two floors linked by a spiral staircase ... Access to the two Towers is via the Gallery ...
- a Gallery, which gives an architectural and functional unity to the new complex by linking all the new and existing buildings.[11]

I leave it to the reader to decide whether and how much this architectural compound resembles Babel or even Tolkien's fantasies, an allusion a recent *European Law Review* editorialist has found difficult to suppress as regards the Towers, but one might find it even harder to repress an allusion to the members as the Lords (and Ladies) of the Ring.[12]

The European Court of Justice (the Court of Justice operating since 1952, the Court of First Instance created in 1988, now General Court since 1 December 2009 and the Civil Service Tribunal created in 2004) ensures that "the law is observed" "in the interpretation and application" of the treaties: It reviews the legality of the acts of the institutions of the European Union, published in the Official Journal in the official languages, it ensures that the Member States comply with their Community obligations and it interprets Community law at the request of the national courts and tribunals, interacting with each of them in their own official language. The Court thus constitutes the judicial authority of the multilingual European Union

10 Ost (2009: Chapters 1–2) has carried out a brilliant exegesis of this passage.

11 Picture of the new architecture can be found at http://www.perraultarchitecte.com.

12 The original is *The Lord of the Rings*. See *European Law Review* (2009).

and ensures the uniform interpretation of Community law in 22 of the official languages (plus Irish,[13] if ever an Irish court made a reference or an applicant lodged a case in that language), in cooperation with the domestic jurisdictions responsible for the application of the Community, now EU, law thus uniformly interpreted. The Court ensures the observance of the law through its judgments (of which, more than 15,000 so far) which contain the Court's legal reasoning, a particular form of discourse used in the interpretation and application of the law. If, as Robert S. Summers claims,[14] "the published justifications appearing in opinions of the higher courts in Western legal systems comprise what is perhaps the greatest repository of recorded practical reasoning known to humankind", then those of the ECJ are the most sophisticated form of institutional practical reason expressed multilingually.

Each Member State of the EU has its own official language(s) and specific legal system(s), and the Court, like the EU as an organization, is a multilingual institution. Its language arrangements have no equivalent in any other court in the world, since each of the official languages of the European Union can be the language of a case. The Court communicates with the parties and courts in the language of the case and ensures that its case law is disseminated throughout the Member States in their official languages. The Court is therefore a multilingual institution, and the judgments of the Court are published in all the EU's official/working languages.[15] The Court's translation service (ensuring up to 506 language pairs) is organized in sections that employ only lawyer-linguists who have both legal training and a command of at least three official languages. The translation service makes up more than 40 per cent of the staff of the institution, and its annual workload exceeds 700,000 pages of translation, more than 500,000 pages of which are published in the *European Court Reports*.

The message of the Court, extracted from its official website, is that it manages the multilingual nature of the EU through its competent translation service. Any proceedings before a domestic jurisdiction will continue in the *Palais* in the same language in which it was initiated, and this will determine "the language of a case" (Article 29 RoP); the hearing will be held in that language or with interpretation into that language, and the Advocate General's opinion and the Court's judgment will be available in that same language. These last documents will eventually be made available in all official/working languages mentioned in Article 1 of Regulation 1. According to Article 31 of the Court's Rules of Procedure, the pleadings and applications, observations and witness declarations will be authentic in the language of the case or in the official language authorized by the Court, but although this provision does not mention its judgments, it is commonly held that

13 Irish is an official language, see Article 29, Rules of Procedures of the ECJ, consolidated version 2008.

14 "Introduction" in MacCormick and Summers (1991: 1).

15 Irish is not a working language.

the language of the case is the *authentic* version of the judgment.[16] In my view, all judgments of the Court are co-official and equally authentic, and this means that domestic courts wishing to know how the Court interpreted any given point of law need only read the judgment in their own official language, even if a better understanding could be gained by reading the French. At any rate and without taking into consideration whether all linguistic versions of the judgment are equal and authentic,[17] it is undisputed that all language versions of the treaties or of secondary law are co-official, and that no single one of them prevails over the rest in case of conflict or ambiguities.[18]

The fact that originality is not as important as officiality has interesting consequences for the theory of statutory interpretation of the ECJ: Since the Community law-making process is one of multiple interpretations in different directions and at different stages of the law-making process, it becomes exceptionally difficult to stick to any notion of "original legislator", "the will of the legislator", or any of the like notions that are common currency in theories of (monolingual) statutory interpretation at the domestic level,[19] even less so *authentic* interpretation. In cases of doubt, there is simply no authentic text of the law to resort to. Referring to the will or intention of the legislator becomes difficult

16 See Arnull (2006: 12): "Ambiguities in other language versions can therefore sometimes be resolved by comparing them with the French version, even though strictly speaking only the version drawn up in the language of the case is authentic". The documents referred to in Article 29, to which Article 31 refers, extend the concept of authentic document to the opinions of the Advocates General, but not to the judgments of the Court. As regards the judgments of the Court of Justice, there is no authentic version in the sense sometimes used in bilingual systems like that of the European Convention on Human Rights (French and English equally authentic), in trilingual systems like the WTO Agreement (French, English and Spanish) and in the international law of treaties.

17 Article 33(4) of the Vienna Convention on the Law of Treaties contains a guideline for the interpretation of *treaties authenticated in two or more languages* where a difference of meaning is disclosed: to reconcile the text with the object and purpose of the treaty.

18 In *EMU Tabac*, Case C-296/95 [1998] ECR I-1605, the Court said that "all the language versions must, in principle, be recognized as having the same weight and this cannot vary according to the size of the population of the Member Status using the language in question" (para. 36).

19 See on this point MacCormick and Summers (1991). The main categories of interpretative argument in this comparative study include legislative intention as their fourth category, called "intentional" together with linguistic, systematic and teleological-evaluative. I witnessed some of the discussions and drafts of the group while working on my thesis on the theory of interpretation and justification at the ECJ and, after initial hesitation, I discarded legislative intention, a category not much used in the reasoning of the ECJ. I believe there might be another explanation: There is simply no monolingual legislator onto whom any intention in the sense of the said theories can be traced and attributed. Similar consideration could arguable be made for the "originalist" constitutional interpretation theories (Scalia) based on the original intention of the drafters of the treaties or the Constitution.

in such a multilingual context. The Community legislation process is complex, cumulative and successive,[20] and it expresses itself through the translators and interpreters. Likewise, the Court expresses itself multilingually, and this fact is too often overlooked by the literature assessing its style and reasoning, especially by the specialized literature produced in dominant languages.[21]

The *Anneau*

The multilingual feature of the Court does not imply that its members, 27 Judges and eight Advocates General, are multilingual. In fact, the only official language they are expected to know is French. They are appointed by common accord by the governments of the Member States and chosen from among lawyers whose independence is beyond doubt and who possess the qualifications required for appointment, in their respective countries, to the highest judicial offices, or who are of recognized competence. The Court may sit and deliberate as a full court of 27 judges (with 23 official languages represented), in a Grand Chamber of 13 judges (five to 13 official languages represented) or in chambers of three (one to three official languages) or five judges (two to five official languages). There might have been some point in time when some, not all, of the Court's members knew all its official languages, but this probably ceased to be true after the first accession and is most unlikely now. A judge fluent in six official languages will certainly stand out as a veritable Herculean judge.[22] The options to ensure effective communication among the members are either to ensure interpretation and translation among them at all times or to find a language in which they are all (reasonably) competent. The choice was to allow the Advocates General to conclude in their official language or any other official language of their choice and to have the Court deliberate and

20 With new accessions, the legislative *acquis* becomes law in the new MS; any further amendments of valid law are made in all the official languages, and legislative intention becomes even more fictitious.

21 Research into the major English language textbooks on EC or EU law has confirmed this impression: They do not mention multilingualism when developing the main features of its legal system or when explaining the Court. A notable exception is Arnull (2006: 608), who deals with "the multi-lingual nature of Community law". But this general neglect is shared with textbooks on jurisprudence and on interpretation; one seldom finds any reference to linguistic skills, and if one does, it will not be with the view to pluri-lingual situations but rather to semiotic skills.

22 A judge who reads in many of the official languages, knows all relevant national and European law, which he or she applies ex officio, but also engages in comparative interpretation of the law, identifies with the European *telos*, in other words, a judge who is faithful to *CILFIT*, would be a veritable European judicial Hercules, as Bobek drawing from Dworkin's *Law's Empire*, labels her (2007–08). But, as Bobek argues, there is a huge gap between the *CILFIT* requirements and the standard methodology, the practice and realistic capacities of national courts.

draft in French: All written documents introduced by the parties to proceedings are then translated into French for the Court (and the AG) to work upon. The weekly administrative meeting, *reunion générale*, of all 27 judges and eight AGs also takes place in French around a vast table in what the *European Law Review* editorial has called a "cavernous room". Even with a common working language, the "possibility for organic, unstructured discussion is impossible to reconcile with the present size of this judicial college", although expecting any discussion at that high level of judicial decision-making to be *unstructured* is perhaps too unrealistic a requirement on the part of the learned editorialist even in the case of three- or five-judge chambers.

Whether it is by reason of its size, or by reason of its language diversity, the fact that the judgments of the Court of Justice of the European Union are translations, except in French, probably contributes to the impression of a distinct style. But even the French version of the judgment, let us call it base-language French version, will be the result of a collective enterprise where not all, perhaps not even one, of the judges deciding the case is a native French speaker. While "it is possible that the style of the Court's judgment is affected by the language in which they are drafted",[23] it is perhaps unfair, and probably incorrect, to say that translation into all the official languages might be a further reason contributing to "the inelegance or obscurity of judgments".[24]

By opting for a common working language, the Court preserves multilingualism as an institution but becomes a monolingual decision-maker. In other words, a common working language is superimposed on a multilingual institution where the language of the procedure (the official language chosen by the applicant in direct actions, or the language of the proceedings in the domestic jurisdiction), the languages of the intervening governments, the language in which the AG delivers the opinion and the working language of the formation (always French) will usually always differ. The new architecture of the Court aptly reflects this situation: a square monolingual *Anneau* encircling the courtrooms and the multilingual interpreters' booths. The Translation Towers adjacent to this compound ensure the connection between the chambers and the courtrooms and the balance between a shared working language and the official multilingualism in which the Court expresses itself.

The machinery works from procedural language of the pleadings, applications or references and observations → to French and from the French

23 Arnull (2006: 13).

24 Craig and de Burca (2003: 96). The authors would have to consider the style in the French language to begin with, and it seems awkward to attribute such shortcomings to translation. To suggest that the judgments of the Court might be inelegant or obscure is to make an assessment from a given legal culture neglecting the fact that the ECJ brings in many different legal and judicial cultures, rituals and styles. But to suggest that this inelegance or obscurity might be explained by translation into all the official languages is a very infelicitous statement based more on hypotheses than on factual support.

projet d'arrêt → back to all official languages. The Court will have produced in French reports for the administrative meeting and reports for the hearing, the *projet de motifs* and the deliberations with their written notes and the finally agreed draft judgment which becomes *projet d'arrêt*. The system is inflexible to such an extent that if a judgment were to be drafted in a language other than French (for example, in English, as has exceptionally been the case), the Court would literally be totally *lost in translation*, and this regardless of the fact that the AG's opinion need not be written in French.

The Influence of Legal (Judicial) Cultures

Not only is the Court to be considered as a multilingual institution, but given its composition, with judges (and AGs) educated and trained in different legal systems and different areas of the law, the Court is a potential laboratory for comparative law and comparative legal cultures.[25] Much needs to be researched in this still unexplored territory of cultural patterns, that is, historically created systems of meaning in terms of which we give form, order, point and direction to our legal (and judicial) experience.[26] It is often assumed that the mere fact of having up to 13 judges from different Member States deciding a case (and exceptionally the whole 27 of them), will bring in a diversity of legal sensitivities unthinkable in domestic jurisdictions, especially considering that they will have specialized in one or several of the many branches of law and jurisdictions, each with their different legal systems, legal traditions, legal cultures and most but not all, of them with careers developed outside EC law. Facing such enormous diversity, it is sometimes tempting to explain the differences in terms of different legal families, but these views can be simplistic.

To begin with, as regards domestic jurisdictions, these are not tucked in their isolated territories; on the contrary, domestic courts are enforcing a new transnational legal order established by the interactions among citizens, corporations and government agencies of increasingly disaggregated and porous states. Often, in a *Marleasing*[27] spirit, they are required to interpret domestic law in conformity with some supranational law, as when the Human Rights Act 1998 requires UK judges to interpret primary and secondary legislation in a way compatible with the Convention rights. National courts increasingly cite judgments from other jurisdictions as part of their own reasoning. Horizontal

25 See Jacobs (2003: Chapter 21). Jacobs makes an interesting correlation between legislative style of law-making and judicial style of interpretation. In the *fuzzy* style of drafting in civil-law systems, the judge is entrusted with pursuing the aims of the legislator whereas in the *fussy* style of legislative drafting, the common-law judge will be reluctant to go beyond the literal meaning of very detailed legislation.

26 This definition comes from Geertz (1973: Chapter 3).

27 Case C-106/89 [1990] ECR I-4135.

transnational interactions among high courts throughout Western Europe are clearly taking place, giving rise to a "transnational judicial dialogue", and judicial activism has increased the opportunities for courts to step in and interpret, for example, citizenship and human rights issues.

The ECJ is not alien to these processes, but it is also involved in its own supranational, as distinct from transnational, process.[28] It will explicitly, openly and publicly engage in comparative analysis only on rare occasions, even if it does so more frequently in camera,[29] but it will be particularly interested in declaring, drawing from and developing autonomous concepts and independent meaning to ensure effective and uniform application of EC law based more on the teleology of the treaties and consequential reasoning than on the urge to link with national legal traditions. This approach can be illustrated with the Judgment of the Court of First Instance of 6 October 2005 in Joined Cases T-22/02 and T-23/02, *Sumitomo and Sumika v Commission*:[30]

> 100. According to the case-law, the terms of a provision of Community law which makes no express reference to the law of the Member States for the purpose of determining its meaning and scope must normally be given an independent and uniform interpretation throughout the Community and that interpretation must take into account the context of the provision and the purpose of the relevant regulations (Case 327/82 Ekro [1984] ECR 107, paragraph 11; Case T-41/89 *Schwedler v Parliament* [1990] ECR II-79, paragraph 27; Case T-43/90 *Díaz García v Parliament* [1992] ECR II-2619, paragraph 36; and Case T-9/92 *Peugeot v Commission* [1993] ECR II-493, paragraph 39).
>
> 101. In particular, in the absence of an express reference, the application of Community law may necessitate a reference to the laws of the Member States where the Community judicature cannot identify in Community law or in the general principles of Community law criteria enabling it to define the meaning

28 See Slaughter and Burke-White (2007: 115): "As the EU's legal system has evolved, the prime purpose of the ECJ and even the Commission has been less to create and impose EU law as international law than to spur national courts and regulatory agencies to embrace and enforce EU law as national law". Still, the ECJ does quote from the ECHR and the AGs do so much more liberally and occasionally also from the US Supreme Court as in cases of discrimination (AG Tesauro's opinion in *Grant*). On Transnational Judicial Dialogue, see McRudden (2000) and Littlepage (2008). Littlepage shows that transnational jurisprudence has been used within a wide range of cases concerning immigration, human rights, discrimination and extradition. Foreign jurisprudence from all over the world is creating a dialogue and allowing transnational judicial dialogue to have an impact on the law.

29 The Court has a competent research and documentation service which upon the request of the Court prepares useful comparative reports on specific points of law. The fact that the Court's judgment shows no trace of comparative reasoning does not mean that such comparative reports have not been produced and used.

30 Joined cases T-22/02 and T-23/02, ECR [2005] II-04065.

> and scope of a Community provision by way of independent interpretation (Case T-85/91 *Khouri v Commission* [1992] ECR II-2637, paragraph 32, and *Díaz García v Parliament*, paragraph 36).
>
> 102. In the present case, the Court held … that the meaning and scope of Article 1(1) of Regulation No 2988/74 … emerge from an independent interpretation of that provision, carried out according to the literal, contextual, teleological and systematic methods of interpretation. Accordingly, there is no need to refer to the laws of the Member States in interpreting that provision.

Members of the ECJ all share the view that the concepts of Community law are autonomous and that their interpretation should be independent. This is, in itself, a feature of European legal culture. It would be an exaggeration to say that the style of legal reasoning, even less so, the decision or ideological choice favoured by a judge in hard cases is determined, in a strict sense, by that individual judge's legal culture. The judge's personal choices and ideological (not only political) outlook are another important factor in situations where leeway is recognized, but these are not unconnected with legal culture: The parameters of legal culture, and not simply judicial ideology, condition what is seen as acceptable use of leeway. Legal culture sets the framework within which the judge will decide, following views presented as coherent with principles of political morality inspiring the law. But what is decisive in a Court composed of so different legal backgrounds and so many ideological nuances, if not full-blown differences, all fused in a single collegiate judgment, is that diversity of legal cultures and plurality of members make it seem futile to try to detect an ideological preference of the Court, clearly distinguishable from the complex institutional and systemic dilemmas routinely debated before it and balanced with a view to enhancing the effectiveness of the Community legal order and the need for its autonomy, coherence and integrity.[31]

Relevant Examples of Multilingual Judicial Reasoning

As we have seen, the fact that the Court as an institution is multilingual does not, however, mean that the legal reasoning of the Court is a multilingual judicial reasoning. My contention is that it remains essentially monolingual reasoning. The exception to the rule is when the Court (including, of course, the *Tribunal*) resorts to a genuine comparison of language versions in order to reach a better interpretation of the norm of Community or EU law. That would be truly multilingual reasoning. The relatively few cases where language comparative analysis is carried out by the Court are those where the parties have signalled some of the possible deviations in

31 This does not imply that ideological preference is not important but rather that, amongst those other factors, its relevance in each given case is not easy to perceive. On integrity and coherence in interpretation, see Bengoetxea, MacCormick and Moral Soriano (2001) and Lasser (2004: 359).

language versions or have referred to the unequivocal terms used by the provision in question.[32] The Court seldom raises the language issue of its own motion, possibly because the Court itself has failed to detect possible discrepancies. I would say the Court has not incorporated the practice of comparing language versions as a matter of routine or as a norm of interpretation, contrary to the very directives the Court enacted for the domestic courts in the *CILFIT* case.[33] The following is an example of the standard Court discourse when comparing language versions:[34]

> 23. The question referred by the national court concerns the treatment of the operations in question in the main proceedings as simple or complex operations. In that regard, in support of their interpretations of Article 7(1)(b) of Protocol 4, the parties to those proceedings referred, essentially, to the divergences between the different language versions of that provision.

---

32 The classical case on comparison of language versions is 100/84, *Commission v UK*, [1985] ECR 1169 on the term "taken from the sea" versus "extraits de la mer" or "gefangen". I have opted for less well known instances in this chapter. Other classics are *EMU Tabac*, C-296/95[1998] ECR I-1605; or *Denkavit*, JC C-283, 291-2/94 [1996] ECR I-5063 where only the Danish version of a directive provision used a past tense; or *Regina v Boucheraeu*, Case 30/77 [1977] ECR 1999, or in *Givane and Others* case C-257/00 [2003] ECR I-345; or *Henke*, case C-298/94 [1996] ECR I-4989 and also *Bosphorous* C-84/95 [1996] ECR I-3953 are cases where language versions confirm an interpretation reached by teleological reasoning. A recent example is Zurita et al., judgment of the Court of 22-10-2009 in Joined Cases C-261/08 and C-348/08, "The Spanish-language version [of the Regulation] imposes an obligation, inasmuch as it provides that the competent authorities of the Member State 'shall expel', from the territory of that Member State, a third-country national if the presumption is not rebutted. By contrast, in all the other language versions, expulsion appears as an option for those authorities" (para. 53). This time the Court resorted to a clear majority argument in paragraph 56, although it was backed by the contextual argument: "In the present cases, as the Spanish-language version of Article 11(3) of Regulation No 562/2006 is the only one which diverges from the wording of the other language versions, it must be concluded that the real intention of the legislature was not to impose an obligation on the Member States concerned to expel, from their territory, third-country nationals in the event that they have not succeeded in rebutting the presumption referred to in Article 11(1), but to grant those Member States the option of so doing". AG Kokott's opinion is, as usual, worth reading, and the divergent version is attributed to an error in translation. The explanation could be that an older version was overlooked when the Spanish version of the Borders Code was being prepared. This may have been due to the fact that the incorporation of an existing provision is not apparent from the recitals or from the publicly available documents concerning the drafting of the Borders Code (No.s 39–45 and also 47–9).

33 *CILFIT*, Case 283/81 [1982] ECR 3415, re-explored and reconfirmed in *Lyckeskog* C-99/00 [2002] ECR I-4839.This point is drawn from personal experience and from analysis of its judgments, but it would require statistical verification. As Derlén (2009) holds, the *CILFIT* requirements are perhaps no more than "Castles in the Air": the ECJ has created extensive obligations for domestic courts without offering any genuine guidance.

34 *Euro-Tex*, C-56/06 [2007] ECR I-04859 judgment of 14 June 2007.

24. It is true that certain language versions of that provision could be interpreted as well in the sense suggested by the applicant in the main proceedings as in that suggested by the Commission. That is the case particularly with the German ("einfaches"), French ("les opérations simples de"), Spanish ("las operaciones simples de"), Italian ("le semplici operazioni di") and Portuguese ("simples operações de") versions.
25. It appears, however, from other language versions that the operations referred to by that provision are, by definition, 'simple'. Such is the indication which can be deduced from the following expressions, namely 'simple operations consisting of' in the English version, "enkle foranstaltninger som" in the Danish version, "eenvoudige verrichtingen zoals" in the Dutch version, and "enkel behandling bestående i" in the Swedish version.
26. Consequently, as the Commission argued, the interpretation consisting in regarding as simple all the operations mentioned in Article 7(1)(b) of Protocol 4 is not contrary to any language version of that protocol, whereas the interpretation suggested by Euro-Tex – involving distinguishing between simple and complex matching operations – is inconsistent, at the very least, with the language versions mentioned in the preceding paragraph.
27. In any event, it must be recalled that it is settled case-law that the different language versions of a Community text must be given a uniform interpretation and hence, in the case of divergence between the language versions, the provision in question must be interpreted by reference to the purpose and general scheme of the rules of which it forms a part (see Case C-236/97 Codan [1998] ECR I-8679, paragraph 28; Case C-420/98 W.N. [2000] ECR I-2847, paragraph 21; and judgment of 16 March 2006 in Case C-332/04 *Commission v Spain* of 16 March 2006, not published in the ECR, paragraph 52).

The comparison of language versions seems to be more of a burden than a tool to clarify points of interpretation. At best, it will confirm an interpretation reached by other means. The test is probably to ask whether the comparison of language versions adds any value, or is rather a requisite of procedural justice requiring the Court to address the points raised by the parties. In the following, I provide two examples of excellent reasoning, one purely monolingual from AG Kokott, the other multilingual from the CFI. By comparing them we realize that the Court draws little value from comparison.

AG Kokott's opinion of 14 December 2006 in case *Mickelsson and Roos* (C-142/05), deals with the interpretation of the term *Inbetriebnahme* (EN="putting into service") within the meaning of Article 4(1) of the Recreational Craft Directive 94/25/EC: "Member States shall not prohibit, restrict or impede the placing on the market and/or putting into service in their territory of products referred to in Article 1(1)" including personal watercraft. This interpretation is carried out in points 29 to 36 of the opinion, according to its wording, context and objectives, and the interpretation is confirmed by the *travaux préparatoires* of the directive. But, possibly, because the argument was not put before the Court by any of the parties, referring court or intervening parties, in her German language opinion, the AG does not deal with the question whether the term *Inbetriebnahme* (DE) can in any way be clarified by looking at other language versions *putting into service* (EN), *ibrugtagning* (DA), *tas I bruk* (SV language of the case), *mise en service* (FR), *puesta en servicio* (ES) and *messa in servizio* (IT).

An example of good multilingual interpretation is the CFI (Fourth Chamber, Extended Composition) judgment of 6 October 2005 in Joined Cases 22/02 and 23/02, *Sumitomo and Sumika v Commission*, a case concerning a Commission decision finding infringements concerning cartels in the vitamin sector. The infringements had ceased long before the Commission began its investigation. The Commission could not impose fines because of the time limit imposed by Article 1 of Regulation (EEC) No 2088/4 of the Council of 26 November 1974 concerning limitation periods in proceedings and the enforcement of sanctions under the rules of the EEC relating to transport and competition. The case raises many issues, not least those of interpretation, but also issues of general principles of law, and the reasoning of the CFI is commendable on all fronts. The following, however, is an adaptation of the multilingual judicial reasoning on the interpretation of Article 1 as to whether the limitation to impose sanctions also extended to a limitation on finding infringements, that is, whether the very finding of an infringement already constitutes a "penalty" within the meaning of Article 1, even if no actual fine is imposed since the limitation period has expired. For reasons of space, the arguments of the parties are not presented although they are certainly worthwhile. This is the CFI's reasoning:

40. It is … necessary in the first place to determine whether, as the applicants allege, the limitation period laid down by Article 1(1) of Regulation No 2988/74 applies to the Commission's power to find an infringement of Article 81(1) EC.

41. Article 1(1) of Regulation No 2988/74 provides that "[t]he power of the Commission to impose fines or penalties for infringements of the rules of the European Economic Community relating to transport or competition shall be subject to the following limitation periods:

a) three years in the case of infringements of provisions concerning applications or notifications of undertakings or associations of undertakings, requests for information, or the carrying-out of investigations;
b) five years in the case of all other infringements".

42. For the purposes of a literal interpretation of that provision, it must be borne in mind that Community legislation is drafted in various languages and that the different language versions are all equally authentic. An interpretation of a provision of Community law thus involves a comparison of the different language versions (Case 283/81 CILFIT [1982] ECR 3415, paragraph 18).

43. In that respect, it should be noted that the wording of Article 1(1) of Regulation No 2988/74 in almost all its language versions states that what is subject to limitation is the Commission's power to impose fines or penalties. None of the language versions refers to a limitation period for acts or infringements or the Commission's power to find infringements. It is appropriate therefore to consider the scope of the term "penalties", which appears alongside the term "fines" in that provision, to determine whether, as the applicants submit, that term also covers a decision finding an infringement.

44. Whilst in the majority of language versions that term, considered on its own, is capable of bearing a wider meaning than the term "fines", which only refers to pecuniary penalties, there are language versions (namely, the Finnish and Swedish versions) in which that term, like the term "fines" which precedes it, necessarily refers to pecuniary penalties.

45. An interpretation based on the title of Article 1 is also somewhat problematic in view of contradictory indications. In certain language versions of Regulation No 2988/74, that title refers to the limitation period in respect of the action or procedures, which could suggest that the scope of the limitation period referred to in the provision in question exceeds the mere power to penalise the infringements, so as to cover the possibility even of bringing an action or initiating a procedure seeking merely to establish infringements. In other versions, the title contains terms – such as "poursuites" (French version) or "vervolging" (Dutch version) – which, unlike the terms "action" or "procedures", clearly evoke the idea of punishment. In the Danish language version, the title refers to the limitation period of the power to impose "economic" penalties.

46. According to settled case-law, whilst the need for a uniform interpretation of Community regulations means that a particular provision should not be considered in isolation but, in cases of doubt, should be interpreted and applied in the light of the other official languages, in the case of divergence between language versions, the provision in question must be interpreted by reference to the purpose and general scheme of the rules of which it forms part (Case 9/79 Koschniske [1979] ECR 2717, paragraph 6; Case 100/84 *Commission v United Kingdom* [1985] ECR 1169, paragraph 17; Case C-152/01 Kyocera Electronics Europe [2003] ECR I-13821, paragraph 33; and Case T-80/97 *Starway v Council* [2000] ECR II-3099, paragraph 81).

47. More generally, however, in interpreting a provision of Community law, it is necessary to consider not only its wording but also the context in which it occurs, the objects of the rules of which it is part (Case 292/82 Merck [1983] ECR 3781, paragraph 12), and the provisions of Community law as a whole (CILFIT, paragraph 20).

[Paragraphs 48 to 59 analyse the *travaux préparatoires*, although referred to in the larger category of contextual and teleological interpretation, the recitals of the Regulation, and other related instruments, in a systematic interpretation including an a contrario argument from the ECSC Treaty. The CFI concludes this part of the argument]

(...)

61. A decision finding an infringement is not a penalty within the meaning of Article 1(1) of Regulation No 2988/74 and is not therefore covered by the limitation period laid down by that provision.

In this case, the difference in language versions was such that literal, ordinary meaning interpretation was inconclusive, but it helped clarify the debate: If the provision added the term *penalties* to that of *fines*, the reference of the class or category of penalties needed clarifying: The applicants extended the reference to include the mere finding of infringements, arguing that this finding itself could have consequences similar to sanctions whereas the defendant and the CFI opted for a restriction of the reference of *penalties* to sanctions other than fines but excluding from the *penumbra* the findings of infringements.

Jerzy Wróblewski classified arguments or sources of interpretative arguments as must-sources, should or ought-sources, may-sources and ought-not sources.[35] They differ in the normative expectations, which they generate in the juristic community, depending on the legal culture surrounding the jurisdiction concerned. If we apply these categories to the comparison of language versions at the Court of Justice, I would say that multilingual analysis is a *must-source* only when the parties have raised such argument and derive different claims from the comparison of different versions, and in that case, the Court will be expected to look at all versions and not only those invoked by the parties. Multilingual comparison is a *should-source* when the parties have made reference to the clear meaning of the words in only one language version but have not compared the versions. In that case, the Court should look at all versions to see if the meaning strikes out as clearly as the parties claim. Comparison of language versions is only a *may-source* when the parties have not raised any claim based on ordinary meaning or literal interpretation. Comparison of language versions is never an *ought-not* argument; it is never wrong or incorrect to compare versions of the *intepretandum*.

Multilingual reasoning will therefore be useful if genuinely carried out, with a view to clarifying meaning. Checking language versions of the *interpretandum* is always a salutary practice in case there might be divergence, but it will still be crucial to have what Twining and Miers call linguistic skills, "such as ability to spot ambiguities, to recognise vagueness, to identify the emotive pull of a word and to make appropriate allowances for it, and to analyse and elucidate class words and abstractions".[36] These skills are a prerequisite to both multilingual and monolingual reasoning.

35 Wróblewski (1987). See generally his posthumous work, *The Judicial Application of Law*, edited by Bankowski and MacCormick (Wróblewski 1992).

36 Twining and Miers (1976: 197).

What is Multilingual Judicial Reasoning? *CILFIT* Reconsidered

It would be necessary first of all to address the question what a multilingual judicial reasoning would be like, and this is a difficult task. It is more than mere comparison of language versions although it cannot possibly neglect or elude such comparison. It would involve deploying all linguistic techniques or skills and interpretation methods to all language versions and being aware, when drafting the terms of its own reasoning, of how such terms would be translated into the other official languages so that the message is clearly understood and, as the case might be, any possible ambiguity is properly preserved. It must draw some conclusion as to the reference (extension and intension) of the terms used by those versions and decide whether there is equivalence or divergence. But it probably does not require any exercise in linguistic pragmatics of the sort suggested by the Court in *CILFIT*, which went as far as requiring domestic courts to be aware not only of the linguistic diversity of the norm to interpret but also of the possible intuitive interpretation such versions would receive from other courts in other Member States, something the very ECJ itself could not probably do.

The *CILFIT* guidelines, as reconstructed by Michal Bobek,[37] give us a view of what truly multilingual and multicultural judicial reasoning would look like, not only as regards the ECJ but for all courts of the EU:

1. Do not read one version in isolation; all language versions are equally authentic and correct legal interpretation of any one piece of EU legislation involves the parallel reading of all versions;
2. Do not majoritize from a number of confluent language versions; and
3. Take into account other methods (system and *telos*).

A further criterion can be added to number 2, following from the *Euro-Tex* judgment: (2-B) Do not choose a meaning that is incompatible with some language versions; go for a minimum common denominator.

Bobek believes that if the national judges were genuinely to adhere to these guidelines, the entire Community judicial system would collapse within months. Mattias Derlén,[38] also claims that these guidelines are impossible to follow. In my *Legal Reasoning of the ECJ*, I tried to find a way out of this paradox by appealing to the regulative ideal character of the *CILFIT* criteria: If we were to try to make the best possible justification of a genuine question of interpretation in a hard case, we would find guidance in these criteria instead of deciding unilaterally that the case was clear. The context in which the guidelines came about was a direct contestation on the part of some higher Member State courts, namely the *Conseil d'Etat*, towards the Court's doctrine of the vertical direct effect of

37 Bobek (2007–08).

38 Derlén (2009).

rights contained in non-implemented directives. The excuse not to refer cases to the Court and to prevent such direct effect was the *acte clair* doctrine. The *CILFIT* judgment can be seen either as a punishment to proud courts similar to that of Babel – if you dare contest my authority and contradict clear precedents by resorting on your clear understanding of the law (*acte clair*) I shall have you read all language versions and confuse you! – or as a strategy to defend its own record of interpretation, as when squids squirt ink and blur the waters around them in order to hide from predators – by following the *CILFIT* guidelines you realize the difficult predicament of the Court.

Multilingual Judicial Reasoning would need to face the challenge that different language versions interpreted according to the same methods and canons might lead to diverging interpretations because legal concepts belong in different legal cultures. Even when the concepts are autonomous in EC law, like direct effect and direct applicability,[39] there might still be confusion about their meaning (their intension and extension). Legal terminology used in the various legal systems, both European and non-European, expresses not only the legal concepts which operate there, but further reflects the profound differences that exist among the various systems and the differing legal conceptions of the jurists in each system. Take the term *tribunal* in the French, as opposed to *cour*. *Tribunal* in English has a more specific reference to a type of judicial decision-making body distinguishable from a *court*. The Civil Service Tribunal (EN) of the Court of Justice is closer to such type, whereas the former *Tribunal de première instance*, now simply *Tribunal* (FR) is in English the *General Court*. On the other hand, in Spanish the *Cour de justice* (FR), *Gerichtshof* (DE), *Domstolen* (DA) and the *Tribunal* (FR), *Gericht* (DE), *Retten* (DA), are both called *Tribunal* (ES).

Since legal language is domain specific, translation cannot consist in ascertaining correspondences or “term equivalences” between legal terms used in different languages: There is no strict semantic correspondence of the concepts denoted by the terms and even more significant, the universe denoted by the concepts (the conceptual ontology) is regulated differently in the different legal systems. Even if we translate “direct effect” or “procedural equivalence” verbatim into other languages, the terms might not convey the same meaning when we do not share a common theory of direct effect or of the Rewe/San Giorgio conditions for procedural autonomy, that is, that the procedural remedy available for the claim based on Community law is not treated less favourably than the claim based on domestic law and that the remedy available is effective. It is not simply a question of terminological equivalence or proximity; it requires background knowledge of

39 By way of example, the following can be seen as autonomous EC law concepts: abuse, selling arrangements, marketing rules, market access, parallel imports, measures having equivalent effect, obstacle, barrier, distortion of competition, discriminatory taxation, risk of confusion, provision of cross-border services, unemployed, worker, service transactions, establishment, judicial review, selectivity, social benefit, self-employed, and equal pay.

a legal system. Any legal translation needs to take this into account, and when in doubt, stick to the verbatim translation, instead of correcting the confusion in the original with the help of background knowledge of the concept the translator might have.

On top of that, as we have seen above, Community or EU law goes for conceptual autonomy, even if its terms are the same terms which, in domestic law, convey different concepts, rooted in national legal traditions.[40] In this sense, the ECJ and the ECHR have devised similar consensus seeking strategies:[41] like waiting for a consensus to emerge or else forcing new definitions based on some autonomous meaning on top of differing language versions.

Yet, there is a deeper hermeneutic challenge to multilingual reasoning: Is there a meaning independently from the concrete language version? Is there any pre-interpretative meaning? We come to the heart of the theory of interpretation. This is perhaps what Bobek has in mind when he says, in a critical vein, that the comparison of the language versions releases the interpreter from the text of the rule itself; it allows the interpreter to detect discrepancies and to set aside the wording and rely upon a different method. But how can the text of the rule itself be separated from the language version in which it is expressed, and how can the text (in one version) not be defied if the other language versions differ? Is there an ontology of the rule that goes beyond its formulation in the form of a provision in a given language version? If we are confused by the language versions, how can we know what is the true norm hiding behind them, the meaning that some of the language versions, attempting to capture it, fail precisely to reveal? And what if all versions fail to reveal the *true* norm? Shall we still claim that there is such a thing as a *true* norm? Or is the norm perhaps just the result of a socially and institutionally meaningful intellectual construction of the interpretandum, a joint enterprise of interpretation where complex norm-makers, translators, parties and their lawyers, domestic courts, more translators and reviewers and correctors, the Court's lawyers and members and yet more translators are all involved and where some of these actors have final deciding authority?

Found in Translation

This takes us to the final point in the argument: It might be precisely thanks to translation that we come to understand that meaning is constructed in a different

40 Case 11/70, *Internationale Handelsgesselschaft* [1970] ECR 75, and Case 69/79, *Jordens-Vorsters* [1980] ECR 75.

41 See Gerards (2009: 20): "Just like the meta-principle of teleological interpretation is rather effectively used by the ECJ to respond to its problematic, the ECHR makes use of the principle of evolutive and dynamic interpretation". Sometimes the Court will wait for a natural convergence of national case law to occur; other times it forces new definitions based on an autonomous Convention concept or meaning.

way from the exact term equivalence. When the French language version of the judgment has been drafted and agreed in deliberation and proofread, it is sent to all the translation sections in the other official languages. Interesting phenomena of interpretation are obtained at this stage. An expression that might have seemed obvious in the French language might by contrast be difficult to translate into one or more of the other languages. Intended ambiguities are a case in point, but unintended ones can be even more telling.

Genuine multilingual legal reasoning occurs at the stage of translation much more so than at the stage of drafting or even deliberation. Here the interpreter-translator is bound by a closed and circumscribed universe of meaning, by an immediate intention:[42] the will of the Court as expressed in the final draft French language version judgment or the intention of the Advocate General, which is even more reliable since it involves only one person, one chamber. This meaning is to be matched exactly by the remaining language versions. One initial and obvious inclination will be to consult the original source of the judgment: the chambers of the judge who took part in the elaboration of the judgment. The translator will try to produce an exact replica of the base-language judgment in the French version or of the opinion in any of the official languages. When the judge who has taken part in the decision-making process, in the deliberation, knows the language into which the decided text is to be translated, there might be mechanisms to make the target language replica as exact as possible.[43]

As an illustration of the importance of conceptual translation, it is worth looking at point 25 of AG Kokott's opinion in *Mickelsson*, (above) concerning the term (noun) *Direct Applicability*: "Einer Richtlinie kommt vor Ablauf der Umsetzungsfrist keine unmittelbare Anwendbarkeit zu". The different translations confuse the terms *direct effect* and *direct applicability*, but perhaps the confusion of *concepts* is already in the original German version.

Versions Favouring Direct Applicability as in German Original

- En richtlijn is vóór het verstrijken van de omzettingstermijn niet rechtstreeks toepasselijk (NL: adjective)
- A directive is not directly applicable before the end of the implementation period (EN: adjective)
- Innan tidsfristen för införlivande har löpt ut, är ett direktiv inte direkt tillämpligt (SV: adjective)
- Et direktiv er ikke umiddelbart anvendeligt før udløbet af gennemførelsesfristen (DA: adjective)

42 Intention and meaning are closely connected in the English language as when one asks "What do you mean to do?" In other languages this intention is linked to understanding: "Au'entends tu faire?".

43 On legal translation theory, see Sarcevic (1998). I am grateful to Anne Lise Kjær for directing my attention to this discipline.

Intermediary Version

- Ad una direttiva non è attribuita efficacia diretta prima della scadenza del termine per la trasposizione (IT: new concept: direct effectiveness?)

Versions Favouring Direct Effect (Wirkung)

- Une directive n'a aucun effet direct avant l'expiration du délai de transposition (FR)
- Antes de que expire el plazo de adaptación del Derecho nacional a una Directiva, ésta no tiene efecto directo (ES)
- Uma directiva não produz efeito directo antes do decurso do prazo de transposição (PT)
- Przed upływem terminu transpozycji dyrektywa nie jest bezpośrednio skuteczna (PL)

Have the translators or the reviewers confused the concepts, have they corrected the confusion of the AG, is there a distinction without a difference after all?

In the *Mickelsson* opinion, let us imagine a situation where one translator contacts the chambers of AG Kokott and inquires into her intention in using the term *Anwendbarkeit* instead of *Wirkung*; perhaps such interaction can lead the AG to rethink her own choice of the term and to confirm it or reject it upon consideration. After engaging with such interpretative challenges, discourse acquires a new critical dimension. Such discursive interactions do take place at the Court at different stages: control by some excellent francophone secretaries in the chambers of the drafts produced by *référendaires* whose mother language is not French,[44] oral and written deliberations, informal exchanges among *référendaires* of the same or different chambers, queries originating in the reader of judgments (*lecteur/lectrice d'arrêts*) and/or the *correcteur/correctrice* and last, not least, interactions with services of translation. In an ideal situation, the members of the Court should be encouraging such dialogues and spend good time on the translations into their official language(s). The Court's members and chambers can only profit from such interactions, which should be encouraged from the presidency to ensure excellence of the Court as an organization.

A good practice is the *Gebhard*[45] judgment where the Court struggled to stick strictly to terms that have no equivalence: *Rechtsanwalt, abogado, avvocato, avocat* or *lawyer* (solicitor/barrister-advocate). The Milan Bar had insisted that as a foreign lawyer, Mr Gebhard should operate under the provision of services

44 An example based on personal experience, since I benefited enormously from the competence of the clerical staff at the Chambers of Judge Edward.

45 Case C-55/94 [1995] ECR I-4165.

(lawyers) directive[46] and could not be allowed to practice under establishment unless he registered as an *avvocato* in the Milan Bar. Gebhard himself argued under the category of services and relied on his collaboration with a local Milan legal office. But the Court analysed the case as the establishment of a *Rechtsanwalt* in Italy, which did not recognize the profession of *Rechtsanwalt* but only the different one of *avvocato*. Thanks to these impossible translations, the Court found that it would be possible in principle, and subject to the famous four *Gebhard* conditions,[47] to practice a profession, or important professional activities like giving legal advice to clients, in a Member State that does not recognize or *name* such profession. The judgment in the language versions of the time shows extreme care to avoid confusion of terms. This is largely thanks to a note that the *rapporteur* sent to all translation divisions warning them of the need to keep some of the terms in the original official language and thanks to the care that was taken at the judge's chambers to check the translations.

By Way of Conclusion

> La langue d'Europe, c'est la traduction; le multinguisme est un atout et non un obstacle por l'Europe [The language of Europe is translation; multilingualism is an asset, not an obstacle for Europe].[48]

The Court is clearly a multilingual institution; it receives inputs and delivers its outputs in all the official languages of the EU. Two tools make the processing of those inputs to deliver the outputs possible: translation and a common working language. The multilingual system of EU law and of the Court is operating reasonably well. Budgetary implications may be a constant concern, but EU law is official and equally valid in all official languages, like domestic law. Working in a multilingual system and environment does not however make the Court a multilingually operating organization. As we have seen, the Court does not approach EU law multilingually and it does not reason multilingually by constantly and systematically contrasting language versions. In spite of its own admonitions

46 Council Directive 77/249/EEC of 22 March 1977 to facilitate the effective exercise by lawyers of freedom to provide services (OJ 1977 L 78, 17).

47 Stated in paragraph 37 of the judgment: "National measures liable to hinder or make less attractive the exercise of fundamental freedoms guaranteed by the Treaty must fulfil four conditions: they must be applied in a non-discriminatory manner; they must be justified by imperative requirements in the general interest; they must be suitable for securing the attainment of the objective which they pursue; and they must not go beyond what is necessary in order to attain it (see Case C-19/92 *Kraus v Land Baden-Wuerttemberg* [1993] ECR I-1663, paragraph 32)".

48 Ost (2009: 12).

to the judicial elites in the Member States in *CILFIT* where the best was probably made an enemy of the good, the Court has not lived up to expectations.

The Court is yet to become a multilingual court and has enormous potential to do so. Translation is, arguably, still perceived by the Court more as an obstacle than an asset. With notable exceptions, as we have seen, a multilingual sensitivity and translation-leaning approach are rare amongst the members. Of the two tools mentioned above, the common working language has clearly carried the day, and the time and energy devoted by chambers to checking the languages versions of the EU legal sources and revising the translation of the French version of the *projet d'arrêt* [draft judgment] into the remaining official versions are scant. The methodological preference for the single, common working language has so far hindered the collective and cooperative development of a genuinely multilingual form of legal reasoning. It is clearly not a problem of skills or competences of the members and staff but rather of attitude and vision.

References

Arnull, A. 2006. *The European Union and its Court of Justice.* 2nd Edition. Oxford: Oxford University Press.

Bengoetxea, J., MacCormick, N. and Moral Soriano, L. 2001. Interpretation and Integrity, in *The European Court of Justice*, edited by J.H.H. Weiler and G. de Búrca. Oxford: Oxford University Press, 43–85.

Bobek, M. 2007–2008. On the Application of European Law in (Not Only) the Courts of the New Member States: "Don't Do as I Say"? *Cambridge Yearbook of European Legal Studies*, Vol. 10. Cambridge: Centre for European Legal Studies, 1–34.

Craig, P. and de Búrca, G. 2007. *EU Law, Texts, Cases and Materials*. 4th Edition. Oxford: Oxford University Press.

Derlén, M. 2009. *Multilingual Interpretation of European Union Law*. Alphen aan den Rijn: Kluwer Law International.

European Law Review Editorial 2009. A Court Within a Court: Is it Time to Rebuild the Court of Justice? *EL Rev*, 2.

Geertz, C. 1973. *The Interpretation of Cultures*. London: Hutchinson.

Gerards, J. 2009. Judicial Deliberations at the ECHR, in *The Legitimacy of Highest Courts' Rulings Judicial Deliberations and Beyond*, edited by N. Huls, M. Adams and J. Bomhoff. Cambridge: Cambridge University Press.

Jacobs, F. 2003. Approaches to Interpretation in a Plurilingual Legal System, in *A True European: Essays for Judge David Edward*, edited by M. Hoskins and W. Robinson. Oxford: Hart Publishing.

Lasser, M. 2004. *Judicial Deliberation: A Comparative Analysis of Judicial Transparency and Legitimacy.* Oxford: Oxford University Press.

Littlepage, K. 2008. *Transnational Judicial Dialogue and the Rising Influence of European Courts.* Paper presented at the annual meeting of the ISA's 49th

Annual Convention, Bridging Multiple Divides, San Francisco, 26 March 2008. [Online]. Available at: http://www.allacademic.com/meta/p251172_index.html.

MacCormick, N. and Summers, R. (eds) 1991. *Interpreting Statutes: A Comparative Study*. Aldershot: Dartmouth Publishing House.

McRudden, C. 2000. Common Law of Human Rights?: Transnational Judicial Conversations on Constitutional Rights. *Oxford Journal of Legal Studies*, 20(4), 499–532.

Ost, F. 2009. *Traduire: Défense et illustration du miltilinguisme*. Paris: Fayard.

Sarcevic, S. 1998. *New Approach to Legal Translation*. Dordrecht: Kluwer.

Slaughter, A.-M. and Burke-White, W. 2007. The Future of International Law is Domestic (or, the European Way of Law), in *New Perspectives on the Divide Between National and International Law*, edited by J. Nijman and A. Nollkaemper. Oxford: Oxford University Press.

Twining, W. and Miers, D. [1976] 1999. *How to Do Things With Rules: A Primer of Interpretation*. 4th Edition. London: Butterworths.

Van Calster, G. 1998. The EU's Tower of Babel – The Interpretation by the European Court of Justice of Equally Authentic Texts Drafted in More Than One Official Language. *17 Yearbook of European Law*, edited by A. Barav, and D. Wyatt. Oxford: Clarendon Press, 363–93.

Wróblewski, J. 1987. An Outline of a General Theory of Legal Interpretation and Constitutional Interpretation, *Acta Universitatis Lodziensis, Folia Juridica* 32, Lodz.

Wróblewski, J. 1992. *The Judicial Application of Law*, edited by Z. Bankowski and N. MacCormick. Dordrecht: Kluwer.

Chapter 7

The Multilingualism of the European Union Law in the National Courts: Beyond the Textbooks

Michal Bobek

Introduction

In a typical book on EU law, the linguistic regime of the EU and its institutions would be briefly addressed in a few lines or tucked away somewhere in a footnote. When addressing the issue of languages in the European Union law, legal scholars would restate the fact that all the official languages of the European Union are equally authentic and that any reduction in the number of languages is impossible for political reasons. Few of them may add various examples from the case law of the Court of Justice of the European Union (hereinafter "Court of Justice" or "Court") as to how the conflicts amongst the various language versions are to be resolved.

Little attention is, however, normally paid to the consequences the multilingualism of European Union law and the equal authenticity of all the language versions have on the application of EU law before national authorities (courts and administrative authorities). This chapter offers some insights into what the multilingual character means in practical terms on the national level and what problems it brings. It does so by focusing on three selected issues, which proved to be the most problematic in this area in the last years.

First, the absence of the publication of a language version is assessed, especially the consequences that the recent decision of the Court of Justice in the *Skoma-Lux* litigation had on the duty to publish EU legislation in all the official languages. Second, the alteration of an already published version of an EU legislative act via the issue of a "corrigendum" is discussed. Third, the duty to compare the various language versions as a method of interpreting EU law is introduced together with some examples from the national practice. Finally, based on these examples, several general conclusions are offered regarding the reality and potential of national authorities in their "multilingual" mandate under EU law.

The Absence of a Language Version – *Skoma-Lux* and its Aftermaths

The 2004 accession was characterized by the failure on the part of the EU institutions to secure timely and correct publication of secondary legislation in the eight languages of the new Member States. The Court of Justice has addressed this issue in several decisions,[1] admitting that there actually were no binding and duly published versions of EU legislation in the languages of the new Member States.

The key holding as far as the language-related issues of publication are concerned is the *Skoma-Lux* case.[2] It concerned enforcement of EC legislation unpublished in the Czech language, in the particular case a regulation, by the Czech administrative authorities. The reference was submitted by the regional court in Ostrava [*Krajský soud v Ostravě*] in the course of the proceedings between the company Skoma-Lux, s.r.o. and the Customs Authority, regarding a fine imposed on Skoma-Lux in respect of customs infringements which it was alleged to have committed between March and May 2004. One of the defences raised by the company for the fine to be annulled was that the Customs Authority could not enforce against it EU legislation that had not yet been published in the Czech language in the Official Journal.

The Court of Justice agreed with this proposition. The Grand Chamber observed that, as far as the position of individuals in a similar situation was concerned, EU law:

> precludes the obligations contained in Community legislation which has not been published in the Official Journal of the European Union in the language of a new Member State, where that language is an official language of the European Union, from being imposed on individuals in that State.[3]

Taking into account the considerable impact the decision could have on the already adopted decisions on the national level, the Court of Justice sought to limit the temporal application of its decision. It stated that its holding should not be applicable to national decisions adopted prior to the judgment in the *Skoma-Lux*

1 Case C-161/06, *Skoma-Lux sro v Celní ředitelství Olomouc* [2007] ECR I-10841 and Case C-273/04, *Republic of Poland v Council of the European Union* [2007] ECR I-8925. Further on the implications of the *Skoma-Lux* decision, see Lasińki-Sulecki and Morawski, "Late Publication of EC Law in Languages of New Member States and Its Effects: Obligations on Individuals Following the Court's Judgment in Skoma-Lux", 45 *CML Rev.* (2008), 705–25. See also judgment of the Court of 4 June 2009 in Case C-560/07, *Balbiino AS v Põllumajandusminister and Maksu- ja Tolliameti Põhja maksu- ja tollikeskus*, n.y.r., paras 27–32.

2 The background to the litigation is described in Bobek (2007).

3 Case C-161/06, *Skoma-Lux sro v Celní ředitelství Olomouc* [2007] ECR I-10841, para. 74.

case with the exception of "decisions which had been the subject of administrative or judicial proceedings at the date of this judgment".[4] It added that Member States were not, under EU law, obliged to call into question already adopted decisions. Such an approach of an "already closed chapter" is, nonetheless, in fact negated in the following paragraph, where the Court of Justice reopens the door to potential litigants by stating that there still remains a possibility of reopening final decisions on the national level in cases of

> exceptional circumstances where ... there have been administrative measures or judicial decisions, in particular of a coercive nature, which would compromise fundamental rights: it is for the competent national authorities to ascertain this within those limits.[5]

The exception is framed very broadly. One could argue that any decision by which national authorities imposed financial penalties for disregarding unpublished EU legislation could be regarded as an administrative measure of coercive nature, which touches upon a fundamental right – the right to property.

One of the first direct applications of the *Skoma-Lux* holding on the national level was, apart from the decision in the original case itself,[6] a decision of the Slovak Supreme Court [*Najvyšší súd*].[7] The factual circumstances in the case at hand were similar to the *Skoma-Lux* litigation: an importer was fined by the customs authorities for wrongful declarations. The court annulled the administrative decision, following the Court's decision in *Skoma-Lux* and the express motion in the pleading of the applicant concerning the absence of publication of the relevant customs legislation in the Slovak version of the Official Journal.

In the original *Skoma-Lux* case, as well as in the Slovak decision mentioned in the preceding paragraph, the fact that EU legislation was not duly published at the material time was invoked in the pleading of the parties. A different situation was addressed in subsequent decisions of the Czech Supreme Administrative Court (hereinafter only "SAC"), which concerned a series of imports made by a Czech importer in the period after the accession in May 2004 but before the publication of the Czech version of the relevant EU customs legislation in September 2004. The importer challenged the customs decisions; the alleged ground for annulment of the administrative decisions was, however, substantive errors of assessment by

4 Ibid., para. 71.

5 Ibid., para. 73.

6 Judgment of the *Krajský soud v Ostravě* [Regional Court in Ostrava] of 10 January 2008, 22 Ca 69/2005-217, published as No. 1548/2008 Coll. SAC. The decision was concise and straightforward; the Czech court followed the guidance of the Court of Justice and annulled the challenged customs decision.

7 Judgment of 18 March 2008, 5 Sžf 59/2007, accessible via the JuriFast database at www.juradmin.eu.

the Customs Authority. The issue of due publication of the EU customs legislation was not raised by the applicant. The question which the SAC was faced with was whether the issue of publication was to be considered only following an express motion in this respect made by the applicant or whether the national courts ought to examine this on their own motion.

The SAC upheld the latter solution: In a decision of 18 June 2008,[8] the court stated that the issue of due publication of applicable legislation is to be assessed by a national court of its own motion. The SAC also stated, in general, that it is the duty of all administrative courts as well as administrative authorities to ascertain, when reviewing an administrative decision that was pending before the administrative courts or administrative authorities at the time of the *Skoma-Lux* decision,[9] whether or not the decision was based on a duly published regulation. If not, the decision is to be annulled.

The decision of the SAC considerably expands the scope of cases to which the *Skoma-Lux* decision might be applicable. The only condition set in the decision itself is that the case must have been pending at the date of the decision, not that the applicant in the case must also have expressly raised the absence of publication. Cases, which were pending at the date of the *Skoma-Lux* decision in which the applicant would have expressly raised the absence of due publication of EU law, were perhaps just tens. Cases that were pending at the same date either before administrative authorities or before administrative courts in which decisions adopted in the immediately post-accession period were challenged on various grounds other than absence of due publication of the applicable EU law are hundreds or perhaps even thousands. They do not concern only customs, but various other types of sanctions, such as a fine imposed on a lorry driver for the disregard of compulsory rest periods.[10]

Two last remarks on the consequences of the *Skoma-Lux* holding shall be made. First, for the purposes of enforcement of EU law, the Court of Justice in *Skoma-Lux de facto* accepted that the territory of the Union is divided into 23 language clusters. If a regulation was not duly published within one of the clusters, it is not enforceable there. Second, from the subsequent case law of the Court of Justice,[11] it would appear that "unenforceability" against the individual

8 Judgment of the SAC of 18 June 2008, 1 Afs 21/2008. Available at: www.nssoud.cz.

9 *Skoma Lux*, cited supra note 1, para. 72.

10 See judgment of the SAC of 24 January 2008, 9 As 36/2007, published as No. 1533/2008 Coll. SAC, where the SAC addressed similar issues with respect to the absence of the Czech publication of the Council Regulation (EEC) No. 3820/85 of 20 Dec. 1985 on the harmonization of certain social legislation relating to road transport, O.J. 1985, L 370/1, on the basis of which a lorry driver was fined for not respecting the compulsory rest periods.

11 Case C-345/06, *Gottfried Heinrich*, judgment of 10 March 2009, n.y.r. For further discussion, see a case note on the decisions published in 46 (6) C.M.L.Rev. 2077–2094 (2009).

became the general sanction for the absence of publication of a EU measure. In other words, a regulation that is not published in one, two or three official languages but also not published in all the official languages, would still be valid EU law. It just cannot impose any obligations on the individual.

The Rewriting of a Language Version via Corrigenda[12]

A corrigendum of a legislative text is conventionally thought of as a mere rectification of obvious typing mistakes. It is done after the publication of a legislative text. Its purpose is to realign the published legislative text with the original will of the legislative body by removing mistakes that occurred in the publication process. A corrigendum does not contain any provisions on validity or entry into force. It derives its authority from the text it rectifies, including its legitimacy, legal force and the provisions on its temporal application.

The legislative reality in the European Union today is, however, very far from this ideal. The duty to publish EU legislation simultaneously in, currently,[13] 22 official languages is a heavier burden than even the best translation service can bear without making mistakes. Corrigenda of published EU legislation are common practice: sometimes minor; sometimes, however, amounting to substantial rewriting of the published EU act.

The Current Practice of Corrigenda in the Official Journal

Corrigenda are being published in the OJ on a rolling basis, in the same OJ series (L, C) as that in which the original document was previously published. A corrigendum always concerns just one language version of a published measure. The length of corrigenda differs – from just one or two correction points to hundreds of correction points. What also differs is the impact that the corrigendum has on the original text. This ranges from slight, genuinely formal rectifications to substantial alteration of the legislative text.

---

12 This section is an abridged version of the argument presented in Bobek (2009).

13 As from 1 January 2007, the European Union has 23 official languages. There were, however, temporal derogations for two of the official languages, Irish and Maltese. The derogations provided for transition periods during which the institutions were not obliged to publish all legislation in these two languages. The transitional period in respect of Maltese passed on 30 April 2007. From this day onwards, all new EU legislation was to be drafted and published in Maltese (see Council Regulation 930/2004 of 1 May 2004 on temporary derogation measures relating to the drafting in Maltese of the acts of the institutions of the European Union, [2004] OJ L 169/1). By way of derogation for a renewable period of five years, which is to end in January 2012, the institutions of the European Union are not bound to draft and publish their acts in Irish (see Council Regulation 920/2005 of 13 June 2005 amending Regulation No. 1 of 15 April 1958 determining the language to be used by the European Economic Community, [2005] OJ L 156/3).

The degree to which the text is being altered in comparison with the version published in the OJ can serve as a yardstick for distinguishing two basis types of corrigenda: (1) purely formal corrigenda and (2) meaning-changing corrigenda.

Purely formal corrigenda are what one could call genuine corrigenda. They rectify typographic mistakes and omissions, obvious flaws in writing or typesetting. They might include things like omitted letters,[14] small instead of capital letters at the beginning of a sentence, incorrect internal references caused by a typing mistake,[15] wrongly typeset sentences or paragraphs and so on. They typically occur in the publication process itself, that is, after the adoption of the measure but before its publication.

Meaning-changing corrigenda are those that substantively alter the content of the legal norm. Their scope is very broad. They might include narrowing or broadening of notions in a legal text, changing the nature of a list of conditions to be fulfilled (from enumerative to exhaustive), turning positive sentences into negative ones or even plainly rewriting substantive parts of a piece of EC legislation. The common denominator for meaning-changing corrigenda in EC law is that, unlike purely formal corrigenda, they are not the consequence of a typing or typesetting mistake. They are typically, as will be discussed in detail below, caused by incorrect translations of EU legislation in the legislative process prior to the adoption of the legal act.

It would appear that the current practice of the Office for Official Publications would also support such a division of corrigenda, albeit just in terms of the process as to who will carry out the corrections. If the error was committed by the printer (for example, wrong date, wrong number, mixed language versions and so on), the Office for Official Publications would itself launch the corrigendum process. The Office's proofreaders prepare the text in the relevant language and the corrigendum would be published within a few days. If the error already existed in the adopted manuscript, it is for the relevant Directorate-General to launch a

14 For instance, the title of the Czech version of Regulation 1408/71 of the Council of 14 June 1971 on the application of social security schemes to employed persons and their families moving within the Community (English special edition: Series I, Chapter 1971(II): 416) contains, as the reference to the legal basis on which the regulation was adopted, "(EC)" instead of "(EEC)".

15 An example of a corrigendum rectifying internal an reference might be a corrigendum of the Czech version of Regulation 261/2004 of the European Parliament and of the Council of 11 February 2004 establishing common rules on compensation and assistance to passengers in the event of denied boarding and of cancellation or long delay of flights, [2004] OJ L 46/1. Article 6(1)(c)(ii) contains an internal cross-reference to Article 9(1)(a) and (c). The Czech version of the regulation, however, referred to Article 9(1)(b) and (c), thus creating a different list of entitlements for passengers whose flights were delayed by more than one day. The internal reference was corrected by the corrigendum of 4 April 2009, [2009] OJ L 92/5.

corrigendum procedure. Once prepared, the corrigendum would be then sent to the Office. This typically takes much more time.[16]

The examples of meaning-changing corrigenda are numerous. The easiest to detect, and later to rectify, are translation mistakes, which result in the absurdity of the legislation in question. An example of this category would include the Czech version of Article 23(1) of Council Regulation 44/2001 on jurisdiction and the recognition and enforcement of judgments in civil and commercial matters.[17] It limited the choice of court only to the Member State(s) in which the parties to the contract are domiciled, thus negating free choice of jurisdiction by the parties within the European Union.[18]

Other examples of meaning-changing corrigenda involve narrowing or broadening the scope of the application of a rule,[19] sometimes generating something quite different[20] and sometimes even the opposite. An extreme example of the latter category is the Czech version of Commission Regulation 865/2006 (laying down detailed rules concerning the implementation of Council Regulation 338/97 on the protection of species of wild fauna and flora by regulating trade therein).[21] The regulation was published in the Official Journal on 19 June 2006. It entered into force 20 days later, and the administrative authorities started applying it. More than a year later, in August 2007, a corrigendum of the Czech version of

16 I am much obliged to Mr Nuno Mesquita of the Publications Office for this information (provided in electronic correspondence with the author, 14 August 2009).

17 [2001] OJ L 12/1.

18 Rectified by the corrigendum of 10 October 2008, [2008] OJ L 269/14.

19 An example of this would be the Czech version of 17(1)(b) of Council Directive 2004/83/EC of 29 April 2004 on minimum standards for the qualification and status of third country nationals or stateless persons as refugees or as persons who otherwise need international protection, [2004] OJ L 304/12. The Czech version excludes a third country national or a stateless person from being eligible for subsidiary protection if s/he committed a "serious crime of non-political nature". Other language versions, however, exclude any individuals who committed "a serious crime" ("eine schwere Straftat"; "un crime grave de droit commun"; "un reato grave", and so on) without any qualification as to its nature.

20 Yet another example from the corrigendum to the Czech version of Regulation 44/2001: Article 24 provides for an additional instance of forum prorogation, namely in cases when the defendant accepts jurisdiction by an active step in the proceedings. The provision reads: "Apart from jurisdiction derived from other provisions of this Regulation, a court of a Member State before which a defendant enters an appearance shall have jurisdiction". The term "defendant enters an appearance", which reads in French "le juge d'un État membre devant lequel le défendeur comparaît" and in German "wenn sich der Beklagte vor ihm auf das Verfahren einlässt", was originally translated into Czech as meaning that the defendant must be indeed physically present at the court's hearing, thus negating the idea that any active (typically written) action by the defendant amounts to implied recognition of jurisdiction.

21 [2006] OJ L 166/1.

the regulation was published in the Official Journal.[22] The corrigendum contains no fewer than 122 correction points in a regulation composed of 75 articles: More or less every article is amended twice, including the title of the regulation itself. The corrigendum points include, *inter alia*, changing singular forms into plural, turning positive statements into negative ones and changing the nature of a list of conditions to be fulfilled (from requiring at least one of the criteria to be met into the requirement that all of the criteria must be met).

This is, unfortunately, not an uncommon example in today's EU legislative practice. Without much exaggeration, the post-corrigendum regulation is, in fact, a different legislative text. It is, however, still entitled "corrigendum", that is, a notice about a rectification of a legislative text.

The Legal Status of a Corrigendum

In strictly legal terms, there are no corrigenda in EC law. That is, at least, the impression one could get when reviewing primary and secondary law concerning the publication of EC legislation. The "constitutional basis" for the publication of secondary EC legislation is Article 254 EC. This provision is fleshed out by three pieces of secondary legislation. First, the decision of the Council of EEC creating the Official Journal[23] established the Official Journal of the European Union. Second, the organization and the tasks of its publisher, the Publications Office of the European Union, are laid down in an inter-institutional decision.[24] Third, the linguistic regime of the publications is provided for in Regulation 1/1958.[25] None of these documents provides, however, for the publication of any corrigenda in the Official Journal. The contemporary practice can thus be said to be just a convention.

Nor does the case law of the Court of Justice shed any light on the legal status of corrigenda. So far, there has been just one instance in which the Court addressed generally the issue of divergence between an adopted version of an EU legislative act and its published version, *United Kingdom v Council*.[26] One of the arguments brought by the UK against the validity of the challenged directive was procedural irregularity. The UK argued that the Secretariat-General of the Council reworded the text of the preamble to the directive after the text was adopted in the Council. The Court of Justice upheld the UK's argument and declared the directive void in its entirety. The Court stated firmly that the Rules

22 [2007] OJ L 211/30.

23 [1958] OJ L 17/390 (French edition).

24 Decision of 26 June 2009 on the organization and operation of the Publications Office of the European Union, [2009] OJ L 168/41.

25 Regulation No. 1 determining the languages to be used by the European Economic Community, [1958] OJ L 17/385 (French edition).

26 Case 131/86 [1988] ECR 905.

of the Procedure of the Council did not empower the Secretariat-General to make any alterations to a measure once approved by the Council. The Court thus underlined the importance of observing legislative procedures and the grave consequences of a failure to do so.[27] However, this case did not concern the issue of corrigenda, but an unauthorized alteration of an approved legislative text within an institution before the publication of the directive. There have been other instances in which the Court faced *ex post* corrections of official EU measures. These concerned, however, mostly Commission decisions, that is, individual administrative acts.[28]

It can thus be said that EU law itself provides very little guidance on what are corrigenda in the Official Journal in legal terms and how should they be approached. Under such circumstances, comparative reasoning and a look into the practice in some of the Member States could be instructive in inducing what is conventionally regarded as a corrigendum of a published legislative text.

Unfortunately, the extent to which the practice of corrigenda is currently (mis-) used in EU law has no parallel in any of the national systems in the Member States.[29] In monolingual Member States, the issue of corrigenda is indeed reserved for the rectification of minor typing, setting or printing mistakes of national legislation. It is not used as a tool for substantively rewriting the content of a legislative measure after its publication. The identification of the authentic text in such monolingual legislative environments appears not to be problematic: There is always one authentic text signed or promulgated by a body participating as the last link in the legislative chain (typically, the head of state), against which the published version of the legislative measure is then examined. The corrigendum is not a self-standing legislative text. It is not promulgated and not published in the same way as a new legislative measure. Normally, the corrigendum will be just in the form of a notice in the Official Journal. It enters into effect at the same time as its "parent-text". The fiction is that it has always been a part of the will of the legislator that just became somewhat lost in the publication process.

Unlike monolingual national systems, it is hard to claim that, in EU law, there is one clear "parent-text" against which rectification of the published text(s) could be carried out. There is, naturally, an original version of the legislative measure adopted. If the legislative measure is adopted in the process of co-decision, then it is the document signed by the president of Parliament and the president of the Council. This source measure is, however, drafted and, prior to publication, available in all the 22 official languages. Due to the principle

27 Case note by Bridge (1988: 741).

28 See, for example, Joined Cases C-48/90 and C-66/90, *Kingdom of the Netherlands and Koninklijke PTT Nederland NV and PTT Post BV v Commission of the European Communities* [1992] ECR I-565 and especially paras 21–25 of the Opinion of Advocate General Van Gerven.

29 Comparative argument offered in Bobek (2009).

of equal authenticity of all the official language versions, however, no single version can be said to be the only authentic one. Thus, no single language version can be picked up and proclaimed to be the authentic one, against which possible correction could then be carried out.

In reality, however, the legislative document is negotiated and adopted in one language version. That version, drafted typically in English,[30] is the result of careful compromises and is not open to much renegotiation; it is then translated into all the other languages and prepared for publication. This often happens under considerable time constraints.[31] It is actually *after* publication that a second round of translation starts, this time with more time and consultation with national authorities. The inflationary (mis-)use of corrigenda in today's EU practice is, in a way, nothing other than *ex post* catching up on translation work which should have been done at the drafting stage.

Meaning-Changing Corrigendum is an Amendment

How to approach the issue of a corrigendum for the purpose of the application of EU law on the national level? First, one should distinguish between the purely formal corrigenda and the meaning-changing ones. Once a corrigendum does not touch upon the meaning of the legal norm, it can be applied retrospectively and with little problems. On the other hand, meaning-changing corrigenda are, in practice, no mere rectifications of obvious typing or typesetting mistakes, but *ex post* alterations of the content of the published EU legal norm. European Union law should thus recognize that meaning-changing corrigenda are amendments in a material sense, which can be applied only prospectively, and even then, with due respect for acquired rights and the legitimate expectations of the individuals concerned.

There is hardly any *per se* approach to all the types of meaning-changing corrigenda. Each case should include a balancing of the two competing interests: on the one hand the EU interest in safeguarding the interpretative unity and equal authenticity of all the languages of the Union and, on the other, respect for legal certainty and the protection of legitimate expectations. The key element in all considerations is the temporal aspect. There is a point at which the protection of legal certainty, legitimate expectation and already created legal relationships take precedence over the obligation to compare language versions.

30 As far as EU legislation produced in the year 2008 is concerned, more than 70 per cent of it is drafted in English, about 15 per cent in French and the rest (15 per cent) in other languages, out of which German is the strongest "small" drafting language. These figures originate from DG Translation Information Booklet *Translating for a Multilingual Community* (Office for Official Publications 2009: 6).

31 See Hakala (2006: 154).

Comparing Language Versions before National Authorities

One of the consequences of the equal authenticity of all the EU languages is the duty to compare the various language versions.[32] When interpreting EU law, national judges are asked to consider other language versions of the relevant EU legislation as well, in order to arrive at the correct interpretation thereof. The task of comparing various language versions of EU law is governed by three basic principles:

1. the prohibition of reading one language version in isolation
2. the prohibition of majoritization
3. overcoming possible discrepancies by taking into account other methods of interpretation, especially the logic, system and purposive reading of the normative text.

How to Do It? The Guidance of the Court of Justice

The prohibition of reading one language version in isolation[33] from the others is an extension of the principle of equal authenticity of all the official languages of the European Union. This principle means that, for instance, an English court cannot seek to "solve" the discrepancy between English and French versions of an EU legal measure by declaring that only the English version is relevant and binding on the territory of the United Kingdom.

The prohibition of "majoritization" – that is, not allowing the majority of language versions to prevail over the minority[34] – is again a logical consequence of the equality of all the official languages. If all the different language versions are equally authentic, then the meaning which is given by the minority, or even by

32 Which is the general consequence of any system in which more than one language is proclaimed to be the authentic language for the publication of legislation; see the comparative assessment of the comparing equally authentic language versions of legislation published in the General Reports of the XVIIth Congress of Comparative Law – *Rapports généraux XVIIe Congrès International de droit comparé*, Utrecht, 16–22 July 2006, Boele-Woelki and van Erp (2007).

33 Most recently in Case C-63/06, *UAB Profisa v Muitinės departamentas prie Lietuvos Respublikos finansų ministerijos* [2007] ECR I-3239, para. 13. For further examples, see: Case 29/69, *Stauder v Stadt Ulm* [1969] ECR 419, para. 3; Case 55/87, *Alexander Moksel Import und Export GmbH & Co Handels-KG v Bundesanstalt für landwirtschaftliche Marktordnung* [1988] ECR 3845, para. 15 or Case C–296/95, *The Queen v Commissioners of Customs and Excise, ex p EMU Tabac SARL, The Man in Black Limited and John Cunningham* [1998] ECR I-1605, para. 36.

34 *UAB Profisa*, ibid.; see also instructive Opinions of the Advocates General in Case C-227/01, *Commission of the European Communities v Kingdom of Spain* [2004] ECR I-8253, paras 22–8 and Case C–371/02, *Björnekulla Fruktindustrier AB v Procordia Food AB* [2004] ECR I-5791, paras 34–43.

just one of them, cannot automatically be outweighed by the meaning given by the majority of the different language versions.

The *Anglo-Polish Fishing Case*[35] affords a classic account of this rule: The case concerned the determination of the precise moment when fish become "goods" for the purpose of customs. Whereas the French, Italian, Greek, Danish and Dutch texts of the relevant EU legislation on the origin of goods referred to the decisive moment as "extraction from the sea" (*extraits de la mer*) – that is, the physical separation of the fish from its natural environment – the German version was satisfied with the moment when the fish is caught (*gefangen*). The English text – "taken from the sea" – appeared to lie somewhere in between these two meanings. The Court of Justice noted that the comparative examination of the various language versions did not enable a conclusion to be reached in favour of any of the language versions, despite the fact that a clear majority of the language versions would hint in the direction of determining the relevant factor to be the moment at which the fish is genuinely separated from its natural environment.[36]

The prohibition of majoritization is absolute; it is applicable not only in situations such as that described above – that is, where there is a genuine divergence in the meaning of a EU rule in various languages – but also in cases of evident shortcomings or mistakes in translation of EU legislation. After the 2004 Enlargement, instances of both phenomena have been numerous. Shortcomings in translation are typically caused by disregard for the established legal terms already extant in legal language or by disregard for already established terminology in the language into which the text is being translated.[37] Mistakes were caused by the hasty translation of tens of thousands of pieces of EU secondary legislation. However, even in cases of clear mistakes in the translation of secondary legislation, the prohibition of majoritization remains.

The *UAB Profisa* case[38] provides the latest example: The case concerned the Lithuanian transposition of the Council Directive 92/83/EEC of 19 October 1992 on the harmonization of the structures of excise duties on alcohol and alcoholic beverages.[39] An erroneous translation of the directive into Lithuanian considerably restricted the grounds upon which an importer of chocolate products

35 Case 100/84, *Commission of the European Communities v United Kingdom of Great Britain and Northern Ireland* [1985] ECR 1169. See also the very helpful and literarily rich opinion of AG Mancini, 1170–76.

36 Opinion of AG Mancini, ibid.: 1182, para. 16.

37 See, for example, Case 55/87, *Alexander Moksel Import und Export GmbH & Co Handels-KG v Bundesanstalt für landwirtschaftliche Marktordnung* [1988] ECR 3845, in which similar problem arose because of a divergence in terminology in German translations of Community Regulations and the introduction of a new term "*Werktag*" without clarifying its relationship to the already extant "*Arbeitstag*".

38 Case C-63/06, *UAB Profisa v Muitinės departamentas prie Lietuvos Respublikos finansų ministerijos* [2007] ECR I-3239.

39 [1992] OJ L 316/21.

containing ethyl alcohol could be exempted from the excise duty. The national implementing law just copied the narrow definition from the wrongly translated directive and denied the importer in question the possibility of exemption from the duty. It appears that, in the particular case, the meaning in all other official languages was clear, demonstrating that a translation mistake had occurred in the Lithuanian version. However, even in this case, the Court of Justice maintained that one language version cannot be "outvoted" by the contrary and clear meaning of the other 19.

The preceding two principles are only capable of detecting problems among the various language versions of the text. They are, however, not able to answer the question: What is the "correct" meaning? In reality, they have quite the contrary effect: After other language versions are considered, a difference in the various texts is detected. This divergence cannot, however, be solved on the basis of simple reassertion of how many languages lean in one direction and how many in the other, that is, by some form of language "voting". If the two preceding principles were to be left on their own, they would create an impasse. The divergence is bridged by resorting to a third principle, which allows us to overcome the stalemate: One is allowed to disregard the conflicting language versions in favour of the systematic or purposive reading of the statute, which is independent of the conflicting texts. In the words of the Court of Justice:

> Where there is divergence between the various language versions of a Community text, the provision in question must be interpreted by reference to the purpose and general scheme of the rules of which it forms part.[40]

This particular approach meant, for instance, in the already discussed case of *Anglo-Polish Fishing*, resorting to the intention of the EU legislature and to systematic interpretation of the rules on the origin of goods in EU law.[41] In the *UAB Profisa* case, the decisive aspect was the objective pursued by the exemptions and the systematic reading of the directive,[42] which meant that the exemption from duty of those products covered by the provision was the rule and refusal to exempt was the exception.

Theoretically, the principles of comparative linguistic interpretation, together with the principle of equal authenticity of all the linguistic versions could, if taken to the extreme, be interpreted as meaning that the content of a EU legal norm is not

---

40 Case C-1/02, *Privat-Molkerei Borgmann GmbH & Co KG v Hauptzollamt Dortmund* [2004] ECR I-3219, para. 25; Case C-437/97, *Evangelischer Krankenhausverein Wien v Abgabenberufungskommission Wien and Wein & Co HandelsgesmbH v Oberösterreichische Landesregierung* [2000] ECR I-1157, para. 42 or Case C-372/88, *Milk Marketing Board of England and Wales v Cricket St Thomas Estate* [1990] ECR I-1345, para. 19.

41 Cited supra, note 35, paras 18 and 19.

42 Cited supra, note 38, paras 17 and 18.

contained in, for example, its French or English version, but only in the aggregate of all the authentic language versions. Correct literal interpretation[43] of any single piece of EU legislation that is drafted in more languages must thus involve the parallel reading of the other language versions.

Whether "other" means "all" or just "some" has never been specifically addressed by the Court of Justice. The Court has never expressly stated that comparing language versions means the obligation to compare all of them; on the other hand, if one were really to believe that the real content of an EU legal norm is contained in the agglomerate of the various language versions, then, implicitly, it would involve the reading of all the authentic language versions.

How is it Actually Done?

National judges do not normally read any language versions other than their own, not even (or perhaps especially not) the judges of last instance courts, upon whom the Court of Justice has laid a specific duty in this respect.[44] There would typically be two instances in which national judges would consider some of the other language versions of EU legislation. First, if an argument based on inconsistency amongst several language versions would be (sometimes very persistently) raised by a party that would seek to rely on a different – for it more favourable – reading of a piece of EU legislation before the national court. Second, a judge would look into other language versions of his or her own motion typically only if the degree of incomprehension of the national version of a EU piece of legislation reaches the stage at which the interpretation of the piece of legislation in the national language alone would lead to absurd results. Comparing language versions could thus be conceived of as an alternative to a "mischief rule" or a "rule against absurdity".

The reasons why national judges would only rarely follow the guidance given by the Court of Justice are varied; there are obvious time constraints and the issue of linguistic competence itself.[45] In those few cases in which other language versions would be compared, the genuine comparison would be quite different from the visions of the Court of Justice. National judges would, first, limit themselves to one or only few of the more significant languages within the Union (English, French and German). Second, the reference to other language versions would be used as a confirming argument in support of the conclusion already

43 One should be mindful that the comparison of the various language versions of the EU legislation forms a part of literal interpretation of the rule. It is not, for which it is commonly mistaken, comparative reasoning as such.

44 Case 283/81, *Srl CILFIT and Lanificio di Gavardo SpA v Ministry of Health* [1982] ECR 3415, para. 18.

45 Which is more assumed than real; to the knowledge of the author, the proof of the proficiency in least one foreign language is not a condition for the appointment to the judicial office in any of the Member States.

reached via interpretation of the text in the national language. Additionally, the depth of the argument tends to be quite far from genuine language comparison; the practice is just to place two or three notions in the foreign language in parentheses next to the word or notion in the original language. The persuasive value of such an enterprise is questionable.[46]

An example of the reasoning schema described above might be the series of decisions handed down by the Czech Supreme Administrative Court[47] concerning the interpretation of the Protocol on Asylum for Nationals of Member States of the European Union.[48] The comparison of various language versions was carried out by the SAC in the effort to identify what precisely is the procedural duty a national administrative authority has when dealing with a request for asylum filed by the national of another EU Member State. In its reasoning, the SAC used references to the English, German and French versions of a provision of Article 1 of the Protocol just to confirm that the meaning of the provision was equally vague in the other languages as well.

A more positive argument out of comparing various language versions was recently made by the *Krajský soud v Ostravě* [Regional Court in Ostrava]. The issue addressed by the court was whether or not a list in a sub-section of the Community Common Customs Tariff[49] is an enumerative or closed one. The court has consulted the English, French, German and Slovak versions of the same provision and has found that in all of these language versions, the list is indeed supposed to be an enumerative, that is, a non-closed list.[50]

A rather questionable example of "comparing language versions" of EU legislation is a recent decision of the Czech Supreme Court.[51] The case concerned the interpretation of the term "establishment" contained in Article 2(h) of the Council Regulation No. 1346/2000 on insolvency proceedings.[52] The scope of this definition was crucial for the purpose of defining where the debtor's main interest was located and where should, in accordance with the regulation, insolvency proceedings against him be opened. At the beginning of its reasoning on merits, the Supreme Court summarized the applicable law. In doing so, it also cited the full definition of the term "establishment" in Czech as well as in all the other (then) 19 official languages of the European Union. Without further using these 20 aligned versions of the definition for its reasoning, the Court just later stated, "It

46 For many further examples and a detailed discussion on the instance of comparative linguistic reasoning before national courts, see Derlén (2009).

47 Judgment of 19 July 2006, case no. 3 Azs 259/2005, no. 977/2006 Coll. SAC

48 [1997] OJ C 340/103.

49 Council Regulation (EEC) No. 2658/87 of 23 July 1987 on the tariff and statistical nomenclature and on the Common Customs Tariff [1987] OJ L 256/1.

50 Judgment of 4 December 2007, case no. 22 Ca 167/2007, unpublished.

51 Judgment of 31 January 2008, case no. 29 Odo 164/2006, published as no. 48/2008 of the Collection of Judicial Decisions.

52 [2000] OJ L 160/1.

entertains no doubts" that all the language versions mean the same, that is, that the debtor indeed has his "establishment" on the territory of the Czech Republic in the sense of the regulation.

One cannot but appreciate the quality and the depth of argument of the court when addressing the applicable EC law, including also detailed review of the case law of the Court of Justice and also decisions of higher jurisdictions of other Member States. However, the part in which the Court seeks to compare the various language versions of the EU legislation simply by reproducing their content in 20 official languages and then just stating, without any further reasoning, that they all mean the same is a rather questionable enterprise. On the other hand, it shows the limits of any use of comparing the various language versions by national courts, which will be addressed in the concluding part of this chapter.

Conclusions: The Limits of Multilingualism in the National Forums

The Creation of De Facto Reference Languages

Although the EU law still formally labours under the assumption that all the official languages of the EU are equally authentic, one may observe that on the national level, the practice arrived at the use of reference languages. These typically are the major languages of the Union (English, French and German). In their use and selection, the national legal cultures follow the previous cultural patterns: For instance, in Central Europe (Czech Republic, Slovakia, Hungary and Poland), the first reference language would be either English or German.

To these "primary" languages, the practice would add the consultation of other "neighbouring" languages. For instance, a Czech judge trying to look at a piece of EU legislation in other official languages would, apart from one of the "major" languages listed above, consult also the Slovak or the Polish versions. Both of these languages are West-Slavic languages, which can be read and understood by a Czech native speaker without additional linguistic knowledge.

In a way, therefore, the national level is, rather intuitively and for practical reasons, that is, not deliberately, mimicking the development on the EU level. After the 2004 Enlargement, the EU institutions accepted that direct translations may no longer be possible in all situations and started pivotal translations via five major languages – English, French, German, Spanish and Italian. Similarly on the national level, the number of "reference" languages tends to be limited to the same languages, perhaps enriched by a related language or languages within the same language family. At both levels, therefore, there is a difference between the proclaimed linguistic equality and the practical reality.

Comparing the Language Version as an Instrument of Confusion?

It is clear that the principal reason for reaffirming the need for the comparison of the various language versions is the equal authenticity of all the official and working languages of the European Union. However, there are two elements that make this interpretative approach somewhat constitutionally suspicious: the end at which it traditionally arrives and the unpredictability as to when it will be used by the EU institutions, especially by the Court of Justice.

As to the ends to which it arrives: Conventionally, one understands methods or "canons" of legal interpretation as the way of eliminating uncertainties in the interpretation of a legal provision. In other words, the methods of interpretation are there to help, in cases of doubts, the interpreter to arrive at a reasonable reading of the norm. Their aim is not to create additional problems. The requirement of a comparative linguistic exercise in 23 languages (or even in any lower, more manageable number of languages) does little but create problems. Considered from this perspective, the comparative language exercise is not a "method of interpretation", but instead a "method of obfuscation" of a legal provision.

The comparison of the various language versions typically leads to greater confusion and legal uncertainty. Its impact is to release the interpreter from the text of the rule itself: The interpreter detects, with the reference to divergence among the various language versions, an inconsistency in the various language versions. The only way of overcoming the inconsistency is by setting aside the wording and, by relying upon a systematic or purposive reading of the text of the law, reformulating the rule. The requirement of the comparative language exercise thus can, in some instances, operate as a tool for defiance of the text of the legal provision.

An example of such reasoning might be one of the first instances in which the Court of Justice used the comparison of various language versions, the *Robert Bosch* case.[53] The case concerned, *inter alia*, the interpretation of the term "agreements … which may affect the trade between the Member States". This term, contained in Article 81(1) EC, is the key jurisdictional criterion for the allocation of competence between the Communities and the Member States in the area of competition law. The issue which arose in the then four official languages was whether to "affect" should be interpreted negatively (to restrict) or neutrally (to influence, without distinction whether positively or negatively). The respective languages were split on this issue: whereas the French "*affecter*" was neutral as its meaning, the German "*beeinträchtigen*" or the Italian "*pregiudicare*" were negative in their meaning.

The Advocate General Lagrande in his opinion[54] suggested to the Court, following a very similar argumentative process to that one described above,

53 Case 13/61, *Kledingverkoopbedrijf de Geus en Uitdenbogerd v Robert Bosch GmbH*, English special edition, 45.

54 Opinion of 27 February 1962.

that it should adopt a broad reading of the provision. The notion should include any affectation of the internal market, be it positive or negative. The Court of Justice silently followed the Advocate General, without conducting a similar linguistic study itself; it simply asserted that "affecting" means influencing in whatever way.

The *Bosch* case provides the example in which comparing language versions was used in the way described above – as a tool of untying the interpreter from the text of the treaty and "reinterpreting" it in a more Euro-friendly way, typically giving broader competence to the EU institutions, based on the aims and purpose of the treaty or secondary legislation. Is such approach constitutionally sound?

One may, of course, claim that it is the inevitable consequence of equal authenticity of all the language versions. That is not entirely true; its consequence might be the duty to compare the language versions, not the fact that the comparison will always lead to an interpretation that empowers, not restricts, the European Union.

The second objection raised is the unpredictability as to when the Court of Justice will use comparing the various language versions. Despite having read hundreds of decisions of the Court of Justice, one is still not able to discern any visible patterns as to when comparing various language versions will be employed. If the method was indeed a necessary instrument in realizing the multilingual character of EU law, then its employment would be compulsory in every single instance. If not, then at least there should be a visible rule as to when the Court of Justice will consult the various language versions. Absent either of the two solutions, the question is whether the procedure might not just be used in cases where detachment from the text of the legal rule and its "reformulation" with the help of the aims and the purpose fits the interpreter?

Language Comparison and the Institutional Balance

There is yet one other problematic element of the duty to compare the various language versions: the fact that it reallocates the responsibility for correctly translating EU legislation and may potentially upset the institutional legislative balance between the Union and the Member States.

From the legal point of view, there is no doubt that the correct translation and due publication of EU legislation is the duty of EU institutions. It is also clear that the Union bears the responsibility for absent translations as well as wrongful translations, the two scenarios discussed earlier in this chapter. At the same time, however, the Court of Justice consistently held that all the institutions of the Member States, including the national legislator, are obliged, when working with EU law, to compare the various language versions. If the national authorities, however, fail to do so, who is liable for potential damages, provided that, for instance, the absent or wrongful translations of EU legislation caused damage to individuals?

Such question, which arose at the hypothetical level in the *Skoma-Lux* scenario,[55] is also present in the cases of the issue of corrigenda or the duty to compare the various language versions generally. An example of the latter is provided in the already-discussed *UAB Profisa* case.[56] There, the wrongful transposition of a EU directive was caused solely by the original incorrect translation of the directive into Lithuanian by the EU institutions. However, even under such circumstances, the Court of Justice held that the national legislator should have also read the other language versions. Implicitly, therefore, it was saying that the national legislator is obliged to read the other language versions in order to detect any potential mistakes.

By stating that all the national authorities have the duty to compare various language versions, even in cases of translation mistakes committed by the Union, the EU institutions are passing on their responsibility to translate and publish correctly. If put to an extreme, an EU institution, irrespective of the fact how poorly a legislative measure was drafted or translated, would be never wrong: It is the duty and possibly then also the responsibility of the national application "filter" to detect mistakes made by the EU institutions. One may only wonder whether the interpretation of the duty of sincere and loyal cooperation between the Union and its Member States could be stretched so far.

The Outlook – Language Clusters, Particularization and the Status Quo?

Despite the various problems with the multilingual character of EU law in the Member States described in this chapter, it is quite unlikely that anything would change in legal terms in the foreseeable future. Although the Court of Justice stated that linguistic regime of secondary law introduced by Regulation 1/1958 does not represent any permanent principle of overall language equality in EU law,[57] Article 342 TFEU [ex Article 290 EC] and the requirement of unanimity in the Council for any changes to the general linguistic regime of secondary law contained therein set clear limits to potential change.

It is thus quite likely that the current linguistic regime will continue, at least on the surface, the formal principle of the equal authenticity of all the official versions. At the same time, however, the reality will evolve into an even greater particularization and the *de facto* creation of language clusters within EU law, while formally preserving the status quo. On the other hand, this is perhaps as good as it gets. To start reducing the number of official language and thus depriving the national authorities and courts of direct access to EU legislation and decisions of the Court of Justice would negate one of the basic foundations of the Union. It might also put in question some of the key constitutional principles: For

55 For a detailed discussion, see Bobek (2007: 71–74).

56 Discussed above, text to the notes 38–40.

57 Case C-361/01 P, *Christina Kik v. Office for Harmonisation in the Internal Market* [2003] ECR I-8283. Case note Nic Shuibhne, Niamh (2004): 41 *CML Rev* 1093-1111.

instance, could there be direct effect and primacy of EU law in the absence of the access to the law in the language of the Member State in which it is to apply? One may only speculate whether the acceptance of these and other basic tenets of the domestic application of EU law would be so smooth if the national constitutional or supreme judges would be faced with a mass of legislation which is not available in their national language. The problems relating to the varieties of the domestic application of the European Convention for the Protection of Human Rights and the case law of the European Court of Human Rights, which are only available in English and French, provide a good example in this respect.

References

Bobek, M. 2007. The Binding Force of Babel: The Enforcement of EC Law Unpublished in the Languages of the New Member States. *Cambridge Yearbook of European Legal Studies*, Vol. 9. Oxford: Hart Publishing, 43–80.

Bobek, M. 2009. Corrigenda in the Official Journal of the European Union: Community Law as Quicksand. *European Law Review*, 34, 950–62.

Boele-Woelki, K. and van Erp, S. (eds) 2007. General Reports of the XVIIth Congress of Comparative Law – *Rapports généraux XVIIe Congrès International de droit comparé*, Utrecht, July 16–22, 2006. Brussels/Utrecht: Bruylant/Eleven International Publishing.

Bridge, J. 1988. Case 68/86, *United Kingdom v Council*, Judgment of 23 February 1988; and Case 131/86, *United Kingdom v Council*, Judgment of 23 February 1988. *Common Market Law Review*, 25, 733–42.

Derlén, M. 2009. *Multilingual Interpretation of European Union Law*. Alphen aan den Rijn: Kluwer Law International.

Hakala, P. 2006. Legislative Process from a Parliament Perspective – Past Practice in 11 Languages and Current Challenges in 20, in *Multilingualism and the Harmonisation of European Law*, edited by B. Pozzo and V. Jacometti. Alphen aan den Rijn: Kluwer Law International, 147–64.

Chapter 8

In Defence of (Limited) Multilingualism: Problems and Possibilities of the Multilingual Interpretation of European Union Law in National Courts

Mattias Derlén

Introduction – Why the Long Faces?

The multilingual regime of the European Union can be analyzed from many different perspectives, as demonstrated by the present book. This chapter concentrates on the multilingual interpretation of European Union law. In other words, how does the equal standing of the now 23 official languages affect the Union legal system? The most striking aspect of this discussion is the prevailing feeling of gloom. Multilingualism is perceived as a problem, a difficulty and an obstacle. It should be readily admitted that I have myself stressed the complexity of the multilingual interpretation of European Union law (Derlén 2007). No doubt it is a challenge to maintain an extensive multilingual regime, such as the Union's, and make it a natural and effective part of the legal system. However, in this chapter I will argue that the situation is far from hopeless. First of all it is important to understand where the problem truly lies. It is not multilingualism *per se* that is excessively difficult but the conflicting and unclear directions concerning the relationship between multilingualism and the interpretation of Union law emanating from the European Court of Justice in Luxembourg. The lack of clarity on the part of the Court of Justice has created substantial confusion among national courts, as will be demonstrated below. Multilingualism proper, that is, the existence of several language versions[1] of a given provision of European Union law is, I will argue, an asset rather than a problem, at least when approached in a reasonable way.

This chapter is divided into five parts. In the second part, the approach of the European Court of Justice *vis-à-vis* the issue of multilingualism and the interpretation of European Union law is described in outline. The third part relates how national courts have responded to the guidelines (or rather, lack thereof) from

1 For practical reasons, I use the concept 'language version' when referring to the wording of a Union provision in an official language. On issues of terminology, see Tabory (1980: 170–71).

the Court of Justice on this issue. After having discussed the present application of multilingualism in the courts, the part then turns to the issue of reform. The fourth part sets out the alternatives and suggests a way forward. Finally, the fifth part delivers the conclusions.

The Root of the Problem: Fairytales from Luxembourg

Introduction: The Available Options

The explicit rules on multilingualism in European Union law are limited. Obviously, the treaties are declared to be equally authentic in all the official languages.[2] The language regime of the institutions was famously decided by the very first regulation (Reg. 1/58)[3] of the Community, which in its amended form declares all 23 official languages to be working languages in the institutions. The language regime of the European Court of Justice is determined separately but follows the approach of the other institutions, making all the official languages available before the Court.[4] Important as these provisions are, they provide only a part of the picture. They establish the fact that the treaties, as well as secondary legislation, are equally authentic in all 23 languages. However, it is important to note that they do not say anything further when it comes to the impact of multilingualism on legal interpretation in a European Union context. The decision as to how multilingualism is to affect legal interpretation has been left to the European Court of Justice.

In theory, the Court of Justice had three main alternatives when it came to the use of multilingualism in the application and interpretation of Union law. In other words, the notion, established by the Union legislator, that all official language versions are equally authentic could have (at least) three different meanings. First, it could mean that all languages must always be used, as they form the meaning of the provision together, not separately. In other words, the legal provision has a single meaning, which is expressed by all the language versions taken together. Secondly, it could indicate a general right to use, and rely on, a single-language version. The Swedish version of a Union provision is as authentic and authoritative as the French or English version, and, therefore, could be used on its own, without consulting other language versions. This line of thinking would correspond to the

2 Article 225 of the EURATOM Treaty and, following the changes by the Treaty of Lisbon, Article 55 of the EU Treaty and Article 358 of the Treaty on the Functioning of the European Union (henceforth TFEU), where the latter now only refers to Article 55 EU.

3 EEC Council Regulation No. 1 of 15 April 1958 determining the languages to be used by the European Economic Community, OJ 17, 6.10.1958, 385–6.

4 See Article 342 TFEU and Article 29 of the Rules of Procedure of the European Court of Justice as well as Article 64 of the Statute of the Court of Justice.

idea behind Article 33.3 of the 1969 Vienna Convention on the Law of Treaties.[5] Article 33 concerns the interpretation of multilingual treaties and paragraph 3 states that '[t]he terms of the treaty are presumed to have the same meaning in each authentic text'. While the meaning of this paragraph is disputed (Kjær 2003: 54, Hilf 1973: 54), it could be seen as granting a right to rely on a single-language version of a provision, given the presumption of equal meaning (Tabory 1980: 198–9). The same logic could be applied to Union law. The equal authority of the various languages could be regarded as granting a right to rely on a single-language version. Finally, one could imagine a middle-of-the-road alternative, where a right to rely on a single-language version would persist as long as this version is unambiguous and free from doubt. This alternative can also be illustrated with Article 33.3 of the Vienna Convention. It has been discussed how long the presumption in Article 33.3 holds and when other language versions should be consulted. Clearly, when a divergence of meaning is discovered among different language versions, the presumption ceases to hold. However, as classically observed by Tabory (1980: 199), here we enter a catch-22 situation. How are we to discover the differences of meaning if we consult only one language version, relying on the presumption of equal meaning in Article 33.3? Presumably we will have to abandon Article 33.3 when faced with an allegation of discrepancy, or when the meaning of the national language version is unclear or ambiguous (Hilf 1973: 80, Kuner 1991: 962). This would amount to a criterion of doubt – granting a right to use a single-language version in the absence of interpretative doubt. Again, the same approach would be possible in European Union law. The treaties grant all official languages equal authority, thus implying that the meaning of each version is correct and can be relied upon. However, in the face of a potential divergence of meaning, the interpreter would have to move on to consult other versions, as varying interpretations of a provision of Union law in different Member States would undermine the uniform nature of Union law. The fact that a version is unclear or ambiguous would be an indication of a potential divergence of meaning.

These were the fundamental options open to the Court of Justice regarding the application of multilingualism to legal interpretation. The problem, which will be explored below, is that the guidelines supplied by the court are vague, sometimes contradictory and very far reaching (to say the least).

A Criterion of Doubt – Doubtful!

For a long time it appeared as if the Court of Justice had chosen the third option outlined above by introducing a criterion of doubt. This was famously adopted in case 19/67 *van der Vecht*.[6] Here the Court of Justice concluded that:

5 Done at Vienna on 23 May 1969. Entered into force on 27 January 1980. United Nations, *Treaty Series*, Vol. 1155: 331.

6 Case 19/67 *Bestuur der Sociale Verzekeringsbank v J.H van der Vecht* [1967] ECR 345.

> the need for a uniform interpretation of Community regulations necessitates that this passage should not be considered in isolation, but that, *in cases of doubt*, it should be interpreted and applied in the light of the versions existing in the other three languages.

In other words, in cases free from doubt, a language version could be interpreted in isolation. Thus, the interpreter could rely on a clear and unambiguous wording as expressing the correct meaning. Only if the national version was unclear or ambiguous would there be a need to consult other languages, in order to determine the meaning of the provision in question. Naturally, one could argue that this is placing too much weight on the four little words in *van der Vecht*, and that it is generally unwise to interpret judgments of the Court of Justice *a contrario*. It is, therefore, appropriate to examine the *van der Vecht* judgment in a bit more detail, to see if a criterion of doubt was actually employed. The case concerned an early regulation (Reg. 3/58)[7] relating to social security for workers using the right to free movement. One of the issues of the case concerned the interpretation of Article 13 A of the regulation. Article 13 A constituted an exception to Article 12, the main rule of the regulation according to which the worker was subject to the social security rules of the state in which he or she was employed. The question was whether Article 13 A should be applied to workers who were engaged solely to work in a Member State in which they did not reside permanently and in which the employing undertaking was not established. The Court of Justice concluded that the Dutch language version of the regulation 'might suggest' that such situations would fall outside of Article 13 A and thus be covered by the main rule in Article 12. However, a comparison with the other language versions demonstrated that the above-described situation was indeed covered by Article 13 A. In conclusion, the Court of Justice could be said to have not only spoken of but also made use of a criterion of doubt, in the sense that the Court indicated that the Dutch language version was somewhat unclear.[8]

However, while many cases imply the existence of a criterion of doubt, an approach that is perfectly in line with Article 33.3 of the Vienna Convention, other judgments point in a different direction. The most obvious example is case C-219/95 *Ferriere*,[9] concerning the interpretation of what was then Article

7 Regulation No. 3 of the Council of the EEC concerning social security for migrant workers, OJ 16 December 1958, 561 et seq.

8 This approach was confirmed in later cases, most notably in case C-372/88 *Milk Marketing Board of England and Wales v Cricket St. Thomas Estate* [1990] ECR I-1345. Here the Court of Justice observed a number of terminological discrepancies in the English version before it moved on to examine the other language versions, *Cricket St. Thomas*, paras 13–16.

9 C-219/95 *P. Ferriere Nord SpA v The Commission of the European Communities* [1997] ECR I-4411.

85 in the EC Treaty, on agreements limiting competition.[10] The Italian version of Article 85 indicated that an agreement would have to have both as its object and effect to limit competition in order to be caught by Article 85, while all other language versions made it clear that the conditions were alternative, not cumulative. The Court of Justice emphasized that the provision should be interpreted in the light of all the language versions. It expressly concluded that the need to engage in multilingual interpretation was not affected by the fact that the Italian language version was – read in isolation – clear and unambiguous (*Ferriere*: paras 13–15).

However, even after the *Ferriere* case, the situation is far from clear. The Court of Justice continues to employ the 'in cases of doubt' expression,[11] sometimes even varying the terminology among various language versions of the judgment in question.[12] So, where does this leave us? The *Ferriere* case makes it clear that no reliance can be placed on a single-language version, if a divergence of meaning is detected. Given the fact that the Court of Justice in *Ferriere*, paragraph 15, refers to *van der Vecht*, the Court might be trying to say that a provision cannot be regarded as clear and unambiguous unless all language versions have been consulted. Thus, 'doubt' should be understood as general interpretative doubt. However, this would deprive the expression 'in cases of doubt' of any real and independent meaning. Another, slightly more cynical interpretation, is that a single-language version can be relied upon as demonstrating the correct meaning of a provision, as long as no discrepancy of meaning is later discovered. This would explain both the strict stance in *Ferriere* and the continued use of the 'in cases of doubt' phrase in later cases. It is simply two different matters. As a working method, a clear and unambiguous wording can be presumed to express the correct meaning of the provision, but if a divergence of meaning is detected, the clear meaning cannot be allowed to take precedence over other versions. Naturally, as with most questions concerning the Court of Justice, a final alternative is that no particular reliance can be placed on what the Court says, rendering the 'in cases of doubt' expression useless. While this is an easy way out of the problematic situation, it is also deeply unsatisfying. If we are to give up on the basic premise that the Court of Justice

10 Now Article 101 TFEU.

11 For some recent examples, see cases C-199/08 *Erhard Eschig v UNIQA Sachversicherung AG*, not yet published, judgment of the Second Chamber 10 September 2009, para. 54, C-263/08 *Djurgården-Lilla Värtans Miljöskyddsförening v Stockholms kommun genom dess marknämnd*, not yet published, judgment of the Second Chamber 15 October 2009, para. 25 and C-347/08 *Vorarlberger Gebietskrankenkasse v WGV-Schwäbische Allgemeine Versicherungs AG*, not yet published, judgment of the Third Chamber 17 September 2009, para. 26.

12 See case C-296/95 *The Queen v Commissioners of Customs and Excise, ex parte EMU Tabac SARL, The Man in Black Ltd, John Cunningham* [1998] ECR I-1605, where a criterion of doubt is used in para. 36 of the German and French language versions of the judgment while the English language version of the same paragraph contains no such phrase.

means to relay some meaning with the chosen language, we might as well turn out the lights and go home.

Rule of Law and Legal Uncertainty

While the general use of a criterion of doubt was unclear, the right to rely on a single-language version could still be claimed as part of the principle of legal certainty, at least in cases with financial or criminal law consequences. The Court of Justice has made it very clear that it regards the principles of legal certainty and legitimate expectations as important aspects of the Union legal system.[13] Following this case law, we know that Union law with financial or criminal law consequences must be clearly and precisely drafted. Furthermore, we know that reasonable expectations on the content of the law will be protected. How does this then translate to multilingual interpretation? It would be reasonable to assume that the principles of legal certainty and legitimate expectations grant a right to rely on the wording of a single-language version in criminal or taxation law contexts, or at least impose certain limitations on acceptable interpretations in such situations. A number of judgments from the Court of Justice would seem to support this assumption. In the well-known case C-161/06 *Skoma-Lux*,[14] paras 32–51, the Court of Justice declared that a regulation not published in Czech in the Official Journal could not be enforced against individuals in the Czech Republic, even though a Czech version was available for example by way of the EUR-Lex database. The Court here adopted a formal standpoint: arguing that publication in the Official Journal is the only acceptable option. This could be regarded as a strong voice in favour of rule of law and legal certainty. Union legislation creates not only rights but also obligations for the citizens of the Member States, who must, therefore, be able to inform themselves of the content of that legislation in their own language. Naturally, the situation in *Skoma-Lux* was extreme in the sense that no official Czech version existed. The more common problem would be how much reliance can be placed on a single, existing language version. Also in this regard, the case law of the Court of Justice offers hope, most notably in case C-1/02 *Privat-Molkerei Borgmann*.[15] Here the Court of Justice emphasized the

13 See, regarding legal certainty, for example, case 13/61 *Kledingverkoopbedrijf de Geus en Uitdenbogerd v Robert Bosch GmbH and Maatschappij tot voorzetting van de zaken der Firma Willem van Rijn* [1962] ECR 45, case 10/69 *S.A. Portelange v S.A Smith Corona Marchant International and others* [1969] ECR 309 and case 325/85 *Ireland v Commission of the European Communities* [1987] ECR 5041. Regarding legitimate expectations see for example case 112/77 *August Töpfer & Co. GmbH v Commission of the European Communities* [1978] ECR 1019 and case 31/80 *NV L'Oreal and SA L'Oreal v PVBA 'Die Nieuwe AMCK'* [1980] ECR 3775.

14 Case C-161/06 *Skoma-Lux sro v Celní ředitelství Olomouc* [2007] ECR I-10841.

15 Case C-1/02 *Privat-Molkerei Borgmann GmbH & Co. KG v Hauptzollamt Dortmund* [2004] ECR I-3219.

importance of the principle of legal certainty, in particular, as regards rules that may lead to the imposition of charges on economic operators. In a situation where a provision is open to diverging interpretations, as was the case in *Privat-Molkerei Borgmann* due to variations in wording among the different language versions, it should be interpreted in favour of the economic operator that has relied on the provision (*Privat-Molkerei Borgmann*: paras 29–32).

However, this is not the typical approach of the Court of Justice when it comes to the relationship between legal certainty and multilingual interpretation. Two of the most obvious examples of a very different approach will be used to illustrate this point: the cases 238/84 *Röser*[16] and 173/88 *Henriksen.*[17] In the former case, the Court of Justice admitted that the interpretation suggested by the applicant was possible given the wording of the German version of the provision in question. However, the other language versions made it clear that the opposite interpretation had to be adopted (*Röser*: paras 22–25). It is particularly noteworthy that the Court of Justice adopted this approach despite the warning issued by the Commission. The latter argued that a broad interpretation of the provision, as undertaken by the Court, was out of the question since this would have criminal law consequences in Germany (*Röser*: paras 13–14). Similarly, in *Henriksen* the Court of Justice adopted a broad interpretation in a matter of taxation. The question was whether letting of garages was excluded from value added tax. A number of language versions, including the national version relied on by the applicant, indicated that it was. However, the Court of Justice examined other language versions as well as the purpose of the provision and came to the opposite conclusion (*Henriksen*: paras 9–13). Again there were words of warning, this time from Advocate General Jacobs, who favoured a literal interpretation of the provision, given the tax law context.[18]

How to explain these very different attitudes *vis-à-vis* legal certainty? It would appear that it is the *Skoma-Lux* and *Privat-Molkerei Borgmann* cases that deviate from the common approach of the Court. *Skoma-Lux* is different in the sense that it concerns the formal side of legal certainty. Legal certainty and rule of law require the existence of an official version of the provision in the language in question. On this there can be no compromise. However, paradoxically, once that language version is in existence, no reliance can be placed upon it, even in criminal or taxation law situations. While the *Privat-Molkerei Borgmann* case might appear to be saying something else, a closer inspection brings this case into line with *Röser* and *Henriksen.* In the *Privat-Molkerei Borgmann* case (paras 29–32) the Court emphasized that neither the context nor the purpose precluded the adopted interpretation. In fact, the context and purpose offered no interpretative guidance at all. In this situation, the Court of Justice fell back on the principle of legal

16 Case 238/84 *Criminal proceedings against Hans Röser* [1986] ECR 795.

17 Case 173/88 *Skatteministeriet v Morten Henriksen* [1989] ECR 2763.

18 Opinion of Advocate General Jacobs in the *Henriksen* case, delivered the 17 May 1989, paras 11–20.

certainty. To put it somewhat dramatically, the context and purpose rule supreme and take precedence over legal certainty. The applicants in *Röser* and *Henriksen* simply had the bad fortune to be on the wrong side of the purpose, so to say. The limited weight given to legal certainty in these situations may be seen as an abdication on the part of the Court of Justice. The uniform nature of Union law apparently makes it impossible to deviate from a broad interpretation of the provision, considering all language versions as well as the purpose. This is simply how the Court determines the meaning of Union law. The kindest interpretation would be that the Court of Justice thereby leaves the application of legal certainty and other fundamental principles to national courts.

All Languages? Really?

If there is no criterion of doubt, and thereby no right to rely on a single-language version, in general or in criminal and taxation law contexts, the question naturally arises how many languages the national court is expected to consult. This was famously addressed in the context of preliminary rulings in the seminal case 283/81 *CILFIT*.[19] Here the Court of Justice stated that the interpretation of Union law could be left for national last instance courts, even in the absence of a previous ruling on the issue from Luxembourg. However, that was only possible if the conditions for *acte clair* were fulfilled, requiring the matter to be equally obvious to courts in all Member States as well as to the European Court of Justice. As famously established in paragraph 18, this requirement necessitated a comparison of the different language versions of the provision in question.

The *acte clair* criterion in *CILFIT* was heavily criticized, not only in the literature but also by a number of Advocates General.[20] However, despite the heavy criticism the European Court of Justice has not backed down from the requirements of *CILFIT*. In fact, the Court simply did not discuss paragraph 18 of *CILFIT* when it was challenged by the Advocates General. Thus, the requirement to consult all language versions is still law, in all its absurdity. The silence from the Court of Justice might, at best, indicate that the Court is locked down in disagreement concerning this requirement. If that is the case it is be expected that the Court will neither reject nor confirm paragraph 18 of *CILFIT*.

19 Case 283/81 *Srl CILFIT and Lanificio di Gavardo SpA v Ministry of Health* [1982] ECR 3415.

20 For an overview of the discussion in the literature, see Derlén (2009, Chapter 4.5.2). Regarding the critique from within the Court see Opinion of Advocate General Jacobs in case C-338/95 *Wiener S.I. GmbH v Hauptzollamt Emmerich* [1997] ECR I-6495, delivered 10 July 1997, paras 64–5, opinion by Advocate General Stix-Hackl in case C-495/03 *Intermodal Transports BV v Staatssecretaris van Financien* [2005] ECR I-8151, delivered on 12 April 2005, para. 99 and opinion of Advocate General Ruiz-Jarabo Colomer in case C-461/03 *Gaston Schul Douane- Expediteur BV v Minister van Landbouw, Natuur en Voedselkwaliteit* [2005] ECR I-10513, delivered 30 June 2005, paras 44–59.

Obviously, the *acte clair* doctrine as established in *CILFIT* is, in itself, limited in its application to the context of national last instance courts requesting preliminary rulings. However, it is important to note that the requirement to consult all language versions is not limited to this context. The Court of Justice has upheld the requirement also in other cases. The case C-498/03 *Kingscrest*[21] is an excellent example.[22] In *Kingscrest* the VAT and Duties Tribunal in London enquired whether it was permissible to use other language versions in interpreting the Sixth VAT Directive 77/388/EEC.[23] The answer from the Court of Justice highlights the importance of multilingual interpretation. It stated that the directive 'must be interpreted taking account of all the language versions' (*Kingscrest*, para. 27). In other words, consulting all language versions was not only permissible but mandatory, despite the fact that the referring court was obviously not a court of last instance. The Court of Justice is providing a general explanation – stating that Union law simply cannot be properly understood without taking its multilingual character into account.

Reconciliation: Does the Right Hand Know What the Left Hand is Doing?

The final issue to be addressed in this part is the reconciliation of language versions with diverging meanings. Obviously, if all language versions of a given provision of the Union are to be consulted in every instance, situations of diverging meanings will occur. This might depend on human error: The Directorate-General for Translation at the Commission translated 1,805,689 pages in 2008 (European Commission 2009: 5), and it is certainly understandable if mistakes are made occasionally. Furthermore, as has been argued extensively in the literature, expressing legal concepts with the same content in many different languages is challenging, to say the least.[24] The obvious question then is how language versions with diverging meanings should be reconciled. Naturally, this question is not unique to European Union law. It has previously been discussed in international law, not least in connection with the above mentioned 1969 Vienna Convention on the Law of Treaties. Several different methods of reconciling

---

21 C-498/03 *Kingscrest Associates Ltd & Montecello Ltd v Commissioners of Customs and Excise* [2005] ECR I-4427.

22 See also, for example, case C-455/05 *Velvet & Steel Immobilien und Handels GmbH v Finanzamt Hamburg-Eimsbüttel* [2007] ECR I-3225, para. 16, and case C-261/08 *María Julia Zurita García v Delegación del Gobierno en Murcia & C-348/08 Aurelio Choque Cabrera v Delegación del Gobierno en Murcia*, not yet published, judgment of the Third Chamber 22 October 2009, para. 54.

23 Sixth Council Directive 77/388/EEC of 17 May 1977 on the harmonization of the laws of the Member States relating to turnover taxes – Common system of value added tax: uniform basis of assessment, OJ L 145, 13.6.1977, 1–40.

24 Pierre Legrand is the famous champion for the most radical position in this debate, arguing that legal concepts will always be assigned a new, local meaning. Or, as he puts it, 'meaning simply does not lend itself to transmigration', Legrand (2001: 1038).

diverging meanings have been discussed. Traces of such methods can be found in the case law of the European Court of Justice, including preference for the majority meaning, preference for the clear meaning and preference for the liberal meaning.[25] However, the Court prefers no single method. Claims that the Court has one method of resolving diverging meanings are normally easily debunked. For example, it is generally claimed in the literature that the Court of Justice reconciles diverging language versions by using the context and purpose (Stevens 1967: 728, Bredimas 1978: 40, Barents 1997: 53, Brown and Kennedy 2000: 327–9, Müller and Christensen 2003: 223–4). While there is no denying that the context and purpose are important tools for the Court, this claim is an oversimplification of the approach of the Court. As this chapter will discuss further below, the Court does not always resolve diverging meanings by turning away from the wording to the context and purpose. Sometimes the wording of the different language versions can be used to reconcile divergences. The Court of Justice employs a variety of different techniques to reconcile diverging meanings, and no single approach can be found. While this might be practical for the Court, it leaves little to no guidance for national courts trying to perform the same feat.

Confusion in National Courts: Choosing between Theory and Reality

As demonstrated above, national courts are left in a difficult position indeed. The European Court of Justice has made extensive demands when it comes to multilingual interpretation of Union law but has offered very little in the way of practical guidance. In this situation, national courts have been forced to be creative, in essence creating their own approach to multilingual interpretation. Space precludes a thorough discussion of the characteristics of this approach, but a few short examples will be given from the case law of Danish, English and German courts.[26] While some aspects of the illustrated approach might seem unorthodox, it is certainly not my intention to belittle national courts. On the contrary, they have made the best of an impossible situation, and their attempts at creating a manageable approach to multilingual interpretation are admirable.

When Do We Open Pandora's Box?

The most obvious question as regards multilingual interpretation of Union law on a national level is when it is used at all. It is obvious to everyone that national courts do not engage in multilingual interpretation every time a provision of

25 For an overview of the discussion in the literature, as well as a presentation of my own theory, see Derlén (2009: Chapter 3.3).

26 For further discussion, see Derlén (2009: Chapters 5–12).

Union law makes an appearance. In fact, several different factors can encourage a national court to open up Pandora's Box. These include action by the parties, doctrinal debate or case law from the European Court of Justice or from other national courts. However, here we will concentrate on the existence of two other factors encouraging multilingual interpretation on a national level: the criterion of doubt and automatic control. The criterion of doubt, discussed above, may have limited support from the Court of Justice, but it is flourishing in national courts. Many examples can be found of courts consulting one or more language versions due to some vagueness or ambiguity of the national version. Sometimes national courts refer to the case law of the Court of Justice when employing this approach. For example, when the Financial Court in Brandenburg used the criterion of doubt in case 4 K 3025/00 from July 2001 the court referred to the *EMU Tabac* case.[27] Examples can be found of rather extreme uses of the criterion of doubt. For example, in the *Bell Concord*[28] case, the English Court of Appeal suggested that consultation of other language versions was only permissible when the meaning of the English language version was doubtful. Having established doubt, the Court stated that '[i]n such circumstances, it is legitimate to look at the French text of the directive to see if it clarifies the position' (*Bell Concord*: 853).

On the other hand, many examples can also be found of national courts consulting one or more language versions automatically, that is, without being encouraged to do so by any other factor. When using this approach, national courts often acknowledge a duty to consult other languages or at least indicate that this is a prudent course of action.[29] Sometimes this approach is justified by way of reference to the case law of the Court of Justice, including the *CILFIT* case.

Originals: Better than Copies

The second aspect to notice regarding multilingual interpretation in national courts is the limited level of ambition when it comes to language selection. Many examples can be found of national courts consulting only one or two language versions besides the national version. Furthermore, national courts often turn to well-known languages when performing multilingual interpretation. Naturally, as discussed below, this might have practical explanations, in the sense that courts

27 FG Brandenburg 2001-07-05, 4 K 3025/00, reported in *Zeitschrift für Zölle und Verbrauchsteuern* 2002, 2: 60–62. See the discussion above concerning *EMU Tabac* and the criterion of doubt. Obviously, the Financial Court took the German language version of the *EMU Tabac* case as its point of departure.

28 *Bell Concord Educational Trust Limited v Commissioners of Customs and Excise*, Court of Appeal [1989] 1 CMLR 845.

29 An example of the former situation is case BGH 2006-07-25, X ZR 182/05, while the case *National Smokeless Fuels Limited v Commissioners of Inland Revenue*, Chancery Division [1986] 3 CMLR 227, is an example of the latter situation.

can only consult language versions they are able to understand. However, national courts have also demonstrated an awareness of *de facto* originals of Union law. It is well known that secondary legislation in the Union is primarily produced in English and French (European Commission 2009: 6–7). National courts are apparently aware of this state of affairs. For example, in the *Cato*[30] case, the English Court of Appeal referred to the French language version of Directive 83/515[31] as the 'original' (*Cato*: 539–40). Another approach was demonstrated in the *Rxworks v Hunter* case,[32] where the Chancery Division of the English High Court of Justice consulted the languages that were official languages of the Union at the time of adoption of the provision in question, thus in effect regarding them as originals (*Rxworks v Hunter*: 255). Notably, Advocate General Jacobs used the same approach in the above mentioned *Henriksen* case.

Who Has the Babel Fish?[33]

An obvious practical problem for national courts is being able to access the meaning of foreign languages consulted as part of the multilingual interpretation. To some degree, this problem is diminished by the tendency of national courts to consult primarily well-known languages, as we noted above. However, even when limiting the number of languages, understanding across language borders still remains a factor. Again, national courts have demonstrated significant ingenuity in dealing with this problem. Examples can be found of courts using dictionaries as well as expert opinions.[34] However, the most interesting approach is the production of translations. Translations can be arranged either by the parties or by the court itself.[35] While one can understand the practical necessity underlying this approach, it is both peculiar and problematic. It is peculiar in the sense that, for example, an English translation of the French version already exists; it is the English version of the same provision. It is problematic in the

30 *James Joseph Cato v Minister of Agriculture, Fisheries and Food*, Court of Appeal [1989] 3 CMLR 513.

31 Council Directive 83/515/EEC of 4 October 1983 concerning certain measures to adjust capacity in the fisheries sector, OJ L 290, 22.10.1983, 15–19.

32 *Rxworks Limited v Hunter (t/a Connect Computers)*, Chancery Division [2008] E.C.C. 15.

33 In the book *The Hitchhiker's Guide to the Galaxy* by Douglas Adams, a Babel Fish is a universal translator, allowing the bearer to understand the language of any species.

34 See for an example of the former case, OLG Düsseldorf 2004-01-30, I-23 U 70/03, paras 17–19, and for an example of the latter case, *Eamonn Dominic Cunningham and Others v Milk Marketing Board for Northern Ireland*, Chancery Division [1988] 3 CMLR 815, 877–88.

35 See for an example of the former case, *Regina v Secretary of State for the Home Department ex parte Donald Walter Flynn*, Queen's Bench Division [1995] 3 CMLR 397, 409 and for an example of the latter case LSG Baden-Württemberg 1999-02-09, L 13 AL 1733/98.

sense that the parties and the courts are creating unofficial versions of Union provisions, whose potential future use is unclear.

Getting Along – By Any Means

Finally, the confusion concerning reconciliation of diverging meanings in the Court of Justice is mirrored in national courts, in the sense that a variety of approaches can be identified. Naturally, national courts can avoid resolving a discovered divergence of meaning by requesting a preliminary ruling from the European Court of Justice.[36] Another way of, so to say, passing the buck is for the national court to conclude that different language versions support different interpretations of the provision in question, but that the situation at hand is, at any rate, covered by all suggested interpretations.[37] When dealing with a divergence on their own, national courts borrow from the approaches developed by the Court of Justice, sometimes with a direct reference to the judgment where the latter court employed the technique in question.[38] Courts in the Member States have demonstrated significant loyalty when it comes to reconciliation and many examples can be found of national courts adopting a different interpretation than the one indicated by the national language version.

A Way Forward: Giving Up or Keeping the Faith?

The Problems and the Alternatives

The discussion above has outlined the problems associated with multilingual interpretation of Union law. The problems are not created by the existence of several, equally authentic language versions of Union provisions *per se*, but rather by the way the Court of Justice has approached multilingual interpretation. In a sense, the Court of Justice has painted itself into a corner. By endlessly emphasizing the need for uniformity and claiming that uniformity can only truly be realized by taking all languages into account in the interpretative process, the Court has created a paradox. Left with impossible requirements and no real assistance from Luxembourg, national courts have been forced to develop their own approach to multilingual interpretation. Consequently, uniformity has transformed into discretion and the danger of inconsistency. In this situation, a fundamental choice has to be made as to the future of multilingual interpretation. We have, in essence,

36 See for example case BGH 1997-06-26, IX ZB 11/97, reported in English in [1998] ILPR 224, in particular at 227.

37 This was the approach adopted by the Danish Western High Court in case U.1999.1429V.

38 See for example, the English *Nightfreight plc*, VAT Tribunal [1998] BVC 2232, referring to the *Henriksen* case discussed above.

three alternatives. First, we can do nothing, leaving the situation as it is today. As is obvious from the discussion above, I find this alternative unappealing. Multilingual interpretation of Union law in national courts is in many ways the elephant in the room. The discrepancy between rhetoric and reality is obvious, and we can no longer ignore it. The second alternative is to simply give up on multilingual interpretation of Union law in national courts. The importance of the context and purpose of the relevant provision is repeatedly emphasized by the Court of Justice as part of the interpretative process (C-149/97 *Institute of the Motor Industry*,[39] paras 14–21). When analysing the interpretative approach of the Court of Justice, the purpose is regularly awarded pride of place (McLeod 2004: 1125–30). The multilingual character of Union law is often cited as encouraging this approach, in the sense that the presence of 23 official versions precludes finding a clear, literal meaning (Brown 1981: 341, Schulte-Nölke 1999: 157–9). Described thus, multilingualism seems only a needless detour on the road to our ultimate target: the context and purpose of the provision. The logical consequence would be for national courts simply to skip the detour and advance directly to the purpose, without a troublesome and time-consuming consultation of the text of various language versions.[40] The final alternative is to keep the faith and aim for real reform of the issue of multilingual interpretation.

Reforming the System: Mandatory Consultation Languages

After rejecting the first alternative, what is left is a choice between reform and giving up on multilingual interpretation. I will take this opportunity to argue in favour of reform. This will entail a discussion as to why giving up is not an option. However, before getting to that discussion, we need to specify what we mean with 'reform'. Naturally, reform could come in many different ways. In the literature, it is sometimes suggested that the number of authoritative languages should be limited. Obviously, scholars then have different ideas as to how many languages – and most of all which languages – should be authoritative. One, two or three languages, often including English, French and German, are commonly suggested.[41] However, also more imaginative proposals have been put forward.[42] However, while limiting the number of authoritative languages might appear an

39 Case C-149/97 *The Institute of the Motor Industry v Commissioners of Customs and Excise* [1998] ECR I-7053.

40 See in this general direction, for example, Jacobs (2003: 302–5), emphasizing the importance of consulting the purpose in situations of diverging language versions of Community law.

41 See in favour of English, for example, Oksaar (1998: 119–26); in favour of French, for example, Braselmann (1992: 73–4) and in favour of English, French and German, for example, Schübel-Pfister (2004: 497–9).

42 Most well known is perhaps Werner Bormann's argument in favour of Esperanto; see Bormann (1970).

easy solution, it is politically unthinkable (Kjær 2003: 58). The equal status of all official languages – large or small – carries significant symbolic value. Saying that most languages will no longer be authoritative in interpretation will simply not be accepted. In the absence of general, sweeping reforms, we will have to find another way of improving multilingual interpretation. The European Court of Justice obviously occupies a unique position and should be able to handle multilingual interpretation on a broad scale. National courts, on the other hand, are in clear need of a practical approach to multilingual interpretation. The present-day situation leaves them with impossible requirements, beyond the competence of any national court or tribunal.[43] If nothing is done, we run the risk of national courts abandoning multilingualism, turning it into a paper product without connection to legal reality. Both carrot and stick are missing in today's system. The courts of the Member States have no incentive to engage in some form of multilingual interpretation, as they will not be able to achieve the level of ambition required by Luxembourg. Furthermore, the Court of Justice cannot seriously complain about the lack of 'proper' multilingual interpretation, as one cannot expect the impossible.[44] A way out of this mess would be mandatory consultation languages. In such a model, all language versions would remain authoritative *per se*, but certain languages would be generally consulted as part of the interpretative process.[45] I suggest making English and French mandatory consultation languages, consulted together with the national language version when interpreting provisions of Union law in national courts. The English and French language versions would be consulted automatically, not employing a criterion of doubt. The consultation languages would not be decisive for the interpretation. In case of a divergence of meaning, they would carry the same weight as the national language version. The remainder of this part will be devoted to discussing this proposed reform. This will be done in three steps. The first step will discuss whether multilingualism is a value in itself or only an unnecessary complication. Supporting the former, I will argue against the giving up alternative and lay the foundation for the rest of the discussion.

43 That is not to say that national courts cannot be very ambitious when interpreting Union law. For example, the Federal Court for Civil and Criminal Matters in Germany consulted no less than eight different language versions of Commission Regulation 1768/95 in case BGH 2004-05-11, KZR 37/02. However, to consistently examine all language versions, including little-known languages such as Greek and Maltese, of Union provisions is obviously not practically possible.

44 In theory, the Commission could bring an enforcement action according to Article 258 TFEU against the Member State whose courts do not follow the case law of the Court of Justice when it comes to multilingual interpretation of Union law. We know from case C-154/08 *Commission of the European Communities v Kingdom of Spain,* not yet published, judgment of the Third Chamber 12 November 2009, paras 124–7, that Member States can be held responsible when national supreme courts interpret Union law incorrectly. However, such an action is difficult to imagine concerning multilingual interpretation.

45 See, in this general direction, Groh (2004: 268–70), who argues in favour of national courts consulting at least two language versions, representing two different legal cultures.

Second, after having demonstrated the value of multilingualism, the next step will demonstrate the practical importance of multilingualism in national courts. The final step will explain the choice of languages as well as the rejection of a criterion of doubt in multilingual interpretation.

Languages as Added Value or Unnecessary Complications

Naturally, the most fundamental question to be discussed is whether languages are an added value in the interpretative process or simply an unnecessary detour. As described above, the heavy emphasis traditionally placed on the role of the context and the purpose in interpretation could lead one simply to abandon multilingualism. However, it is high time to scrutinize the context and purpose mantra and examine how this interpretative argument is actually employed. More precisely, we need to discuss how the purpose of a provision is determined. It could be argued that the purpose normally has textual roots. In other words, it is derived from the text of the provision itself, from surrounding provisions (the context), from the preamble or from provisions in the treaties (Due 1999: 77, McLeod 2004: 1130–32). In other words, the purpose is not an esoteric entity but dependent on textual support. In such a situation, the multilingual character of Union law is not a problem but a possibility. Solan, drawing on Saint Augustine, argues that the existence of several language versions enables the Court of Justice to compare and triangulate, thus gaining better insight into the intention of the legislator. Even when a comparison of the language versions does not establish the purpose, it is still valuable, as it can demonstrate that the clear wording of one particular version is misleading (Solan 2007: 21–6). Solan's argument is based on the basic premise that 'the language of a statute provides privileged evidence of what the legislature intended' (Solan 2007: 10).

The case law of the Court of Justice supports the points made by Solan. When explaining its own approach, the Court presupposes that a literal interpretation (that is, an interpretation concentrating on the wording of the different language versions) can resolve problems of diverging meanings. For instance, in case C-257/00 *Givane v Secretary of State*,[46] paragraph 38, the Court stated (with emphasis added):

> Since a literal interpretation of the words "for at least two years" … *does not provide an unequivocal answer* to the question referred, it is necessary to place that expression in its context and to interpret it in relation to the spirit and purpose of the provision in question.

Naturally, the emphasized words could be understood simply as indicating a divergence of meaning. In other words, as the language versions deviated in

46 Case C-257/00 *Nani Givane and Others v Secretary of State for the Home Department* [2003] ECR I-345.

meaning, literal interpretation could not resolve the issue. However, the Court had already, in the preceding paragraph, observed the divergence of meaning, and paragraph 38 would then be redundant. On the other hand, the quoted passage could be read as saying that literal interpretation can be used to reconcile diverging meanings, but that this was not possible in the case at hand. Furthermore, when explaining the need for multilingual interpretation, the Court of Justice regularly makes use of a standard phrase, where the importance of the language versions as carriers of the legislature's intention is emphasized. The phrase normally goes something like this:

> It must be borne in mind in this regard that, according to settled case-law, the necessity for uniform application and accordingly for uniform interpretation of a Community measure makes it impossible to consider one version of the text in isolation, but requires that it be interpreted on the basis of both the real intention of its author and the aim he seeks to achieve, in the light, in particular, of the versions in all languages (C-188/03 *Junk*,[47] para. 33).

Thus, the intention is viewed in the light of the different language versions.

This fits with the reality of multilingual interpretation as performed by the Court, as examples can be found of the Court engaging in comparison of the different language versions, finding the meaning of the provision in the language itself. One example is the *Ferriere* case, already mentioned above. Here the wording of the Italian version was rejected 'since all the other language versions expressly render the condition set out in Article 85(1) of the Treaty in the form of an alternative' (*Ferriere*: para. 15). In other words, the other language versions together demonstrated the correct meaning, overriding the Italian version. The *EMU Tabac* judgment has also been mentioned above. Here the Danish and Greek language versions were used to exclude the possibility of excise duty being payable in the country of purchase when an agent had arranged the transport (*EMU Tabac*: para. 33). Finally, the joined cases C-261/08 and C-348/08 *García*[48] are a recent example of this approach.[49] Here the Court of Justice noted that the Spanish wording differed from the wording of the other language versions. The Court gave preference to the meaning expressed by the majority of the language versions, explaining that the Spanish wording could not be regarded as the real intention of the legislature as it was 'the only one which diverges from the wording of the other language versions' (*García*: paras 52–6, the quote from para. 56). This interpretation was confirmed by the fact that the Spanish version suffered from internal inconsistencies (*García*: para. 57). In other words,

---

47 Case C-188/03 *Irmtraud Junk v Wolfgang Kühnel* [2005] ECR I-885.

48 Case C-261/08 *María Julia Zurita García v Delegación del Gobierno en Murcia & C-348/08 Aurelio Choque Cabrera v Delegación del Gobierno en Murcia*, not yet published, judgment of the Third Chamber 22 October 2009.

49 For another recent example, see case C-375/07 *Staatssecretaris van Financiën v Heuschen & Schrouff Oriëntal Foods Trading BV* [2008] ECR I-8691, paras 43–53.

the majority of the language versions expressed the true intention of the legislature. Naturally, the idea of a connection between the wording of the language versions and the intention of the legislator is not novel. In the international law literature, preference for the clear meaning has been defended with reference to the intention of the legislator. The idea is that a clear language version constitutes a reasonable presumption as to what the intention of the legislator was (Hardy 1961: 87–8).

However, while ample support can be found for Solan's argument in the case law of the Court of Justice, it is important not to overstate the point. The literature sometimes claims that the Court only moves on to examine the purpose after a 'thorough semantic analysis' (van Calster 1997: 377). This is refuted by countless examples, where the Court of Justice abandons the level of literal interpretation as soon as a divergence is discovered, without trying to overcome the difference using that technique. One example of this is the above-mentioned *Institute of the Motor Industry* case, where the Court turned to the context and purpose of the Sixth VAT Directive 77/388/EEC directly after finding a divergence of meaning between the French *syndicale* and the English *trade union*, without first trying to reconcile the language versions by way of literal interpretation.[50] However, this tendency of the Court of Justice does not make multilingual interpretation redundant. Naturally, there are situations where a comparison of the different language versions will not solve the interpretative problem. As Solan pointed out (2007: 26), a comparison of the languages will still be valuable in the sense that it can demonstrate that a particular wording is misleading. Furthermore, as demonstrated above, in many situations, the comparison is in itself sufficient to resolve the interpretative problem. Finally, we should remember that the interpretative arguments from context and purpose are normally textually based. When the Court of Justice resolves an interpretative problem by turning to the purpose, it often makes use of the wording of various articles in the act in question and/or its preamble. One example of this is the case 107/84 *Commission v Germany*,[51] which the Court of Justice falls back on in the above-mentioned *Institute of the Motor Industry* case.[52] In the former case, the Court considered both the wording of Article 13 as well as the preamble of the directive in order to establish the purpose (*Commission v Germany*: para. 17). Given that the purpose is often dependent on the text, in this manner, multilingualism can be of value to clarify the wording of the preamble or of other provisions. The next part will

50 See also, for example, case C-280/04 *Jyske Finans A/S v Skatteministeriet* [2005] ECR I-10683 paras 30–32.

51 Case 107/84 *Commission of the European Communities v Federal Republic of Germany* [1985] ECR 2655.

52 See also the above-mentioned *Jyske Finans* case as well as, among many others, the cases C-389/95 *Siegfried Klattner v Elliniko Dimosio (Greek State)* [1997] ECR I-2719, para. 25, C-341/01 *Plato Plastik Robert Frank GmbH v Caropack Handelsgesellschaft mbH* [2004] ECR I-4883, para. 56 and C-72/95 *Aannemersbedrijf P.K. Kraaijeveld BV e.a. v Gedeputeerde Staten van Zuid-Holland* [1996] ECR I-5403, para. 30.

give examples of these various uses of multilingual interpretation and thereby demonstrate its practical significance.

Multilingual Interpretation as an Aid for National Courts

The first, and perhaps most important, manner in which multilingual interpretation is helpful for the courts of the Member States is in examining whether the wording of the national language version represents the true meaning of the provision in question. By consulting other language versions, the national court can discover a divergence of meaning. This divergence of meaning can then be resolved directly by the court or referred to the European Court of Justice. An example of the former is the *McCormack* case,[53] where the French language version clarified the English version (*McCormack*: para. 15). An example of the latter is the judgment of the Federal Financial Court in Germany in May 2001 concerning the interpretation of Article 13.B.d of the Sixth VAT Directive 77/388/EEC. The court observed the potential divergence of meaning between the English and German language versions and requested a preliminary ruling on the correct interpretation.[54] Naturally, the flipside of this discussion is that other language versions can also be used to confirm that the national wording is correct. For example, in a case from April 2008, the German Federal Financial Court consulted the English and French language versions of Article 3.1 of Directive 2003/30/EC[55] in order to confirm that the German word *sollten* indicated a strong recommendation and not a legal obligation.[56]

The second advantage of multilingualism has already been touched upon: the possibility of resolving diverging meanings by using other languages versions. Examples abound of this approach being used in national courts. For instance, in the case *Independent Coach Travel*,[57] the Value Added Tax Tribunal in London observed that the English version of Article 26 of the Sixth VAT Directive 77/388/EEC spoke of 'customers' as well as 'travellers', which created interpretative difficulties in the case at hand. Given the wording of other language versions, the Tribunal concluded that the English concept 'customers' should be interpreted to mean 'travellers', thereby resolving the interpretative question at

53 *Richard McCormack v Tribunal de Grande Instance, Quimper, France,* Queen's Bench Division [2008] EWHC 1453 (Admin).

54 Case BFH 2001-05-17, V R 34/99.

55 Directive 2003/30/EC of the European Parliament and of the Council of 8 May 2003 on the promotion of the use of bio-fuels or other renewable fuels for transport, OJ L 123, 17.5.2003, 42–46.

56 Case BFH 2008-04-14, VII B 216/07. See also, among many others, the English case *R. (on the application of) Anti-Waste Ltd v Environment Agency,* Queen's Bench Division [2007] Env. L.R. 28, 613–16.

57 *Independent Coach Travel (Wholesaling) Limited v Commissioners of Customs and Excise*, Value Added Tax Tribunal in London [1994] 2 CMLR 257.

hand. Another example is the judgment of the German Federal Court for Civil and Criminal Matters in March 2005.[58] Here the German version of Article 9.3 of Regulation 1768/95[59] appeared, by its wording, to grant the holders of plant variety rights a right to obtain certain information. However, this impression was incorrect, as demonstrated by the French, English, Italian, Spanish and Dutch language versions of Article 9.3. Sometimes the courts even explicitly state that the purpose of a Union law provision is demonstrated by a comparison of the language versions.[60]

Finally, as mentioned above, multilingual interpretation can also assist the understanding of the preamble of a Union act, and thereby its purpose. One example of this is the judgment of the German Federal Court for Civil and Criminal Matters in October 2004. The case concerned the interpretation of recital 19 of the preamble of the Satellite and Cable Directive 93/83/EEC.[61] The German wording of recital 19 appeared unreasonable, and was reinterpreted based on the English and French language versions of recital 19.[62]

The Issues of When and Which

Since we have established the value and practical importance of multilingual interpretation, it is time to turn our attention to the issues of *when* and *which*, in other words when multilingual interpretation is going to be engaged and which languages are to be used as mandatory consultation languages. Starting with the latter issue, I have argued above in favour of English and French as consultation languages. There are several reasons favouring this choice. We know that English and French are *de facto* originals in the legislation process of the Union, in the sense that a crushing majority of all documents are drafted first in one of these languages. As *de facto* originals they are potentially better prepared than other language versions and better reflect the intention of the legislator. Furthermore, they represent different legal cultures. If an interpretative problem should turn on the fact that certain concepts are difficult to express in different legal cultures, it is a wise precaution to consult languages from both the civil law and common law traditions. Groh (2004: 268–70)

58 Case BGH 2005-03-30, X ZR 191/03.

59 Commission Regulation (EC) No. 1768/95 of 24 July 1995 implementing rules on the agricultural exemption provided for in Article 14(3) of Council Regulation (EC) No. 2100/94 on Community plant variety rights, OJ L 173, 25.7.1995, 14–21.

60 See, for example, the cases *British United Provident Association Ltd v Commissioners of Customs and Excise*, VAT and Duties Tribunal in London [2002] 2 CMLR 15 and BGH 2006-07-25, X ZR 182/05, paras 14–16.

61 Council Directive 93/83/EEC of 27 September 1993 on the coordination of certain rules concerning copyright and rights related to copyright applicable to satellite broadcasting and cable retransmission, OJ L 248, 6.10.1993, 15–21.

62 Case BGH 2004-10-13, I ZR 49/03. See also, for example, the cases BVerfG 2007-09-20, 2 BvR 855/06 and *Vibixa Ltd v Komori UK Ltd and others, Polestar Jowetts Ltd v Komori UK Ltd and another*, Court of Appeal [2006] 1 WLR 2472.

argues along similar lines when proposing that national courts should consult at least two language versions representing different legal cultures. Groh's proposal is very interesting, but I would recommend a more streamlined approach to the issue. Not only does the choice of French and English have the above-stated advantages, but by having fixed consultation languages, we achieve uniformity. As is well known, the Court of Justice is forever emphasizing the virtue of uniformity in the legal system of the European Union (30/77 *Régina v Pierre Bouchereau*:[63] para. 14, C-372/88 *Cricket St. Thomas*:[64] paras 18–19 and C-187/07 *Dirk Endendijk*:[65] para. 25). The need for uniformity is easily understood, at least if we contemplate its absence. Admittedly, a Union whose rules are interpreted and applied differently in each Member State is a Union on paper only. If we accept the need for uniformity, the next question is how to achieve it. The present system, where the Court of Justice tries to achieve uniformity by rigidly requiring the comparison of all language versions, is obviously untenable. A theoretical option would be for the Court of Justice to take on a bigger role when it comes to multilingual interpretation, by increasing the requests for preliminary rulings and thereby removing the problem from the arena of national courts. However, that is just as practically indefensible as the first alternative. If every interpretative question of Union law not explicitly dealt with in the existing case law of the Court of Justice would be referred to Luxembourg, the system would collapse. This leaves us with the alternative of achieving uniformity in a practically viable way. Using French and English as mandatory consultation languages could be the solution. National courts would interpret Union provisions with their own language versions as a starting point, but with the aid of the English and French versions. Thereby, the same languages would be used throughout the Union, enabling uniformity of interpretation and application.

Finally, a few words concerning when national courts should consult other language version: I advise strongly against employing a criterion of doubt. The idea of the mandatory consultation languages is that they should be consulted automatically, as a natural part of the interpretative process. A criterion of doubt is problematic on many levels. First of all, if multilingualism is viewed as valuable in itself, the criterion of doubt is inappropriate, as we want to encourage more multilingual interpretation, not less. Second, as demonstrated by the discussion above, the application of a criterion of doubt is difficult, and it is likely that national courts will understand the criterion in different ways. Finally, employing a criterion of doubt will tend to mask divergences of meaning and interpretative problems, eliminating one of the key advantages of multilingual interpretation.[66]

---

63 Case 30/77 *Régina v Pierre Bouchereau* [1977] ECR 1999.

64 Case C-372/88 *Milk Marketing Board of England and Wales v Cricket St. Thomas Estate* [1990] ECR I-1345.

65 Case C-187/07 *Criminal proceedings against Dirk Endendijk* [2008] ECR I-2115.

66 Here I agree with Kuner, who argues forcefully against the application of a criterion of doubt in international law. He describes reliance on a single-language version as a 'time

Conclusions: Don't Let Perfection Stand in the Way of Good Enough!

Naturally, no one can deny that multilingual interpretation of European Union law is complex. However, if we are to move forward, we must be clear on what the problems actually are. In this chapter, I have endeavoured to demonstrate that it is not multilingualism *per se*, but rather the uncertain and practically impossible guidelines from the Court of Justice that lead to problems in national courts. Multilingualism in itself is actually an asset of Union law, if used properly. This message should instil hope. Yes, the system is broken, but it can be fixed. National courts have demonstrated significant loyalty *vis-à-vis* the multilingual character of Union law. They deserve practically viable guidelines as to how multilingualism should be used in the interpretation of Union law. The suggestion of using English and French as mandatory consultation languages in national courts could contribute to a truly multilingual Union. Furthermore, it would help achieve uniformity of interpretation and application of Union law. The critics might argue that the suggested solution elevates French and English to a privileged position. However, as demonstrated above, these languages already enjoy a special position. National courts have demonstrated that they are aware of the status of these languages as *de facto* originals in the legislative process of the Union. The suggested solution would simply acknowledge this state of affairs. By using English and French side by side with the national language version, we would encourage more multilingual interpretation and aid national courts in the difficult task of applying European Union law. It makes no sense to forego this possibility, leaving a broken system, simply because some languages will see wider use than others. Finally, the pessimists might argue that even this solution is too difficult and/or burdensome for national courts. However, reality demonstrates the opposite. One of the advantages of the suggested solution is that national courts have demonstrated that they can use other language versions, not only to discover divergences of meaning but also to reconcile such divergences. The different language versions of Union provisions are readily available for national courts, for example, by way of the EUR-Lex database. We can even find examples of national courts making direct reference to EUR-Lex.[67] Even if the comparison of three different languages should prove challenging, some comparison is surely better than none. National courts would retain the possibility to refer the most difficult cases to Luxembourg. This is not the time to give up on multilingual interpretation of European Union law; this is the time to keep the faith in national courts.

bomb', in the sense that differences among languages are concealed for a long time. See Kuner (1991: 962–4).

67 Case BGH 2001-12-17, II ZR 288/99.

References

Barents, R. 1997. Law and Language in the European Union. *EC Tax Review*, 6, 49–55.
Bormann, W. 1970. Sprachenproblem in den europäischen Institutionen. *La monda lingvo-problemo*, 2, 114–26.
Braselmann, P. 1992. Übernationales Recht und Mehrsprachigkeit – Linguistische Überlegungen zu Sprachproblemen in EuGH-Urteilen. *Europarecht*, 27, 55–74.
Bredimas, A. 1978. *Methods of Interpretation and Community Law*. Amsterdam: North Holland Publishing Company.
Brown, L.N. 1981. The Linguistic Regime of the European Communities: Some Problems of Law and Language. *Valparaiso University Law Review*, 15, 319–41.
Brown, L.N. and Kennedy, T. 2000. *The Court of Justice of the European Communities*. 5th Edition. London: Sweet and Maxwell.
Derlén, M. 2007. *A Castle in the Air – The Complexity of the Multilingual Interpretation of European Community Law*. Umeå: Umeå Studies in Law No. 16/2007.
Derlén, M. 2009. *Multilingual Interpretation of European Union Law*. Alphen aan den Rijn: Kluwer Law International.
Due, O. 1999. Understanding the Reasoning of the Court of Justice, in *Mélanges en homage à Fernand Schockweiler*, edited by G.C Rodriguez Iglesias, O. Due, R. Schintgen and C. Elsen. Baden-Baden: Nomos Verlagsgesellschaft.
European Commission 2009. *Translating for a Multilingual Community*. Luxembourg: Office for Official Publications of the European Communities.
Groh, T. 2004. Methodenrelevante Normtexte im Gemeinschaftsrecht, in *Rechtssprache Europas – Reflexion der Praxis von Sprache und Mehrsprachigkeit im supranationalen Recht*, edited by F. Müller and I. Burr. Berlin: Duncker & Humblot.
Hardy, J. 1961. The Interpretation of Plurilingual Treaties by International Courts and Tribunals. *British Yearbook of International Law*, 28. London: Oxford University Press, 74–138.
Hilf, M. 1973. *Die Auslegung mehrsprachiger Verträge – Eine Untersuchung zum Völkerrecht und zum Staatsrecht der Bundesrepublik Deutschland*. Berlin/Heidelberg/New York: Springer-Verlag.
Jacobs, F.G. 2003. Approaches to Interpretation in a Plurilingual Legal System, in *A True European – Essays for Judge David Edward*, edited by Mark Hoskins and William Robinson. Oxford and Portland, OR: Hart Publishing.
Kjær, A.L. 2003. EU's flersprogsordning i praksis: Ret, sprog og virkelighed for de danske fjerkræavlere ved udbrud av Newcastle disease. *Juristen*, 85, 45–59.
Kuner, C.B. 1991. The Interpretation of Multilingual Treaties: Comparison of Texts versus the Presumption of Similar Meaning. *International and Comparative Law Quarterly*, 40, 953–64.

Legrand, P. 2001. The Return of the Repressed: Moving Comparative Legal Studies beyond Pleasure. *Tulane Law Review*, 75, 1033–51.

McLeod, I. 2004. Literal and Purposive Techniques of Legislative Interpretation: Some European Community and English Common Law Perspectives. *Brooklyn Journal of International Law*, 1109–34.

Müller, F. and Christensen, R. 2003. *Juristische Methodik – Band II Europarecht*. Berlin: Duncker & Humblot.

Oksaar, E. 1998. Das Sprachenproblem aus linguistischer Sicht, in *Die Europäische Union und ihre Sprachen – Interdisziplinäres Symposium zur Vielsprachigkeit als Herausforderung und Problematik des europäischen Einigungsprozesses. Gespräch zwischen Wissenschaft und Praxis*, edited by T. Bruha and H.J. Seeler. Baden-Baden: Nomos.

Schulte-Nölke, H. 1999. Elf Amtssprachen, ein Recht? Folgen der Mehrsprachigkeit für die Auslegung von Verbraucherschutzrichtlinien, in *Auslegung europäischen Privatrechts und angeglichenen Rechts*, edited by R. Schultze. Baden-Baden: Nomos Verlagsgesellschaft.

Schübel-Pfister, I. 2004. *Sprache und Gemeinschaftsrecht – Die Auslegung der mehrsprachig verbindlichen Rechtstexte durch den Europäische Gerichtshof*. Berlin: Duncker & Humblot.

Solan, L.M. 2007. *Statutory Interpretation in the EU: The Augustinian Approach*, Brooklyn Law School Legal Studies Research Papers, Working Paper Series, No. 78.

Stevens, L. 1967. The Principle of Linguistic Equality in Judicial Proceedings and in the Interpretation of Plurilingual Legal Instruments: The Régime Linguistique in the Court of Justice of the European Communities. *Northwestern University Law Review*, 62, 701–34.

Tabory, M. 1980. *Multilingualism in International Law and Institutions*. Alphen aan den Rijn: Sijthoff & Noordhoff.

Van Calster, G. 1997. The EU's Tower of Babel – The Interpretation by the European Court of Justice of Equally Authentic Texts Drafted in More than One Official Language. *Yearbook of European Law*, 17. Oxford: Clarendon Press, 363–93.

Chapter 9

Language Rights: The Interaction between Domestic and European Developments

Bruno de Witte

Introduction: Language Rights

Language rights are defined in this chapter as fundamental rights protecting language-related acts and values. The term *fundamental* is taken in a formal legal sense, as denoting the fact that those rights are entrenched in the constitution of a country or in an international treaty binding on that country and, therefore, cannot be freely disposed of by the national or regional legislature or government. In this sense, language rights constitute limits to the ordinary operation of the politics of language within a state or within a region. The main theme of this chapter is that we have witnessed, during the last two decades, a development whereby language rights are no longer only to be found in (some) national constitutions, but that European law (meaning, in this case, primarily the law of the Council of Europe rather than that of the European Union) increasingly sets limits to national language policies in order to protect language rights of individuals. The standard setting at the European level does not directly *aim* at creating new rights, but that might be their *effect* in practice.

The core linguistic right is the right to speak one's language, or, more precisely, the language of one's choice. The core right is, or can be, accompanied by a series of ancillary rights without which the right to speak a language becomes less valuable for its beneficiaries, such as: the right to be understood by others when speaking that language (for example, by public authorities), the right to a translation or an interpretation from other languages (for example, in the course of a meeting or trial at which those other languages are spoken), the right to compel others to speak one's language and the right to learn the language.

In terms of the legal recognition of those rights, a crucial distinction which is often made is that between the *private* and *official* use of the language. It is traditionally considered that states are free to decide whether, and to what extent, they allow the use of a plurality of languages for official purposes, in public administration and the courts, in the public service media and in public educational institutions. States can either opt for a system of rather strict linguistic uniformity (as do France and Germany) or give wide official recognition to regional and minority languages (as do Spain, Italy and the United Kingdom). However, the *private* use of language is not within the control of the state; as the UN Human Rights Committee held in its *Ballantyne* opinion of 5 May 1993:

> a State may choose one or more official languages, but it may not exclude, outside the spheres of public life, the freedom to express oneself in a language of one's choice.[1]

This statement of the Human Rights Committee points to another important legal feature of linguistic rights: namely, the fact that they are sometimes directly and expressly protected as such, but sometimes only indirectly or implicitly, by means of general fundamental rights. Examples of *explicit protection* are Article 18 of the Swiss Constitution stating tersely: '*La liberté de la langue est garantie*' [Freedom of language use is guaranteed] and Article 27 of the UN Covenant of Civil and Political Rights according to which persons belonging to linguistic minorities 'shall not be denied the right, in community with the other members of their group, ... to use their own language'. An illustration of *implicit protection* is provided precisely by the *Ballantyne* case: the Human Rights Committee held, quite rightly, that the *freedom of expression* naturally includes 'the freedom to express oneself in a language of one's choice', for example, in the case at hand, when advertising by means of commercial signs posted outside business premises. Although most constitutional and international fundamental rights documents protect freedom of expression without highlighting the linguistic component of this freedom, that component is inherently part of freedom of expression.[2] The same is true with *equality and non-discrimination.* Although language is, in some constitutions and in some international human rights treaties, singled out as one of a series of 'suspect' grounds of discrimination, the principle of equality logically protects the right not to be discriminated on account of one's language even when this ground of discrimination is not spelled out in so many words. A third major instance of this implicit protection is the fundamental *right of education.* The freedom to establish private schools arguably includes the freedom to use the language of instruction for those schools, whereas the right to education might be considered to include a right to receive at least part of that education in one's mother tongue.[3]

None of the rights mentioned so far is absolute or unqualified, but the general introductory point which we wish to make is that arguments based on *general* fundamental rights can offer *prima facie* protection for language-related claims of persons (often belonging to a linguistic minority) and require the government to

1 Human Rights Committee, 47th session, Communications Nos. 359/1989 and 385/1989, *John Ballantyne and Elizabeth Davidson, and Gordon McIntyre v Canada*, views adopted on 31 March 1993, para. 11.4.

2 For an elaboration of the argument that freedom of expression includes the freedom to express oneself in the language of one's choice, see De Varennes (1994).

3 On the linguistic dimension of educational rights, see the comparative law study by Milian i Massana (1994).

give good arguments why the language-related claim cannot be honoured in a given case.[4] The underlying consideration is that 'language should not be a liability in the enjoyment of one's general status of civil, social, and political rights and opportunities in society'.[5] However uncertain their precise substantive content may be, and however defective their enforcement, those general fundamental rights serve as a 'platform' on which weaker groups and individuals can stand in order to make their voices better heard. They constitute a floor of rights which exists in all constitutional democracies, even those where no express recognition is given to the value of linguistic diversity and the need to protect linguistic rights as expressions of cultural identity.

It is time now to look more closely at the protection of linguistic rights in Europe. I propose to do so in an evolutionary perspective, by highlighting the main lines in the development of the protection of language rights in Europe during the past two decades. In section 2, I will examine the general evolution in national law, focusing on Western European countries. In section 3, I will present the emergence of a Europe-wide supranational standard in relation to the protection of linguistic rights. In section 4, I will seek to combine these two strands by discussing the respective roles of domestic and European developments and their interaction in the evolution of language law in a selected number of Western European countries.[6]

Legal Recognition and Protection of Linguistic Diversity in Western European Countries: General Trends

From the 1970s until now, we have witnessed throughout Western Europe a stream of constitutional and legislative changes giving greater recognition to the multilingual character of countries with sizeable regional and minority languages.[7] The most spectacular case, no doubt, is that of Spain, where this recognition was accompanied by the devolution of powers to newly established regions, and language law is now increasingly being made at the regional rather than at the national level.[8] In Catalonia, Euskadi, Galicia, Valencia and the Balearic Isles,

4 Generally, on the contribution of general fundamental rights to minority protection, see Henrard (2000: Chapter 2).

5 Rubio Marín (2003: 63). This author proposes the term 'instrumental language rights' to describe this category, as opposed to non-instrumental language rights that protect the use of languages for its own sake.

6 The restriction to the Western part of the European continent is primarily prompted by the need to be selective in the framework of this short contribution, but the choice is also inspired by the fact that there is a rich recent literature on the comparative law of minority protection and language rights in Central and Eastern Europe.

7 For a more extensive comparative law panorama than the one that can be offered here, see Mancini and de Witte (2008: 251–70) and also Arzoz (2009: 556 et seq.).

8 For detailed analysis of the evolution of language law in Spain at the central and regional level, see Pérez Fernández (2006); for an overall perspective on the state of constitutional law in this field, see López Basaguren (2007).

regional legislation was adopted in order to restore the use of the respective regional language as a normal means of public and private communication to compensate for the active suppression of these languages under Franco's dictatorship. Hence, these laws were commonly called 'linguistic normalization laws' (*Leyes de normalización lingüística*). In Catalonia, a second-generation *Ley de Política Lingüística* of 7 January 1998 is possibly the most comprehensive piece of language legislation in Europe today. It deals with the 'traditional' subject matter of the use of languages in and with public administration, public education and the public media (all areas in which it now gives some priority to Catalan over Spanish), but it also deals in a rather detailed way with the use of languages in private business and social activities.[9]

There are long-established regimes of official plurilingualism in countries such as Belgium, Finland and Switzerland, where the main principles of language law were set out in the early part of the twentieth century, but their language legislation was further developed and diversified in recent decades. In Switzerland, in particular, the recent global revision of the Constitution in 1998 involved a codification and strengthening of the country's constitutional commitment to linguistic diversity. In Italy, specific language regimes had been in place for many years for the largest territorial minorities in the border areas (mainly South Tyrol and Val d'Aosta); they were complemented in 1999 by a general law on the protection of 'historical linguistic minorities' in Italy. In the United Kingdom, the Welsh Language Act 1993 and the Gaelic Language (Scotland) Act 2005 have strengthened the legal protection of those regional languages. In Finland, existing language rights for the country's minorities were further strengthened by the adoption in 2003 of the Language Act 423/2003 (dealing with the conditions for the official use of Finnish and Swedish in the various parts of the country) and the Sami Language Act 1086/2003, which is modelled on the former in providing for the official use of the Sami language(s) in the northern part of the country. Whereas France has preserved a clearly dominant position for the national language, even there, meaningful legislative reforms occurred that have strengthened the formal status and practical use of some minority languages (in particular, Corsican) and, very recently, the Constitution was modified so as to include a clause affirming that the regional languages form part of France's cultural heritage – a largely symbolic gesture rather than one having concrete legal consequences,[10] but which is nevertheless indicative of a gradual evolution in constitutional thinking.

This Europe-wide trend becomes all the more meaningful when compared with the legal regime that was developed, in the same countries, in response to the

9 For an analysis of this law, see Poggeschi (2002: 134–87), and Milian i Massana (2002: 337). For an account in English of the political debate surrounding the adoption of the new law, see Costa (2003: 413).

10 See the sceptical commentary of the new constitutional provision by Lavialle (2008).

massive immigration that occurred in the same period. The dominant view in most European countries was, and still is, that no specific language rights are needed for the members of those 'new' minorities, even when many of their members have acquired the citizenship of their state of residence. Rather, the existing language laws of their country of residence should apply to them. Special migration-related language rules, such as they exist, often aim at imposing linguistic conditions or duties, rather than rights. Proficiency, or at least adequate knowledge, of the national language is a traditional condition for the naturalization of foreigners, and it tends to be imposed with more rigour in recent years. Recently, a number of countries have also started to develop 'integration programmes' involving duties for migrants to follow training courses in the language of the host country, and they often make access to public benefits dependent on the participation to these language immersion programmes.[11]

The enactment of constitutional and legislative norms that grant new language rights and benefits does not automatically translate into a change in the language choices by individuals. The legal reforms mentioned above may be more or less effective in achieving their stated aim of enlarging effective linguistic choice and promoting the survival and development of minority or regional languages. In fact, there may be good reasons to be sceptical about the extent to which legal reform leads to effective social change in this area,[12] but this is not an issue that will concern us in the context of this chapter. The main aim is, rather, to map the nature of the political or legal mobilization that has produced those changes and has failed to produce other changes. In this respect, the prevailing picture, in all Western Europe, is that processes of *political* mobilization of regional and ethno-linguistic interests have been far more consistently used and have been far more effective, than processes of *legal* mobilization in the narrow sense of that term, namely the recourse to litigation before domestic and international courts.[13] This seems to contrast rather sharply with other legal domains concerning vulnerable groups such as gender equality and immigrant rights. This 'rights without litigation' trend has gone hand in hand, during the past decade especially, with a growing 'Europeanization of language laws'. In section 4, I will discuss the interaction between domestic developments and European influences in a selected number of Western European countries, showing various degrees of formalization of language rights and also various degrees of openness to European influence. First of all, in section 3 below, I will present the essential content and nature of the emerging European standard of protection for language rights.

---

11 See, for a comparative and theoretical approach of the latter question: Hogan-Brun, Mar-Molinero and Stevenson (2009).

12 By way of illustration, see the comparative study of nine countries by Cardi (2007), showing that regional and minority languages are seldom used before judicial authorities despite the existence of legislation allowing for their use.

13 On the distinction, in general, between litigation and the broader notion of mobilization (and the links between the two), see Cichowski (2007: Chapter 1).

An Emerging European Minimum Standard: The Council of Europe Instruments

The developments in national language laws, briefly sketched in the previous section, are situated in a legal context that is common to most European countries, and that consists of the international human rights and minority protection instruments of the Council of Europe: the European Convention of Human Rights and the 'twin conventions' of the Council of Europe that entered into force in 1998 – the European Charter for Regional or Minority Languages and the Framework Convention on National Minorities.[14]

The European Convention of Human Rights contains a provision prohibiting discrimination on grounds of language in the exercise of the rights of the Convention, and it also guarantees a right for an accused to use an interpreter if that individual cannot understand the language of criminal proceedings. However, it does not lay down general standards for the use of languages and does not contain any specific minority rights. Despite this absence of specific attention to languages and minorities, there has been, in recent years, a 'burgeoning' minority rights jurisprudence of the European Court of Human Rights (ECHR).[15] General human rights listed in the Convention are being explored and tested by applicants from minority groups as to their implicit minority protection potential. These minority cases have only rarely addressed questions of language use. In fact, among the many minority-relevant European Court cases that have emerged in recent years, only a few involved the use of languages.

Notwithstanding this relative failure, so far, to test the language rights potential of the European Convention, there is no doubt that such a potential exists. For instance, following the *Ballantyne* doctrine of the UN Human Rights Committee,[16] restrictions on the use of a particular language (say, Kurdish in Turkey) in private domains, including in private broadcasting or print media, would certainly be considered by the Court as restrictions of freedom of expression, a right guaranteed in Article 10 of the Convention. Support for this view can be found in the *Association Ekin v France* judgment of 2001, in which the Strasbourg court held that French legislation allowing for the administrative seizure of foreign publications or publications in a foreign language (as opposed to 'Franco-French' publications) was a violation of Article 10.[17] The Court's most remarkable ruling, so far, on the implied linguistic dimension of general fundamental rights occurred

14 European Charter for Regional or Minority Languages, European Treaty Series No. 148, adopted in Strasbourg on 05/11/1992, and Framework Convention on National Minorities, European Treaty Series No. 157, adopted in Strasbourg on 01/11/1995.

15 The terms are borrowed from the title of Gilbert (2002). For a more recent survey of the Strasbourg Court's minority case law, see Henrard (2008).

16 For the *Ballantyne* case, see the introduction of this chapter.

17 European Court of Human Rights, judgment of 17 July 2001, Appl. 39288/98, *Association Ekin v France*.

in the case of *Cyprus v Turkey*, in which the Grand Chamber held that the fact that the Northern Cyprus government provided Greek-language primary schooling for the Greek minority living in Northern Cyprus, but did not provide any follow-up at the secondary school level, amounted to a breach of the right to education guaranteed by Article 2 of Protocol No. 1 to the Convention.[18]

What is missing, so far, in the Convention system, is a *general right to equal treatment* that could form the basis for various language rights claims, for example, the claim that states that guarantee the official right to use a particular minority language should also recognize the right to use another minority language of comparable size. [19] At present, as is well known, Article 14 of the European Convention prohibits discrimination on the grounds of language (alongside many other grounds) only within the ambit of one of the substantive rights of the Convention. Since the right to use one's language in dealing with public authorities is not protected by one of the substantive provisions of the Convention, Article 14 cannot be used to challenge the unequal distribution of such a right to public language use.

This is precisely the point where the other, more directly language-related Council of Europe instruments, namely the Framework Convention and the Charter on Languages, offer added value compared to the ECHR. With regard to these instruments, the preliminary question arises – before examining their content – as to whether they can really be considered to form a 'European standard'. Both entered into force in 1998 and contain binding obligations for the states parties (the states that have ratified the treaties). Neither of the two is as yet so universally accepted as the European Convention of Human Rights, but the number of states parties is rising. At the latest count (as of 1 January 2010), 24 states had ratified the Charter on Regional and Minority Languages. The Framework Convention is much closer to becoming a genuine pan-European standard. It has now been ratified by 39 states, and the only ones missing, apart from some mini-states, are Turkey and four EU states: Belgium (which has only signed but not ratified), France, Greece and Luxembourg.

Apart from the question of the degree to which these Conventions have been accepted by the European states, there are also doubts about their legal efficacy. It is true that the provisions of these two treaties do not seem easily capable of direct effect in the national legal orders of the states parties.[20] Also, their international supervision mechanisms do not lead to binding judicial or quasi-judicial decisions.

18 *Cyprus v Turkey*, judgment (Grand Chamber) of 10 May 2001, No. 25781/94, para. 278. See further on this point, Ringelheim (2006: 203–7).

19 Protocol No. 12 to the European Convention, containing a general prohibition of discrimination, has entered into force only recently, in 2005, and has so far (as of 1 January 2010) been ratified by 17 Member States of the Council of Europe, so that there is scope for interesting developments in this respect. See, for some reflections on the possible future impact of this Protocol, Wintemute (2004).

20 But see the nuanced analysis of this question by Palermo (2008).

Instead, periodical state reports on the application of the Conventions must be submitted to the committees of experts that were set up under each of the two Conventions. However, the dynamic approach adopted by these committees in fulfilling their monitoring tasks is quite remarkable, perhaps even unprecedented, in international monitoring practice. They have established a dialogue with the governments concerned, they visit the country and meet with spokesmen of minority groups and they do not hesitate to make statements as to whether the states have adequately complied with their obligations and to express detailed views on how to improve the situation. These statements then lead to recommendations adopted by the Committee of Ministers of the Council of Europe and, in fact, the ministers have so far largely followed the views of the experts.[21] Pressure is thus exerted on the states to adopt best practices as formulated by the expert bodies.[22]

In terms of substance, the European Charter for Regional or Minority Languages is the more directly relevant of the two agreements, since it focuses directly and exclusively on the regulation of the use of languages. It applies to 'autochthonous' languages, excluding expressly the languages of migrants. In the Charter system, no distinction is made between regional and minority languages, but both categories are clearly defined in territorial terms, that is, with reference to particular geographical areas in which those languages are spoken by a sizeable group of people.

The Charter's main characteristic is its *à la carte* approach. Not only are state parties free to indicate which regional and minority languages they choose to protect under the terms of the Charter, but they also have considerable discretion in picking and choosing from among the many, rather detailed, substantive provisions of the Charter. The Charter is, therefore, a very flexible instrument, requiring the contracting states to undertake only those obligations that they are positively willing to undertake, with the expectation that a process of emulation among states will get underway. The states are also entitled to distinguish among minority languages, giving more far-reaching protection to some than to others, as long as those distinctions are justified by reasons of the size or geographical concentration of the groups. However, once states have agreed to undertake commitments for the promotion of a given language in a given field (be it education, the media or public administration), then the Committee of Experts will closely check their compliance with those commitments.[23] This is the reason why, despite the cautious formulation of this Charter, which studiously avoids the use of the term 'rights', its

21 These various reports and recommendations can be found on the website of the Council of Europe.

22 For accounts of the monitoring practice developed under the two Conventions, see Eide (2008) and Dunbar (2008).

23 See, for example, the report of the Committee of Experts on Spain, of 21 September 2005, ECRML (2005) 4, which amounts to 170 pages of detailed analysis and recommendations addressed to the Spanish government. The impact of the Charter on Spanish law is examined by Agirreazkuenaga Zigorraga (2006).

content may nevertheless give rise to genuine individual rights in those countries in which it has been transposed into domestic laws that contain clear commitments for public authorities – and the states concerned may be called to task for their failure to respect those commitments.

The Framework Convention on National Minorities, for its part, includes some linguistic rights within the broader context of its minority protection provisions. Article 10(2) is particularly important. It contains a very cautious and qualified *obligation* for states to allow the use of minority languages in relation to administrative authorities. Article 12(1) which contains a much more straightforward *right* for every person belonging to a national minority to learn his or her minority language. These clauses, and some others of lesser importance, have formed the focus of intensive interpretative debates between the governments and the Framework Convention's Advisory Committee during the past decade, with the experts pushing governments to give a more generous interpretation to their obligations under the Framework Convention.

In sum, it can be said that both these Conventions form an important site for the gradual development of a minimum standard with regard to the legal protection of regional and minority languages. In fact, the decision to ratify these two instruments prompted a number of European countries to adopt new laws on the protection of minority languages, so that one could witness a mini-wave of new minority protection legislation in the late 1990s.[24] They also played a distinctive role in the preparation of the recent enlargement of the European Union. They offered benchmarks for assessing whether the applicant countries offered adequate protection to their minorities, which was one of the political criteria for accession formulated in 1993 by the European Council meeting of Copenhagen. In certain cases, the 'carrot' of accession to the EU was instrumental in convincing governments to modify minority-unfriendly language legislation and adopt the new Council of Europe standards.[25] After the accession of 10 new Member States to the European Union in 2004, the minority rights questions became more prominent *inside* the European Union,[26] linking up with the more traditional debate on the recognition and protection of multilingualism within the European Union. [27] The text of Article 2 of the Treaty on European Union, as amended by the Lisbon Treaty, now states that '(t)he Union is founded on the values of respect for human dignity, freedom, democracy, equality, the rule of law and respect for human rights,

---

24 In addition to the already mentioned Italian law of 1999, one may add the Slovak language law of 1999 and the Swedish Law on national minorities of 1999, which was immediately followed by two specific laws providing for the use of the Finnish and the Sami language.

25 There is a vast literature on this theme, including the following: Pentassuglia (2001), de Witte (2002) and Sasse (2004).

26 See various contributions in Toggenburg (2004) and also de Witte and Horváth (2008).

27 On which, see, for example, de Witte (2004).

including the rights of persons belonging to minorities' (emphasis added). Unlike other human rights that are spelled out elsewhere in primary EU law (namely in the Charter of Rights and, through a reference in Article 6, in the ECHR), minority rights are not listed anywhere else in the founding treaties of the European Union nor are they included in its own Charter of Rights (except to the extent that its Article 21, following the wording of Article 14 ECHR, prohibits discrimination on grounds of membership of a national minority). Therefore, the new text of Article 2 points to the existence of rights *outside* the EU legal order that are incorporated into the EU legal order, although only through their inclusion in the generic basic values clause of Article 2. One may wonder whether the European Court of Justice might be encouraged by this provision to insert minority protection rights into the general principles of Union law, finding inspiration, for example, in the Framework Convention on the Protection of National Minorities.[28]

However, the conclusion that the Council of Europe Conventions form an effective and genuinely common European standard of language rights is subject to two major reservations. One is the fact, mentioned before, that several countries have so far consciously refrained from ratifying one or both of these Conventions; in particular, Belgium, France, Greece and Turkey have not ratified either of them. The other limitation is that both Conventions are primarily addressed to the historical minorities of Europe and do not address the question of whether language rights should also be granted to the members of the new immigrant minorities of Western Europe – despite some efforts by the Advisory Committee of the Framework Convention to encourage states to broaden their minority protection standards so as to encompass also, at least in some respects, the community languages spoken by those 'new' minorities.[29]

The Interaction between National and European Protection of Linguistic Rights: Some Case Studies

The impact of the emerging European standard described above has been widely different from one country to another. This difference is related to a number of factors which include, of course, whether the country concerned has signed the various Council of Europe Conventions, and also the pre-existing level of minority protection in each country. It will appear, from the four case studies below, that the European impact has been most significant in those countries where domestic reform movements championing the extension of language rights were able to

28 For discussion of the relevance of the Framework Convention for the development of EU law, see De Schutter (2008).

29 On this evolution in the monitoring practice of the Advisory Committee, see Verstichel (2008) and Ringelheim (2010). For a general discussion of the nature and legitimacy of the legal differentiation between 'old' and 'new' minorities, see Medda-Windischer (2009).

gather additional legitimacy from the Europe-wide legal developments, and where those European standards were not seen, by the political elites, as threatening the country's constitutional identity. As mentioned in the introduction, the case studies relate to four countries of Western Europe, namely the United Kingdom, France, Italy and Belgium. They may be read in conjunction with the more detailed examination of the cases of Spain and Switzerland, marked by sophisticated regimes of language regulation, in separate chapters of this volume.

United Kingdom

In the UK, the legal system had been comparatively slow in responding positively to the linguistic diversity that has traditionally existed in the country. This situation has changed quite dramatically during the last 20 years. This greater recognition of the status and official use of minority languages is only partially related to the devolution of powers to Scotland and to Wales that was enacted in 1998. Although the devolved government in Cardiff has certainly taken an active interest in the protection of Welsh, the main legislative reforms in relation to that language predate devolution. The main milestones are the Education Reform Act of 1988 (introducing Welsh as a compulsory subject throughout the Welsh public education system) and the Welsh Language Act 1993 (providing for a major expansion of the administrative and judicial use of the language). The combined effect of those acts has been to turn Wales into an officially bilingual region. The Scottish Parliament that, unlike the Welsh Assembly, possesses legislative powers, adopted in 2005 the Gaelic Language (Scotland) Act, which follows the model of the Welsh Language Act, though in a much more modest way, as the language itself has become much more marginal than Welsh.[30] In Northern Ireland, the status of Irish has been strengthened in the course of the implementation of the 'Good Friday' agreement of 1998.

A typical characteristic of the various pieces of UK language legislation is that they studiously avoid the use of terms that could convey the sense that minority language speakers have individual *rights* that can be enforced in court. Rather, they formulate extensive and detailed *duties* for the public authorities to adopt measures facilitating the effective use of the minority language in the schools and in public services. This approach is not necessarily less effective in achieving the protection objective (indeed, it may be argued that the Welsh legislation has been quite successful in reversing the secular decline in knowledge and usage of the language), but it virtually eliminates the potential for legal mobilization and litigation before the courts.[31] In this respect, the UK language planning model (which was also adopted in the Irish Official Languages Act of 2003) is quite different from the model adopted in many continental countries (with their recognition of constitutional rights to use the language, even though these rights

30 For a comparison between both Acts, see Dunbar (2005).

31 See, on this point, the detailed analysis by Dunbar (2002/3).

are sometimes qualified by numerical or territorial criteria) and, indeed, from the model adopted by the Framework Convention on National Minorities. Even the Charter on Regional Languages, although it focuses on languages rather on their speakers, tends to use rather more precise legal terms than UK legislation.

The Charter is, in fact, playing a rather important role with respect to the UK. When ratifying the Charter, the UK decided to bring no less than seven languages within its scope: Irish, Scottish Gaelic, Welsh, Scots, Ulster Scots, Manx Gaelic and Cornish, including, therefore, in the latter case, a virtually extinct language. However, the UK government was careful to specify that it would not accord the same status to each language or the same benefits to the speakers of each language but would modulate those in relation to the number of speakers and their territorial pattern of settlement.[32] States are free to make these distinctions. However, once they have decided to undertake commitments for the promotion of a given language in a given field (be it education, the media or public administration), then the Committee of Experts will closely check their compliance with those commitments. This is, indeed, what has happened in the past 10 years. The Committee has expressed detailed criticism of various aspects of the UK language regime, and the UK, in its follow-up reports, has sought to respond to those concerns in a constructive spirit which is quite exemplary. Despite the non-binding nature of the observations by the Strasbourg body, it has effectively acted as an external control on domestic language policy, and minority interest groups have used the opportunities offered to express their views to the Committee.

Italy

Whereas the Italian Constitution, adopted in the immediate post-war years, contained a prominent provision (Article 6) that states that 'the Republic protects linguistic minorities with appropriate measures', it took a very long time before such appropriate measures were indeed adopted for all the country's language minorities. On the one hand, very elaborate regimes of minority protection were adopted, and entrenched through constitutional laws, for the regions of South Tyrol (protecting the German and Ladin language groups there) and Val d'Aosta (protecting the use of French in public life).[33] On the other hand, though, it took several decades of patient political lobbying before the Italian parliament adopted

---

32 See the United Kingdom's second periodical report on its application of the Charter, 1 July 2005, MIN-Lang/PR (2005) 5.

33 Some of those linguistic regimes have been fine-tuned through litigation and, in particular, through a number of judgments of the Constitutional Court, which generally adopted – unlike its French counterpart – a minority-friendly approach. One may also note – in terms of the influence of European norms – that some minor elements of the minority language regime applying to South Tyrol have been successfully contested by the invocation of EU law norms of free movement before local courts and the European Court of Justice in Luxembourg. See, on this point, Toggenburg (2008).

in 1999 (more than 50 years after the constitutional mandate was formulated) a general law on the protection of historical linguistic minorities. It applies to a listed number of small communities speaking the following languages: Albanian, Catalan, Croat, Franco-Provençal, French, Friulian, German, Greek, Ladin, Occitan, Sardinian and Slovenian. The legislator chose not to protect the Romani language, based on the argument that this language is not linked to a particular territory within the country. Also, the law is a minimum standard which does not prevent more far-reaching accommodation of regional languages under other laws, as is the case most obviously for German and Ladin in South Tyrol. The Italian parliament adopted a specific law in 2001 that considerably strengthened the language rights of the Slovene minority based in the northeast of the country (region Friuli-Venezia Giulia).[34]

Although this new legislation of the turn of the century is primarily the result of political mobilization that was eventually successful at a time when the country had a centre-left government, some observers have also highlighted the coincidence of this new legislation with the ratification by Italy of the European Charter on Regional and Minority Languages and of the Framework Convention on National Minorities. The new legislation may thus be seen, in part, as a deliberate effort to put Italy's legal house in order before signing up to European instruments that Italy could hardly reject in the light of its Constitution's traditional commitment to the protection of linguistic minorities.

The 1999 law is a framework document that requires implementation by the national administrative authorities and, above all, by the regions and localities where these often very small minorities reside. It does not use the 'language of rights', and it seems very difficult to envisage that individual litigation could lead to legal changes on the ground. The implementation efforts by the administrative authorities at all levels seem not to be very effective, and this is where Italy's engagement with the Council of European instruments becomes meaningful. One small example, among many, may serve as an illustration of the mild pressure exercised by the dynamic monitoring mechanism established in Strasbourg. Article 9 of the Framework Convention states, in very vague terms, that minorities should have adequate access to the media. However, the Law 482/99 contains a rather more robust commitment to increase transmission time for minority language programmes on public radio and television. The lack of effective implementation of this commitment was criticized by the Advisory Committee in its opinion on Italy of February 2005.[35] This criticism does not have any immediate domestic legal effects, but it 'shames' Italy into improving the situation in view of its next

34 For detailed analysis of those various historical layers of Italian language law, see Piergigli (2001).

35 Advisory Committee on the Framework Convention for the Protection of National Minorities, Second Opinion on Italy, adopted on 24 February 2005, paras 89–91 and para. 154 (first recommendation).

report to the Advisory Committee.[36] Thus, the vague language of the European instruments is fleshed out by their monitoring bodies on the basis of more concrete commitments that states have made in their own domestic legislation, which are then 'turned against them' by the external expert body.

France

More than in any other country, the extension of minority recognition and minority rights in France in the course of the last quarter of a century – an extension which is real, although modest in comparison with other countries – has been entirely due to successful political mobilization, occasionally supported by minority nationalist violence as in the case of Corsica. The role of courts and of international bodies has been negligible.

As regards the role of the courts, we can even find some evidence of the opposite phenomenon, namely of judicial counter-mobilization, that is, successful litigation aimed at stopping governmental initiatives that were likely to weaken the unitary and unilingual character of the French state. Traditionally, regional minority-interest groups have found more political support with the socialist party than with the parties of the centre-right. So, each time a socialist government came to power, in 1981, in 1988 and in 1997, new plans were made to give greater recognition to the country's regional minorities and their languages. In more than one case, though, such plans were thwarted by the intervention of judicial bodies that enforced traditional Jacobin-republican views couched in legal terminology.

For example in 1991, when the then socialist government, supported by its majority in parliament, decided to adopt a new Special Statute for Corsica extending the island's existing autonomy, a number of opposition deputies challenged the bill before the *Conseil constitutionnel*.[37] The *Conseil* reduced much of the new law's symbolic appeal by declaring its Article 1 to be unconstitutional insofar as it referred to the 'Corsican people, component of the French people'; this, the constitutional judges held, was contrary to the principle of the indivisibility of the French people as embodied in Article 1 of the French Constitution.[38] In the

36 The next report was submitted by Italy on 21 December 2009. It seeks to respond to the criticism of the Advisory Committee (*Third Report Submitted by Italy*, 44 et seq.). It remains to be seen whether the Advisory Committee will consider itself satisfied by the response.

37 Until a very recent reform, the *Conseil constitutionnel* could not review the constitutionality of existing statutes but only of bills of statutes that have been adopted by Parliament but not yet officially promulgated. There was, thus, a short 'window for challenge', which, in practice, could only be used by the opposition parties in the Parliament.

38 On the place of the Special Statute of 1991 in the context of the evolution of France's policy on Corsican autonomy, see Daftary (2008: 288–90).

same decision, the *Conseil* also held that the *mandatory* teaching of the Corsican language in schools was similarly unconstitutional. This happened prior to the amendment of the Constitution that was enacted in 1992 in the wake of the Maastricht Treaty and made French the (sole) official language of the country; the Conseil instead invoked a violation of the principle of equality, which is a rather disputable basis for the rejection of the limited mandatory teaching of any given language (be it a minority language or some other language). Indeed, in other countries, and in the new European instruments, it is exactly the other way around: The principle of equality is the basis for a *duty* to provide some degree of minority language education [39]

A similar story unfolded in 1999. The socialist government that was then in power *signed* the European Charter of Regional Languages in May 1999, thus boosting the hopes of regional language activists that accession to the Charter mechanism would lead the French state to devote more resources to the regional languages and recognize enforceable rights to their users. Those hopes were smothered when opposition MPs challenged the proposed ratification law before the *Conseil Constitutionnel* that declared, on rather spurious grounds, that such ratification of the Charter for Regional or Minority Languages would be contrary to the Constitution.[40] Thus, the signature of the Charter was never followed by ratification, although some commentators have drawn new hope from the recent constitutional amendment proclaiming regional languages to be part of the country's cultural heritage. The Framework Convention on National Minorities, which is a rather more radical instrument than the Charter of Languages, was not even signed by France, after the *Conseil d'Etat* (the legal advisory body of the government) opined that its ratification would also be contrary to the Constitution.

Thus, the potential impact of the new European minority instruments adopted in the 1990s was not felt because France did not ratify either the Framework Convention or the Charter of Languages. Mobilization of judicial and international resources has thus been pretty unsuccessful in the case of France. Quite to the contrary: The courts have been successfully mobilized by the defenders of French unity and uniformity to stop at least some of the reforms designed to enhance the legal status of France's regional communities and languages. Whereas the examples mentioned above are drawn from the case law of the *Conseil constitutionnel,* the *Conseil d'Etat* (which, in addition to being the government's legal advisor, also acts as France's supreme administrative court) has similarly adopted, throughout this whole period, a rigid position of defender of the primacy of the French language.[41]

39 For an (approving) comment of the *Conseil constitutionnel's* decision, see Favoreu (1991).

40 Among the many commentaries of this salient decision, see Mélin-Soucramanien (1999) and Fraisseix (2001).

41 As exemplified by its restrictive rulings on the Breton-language *Diwan* schools; see Viola (2002).

Belgium

The peaceful coexistence of Belgium's traditional ethnic and linguistic groups – the Dutch-speaking Flemings, the French-speaking Walloons and the small German-speaking community in the East of the country – has been framed by complex legal arrangements, combining federal solutions, consociational arrangements and, occasionally, also the protection of the individual rights of the members of those communities. Elements of this complex package deal, which was gradually revamped and constitutionally entrenched in the period 1960–80, have been contested before the domestic courts and at the international level. Remarkably enough, members of the 'real' minority, namely the German-speakers, have never – as far as I can see – resorted to judicial or international mobilization for the advancement of their rights and interests; the political process has produced, in their regard, a legal regime that offers adequate or even optimal protection for their regional and cultural identity (to a large extent, they have been free-riders of the federal reforms that were primarily aimed at solving the Flemish-Walloon conflict). Contestations of the Belgian regime have rather emerged from the side of those who considered themselves to be the victims of the system of territorial unilingualism that was enacted. The formation of large areas with a single official language (namely the Dutch-language area in the North and the French-language area in the South, with only the central area around Brussels being officially bilingual) created linguistic minorities on both sides of the 'language border'; the claim of members of those minorities to use their own language in dealing with public authorities and in public education was denied for the sake of the overall 'linguistic peace' in the country.

The language areas regime, and the resulting curtailment of minority language use in those areas, was established in its present form in the early 1960s. At that time, there was no constitutional review of formal legislation in Belgium, so that the only available arena for judicial challenge was situated abroad, namely in Strasbourg. The famous *Belgian Linguistics* judgment of 1968 was one of the first important judgments of the European Court of Human Rights. Although the Court found a breach of the Convention on some minor points, the main features of the Belgian language legislation were upheld by the Court, and the litigants were effectively defeated. The Court adopted interpretations of the right to non-discrimination, of freedom of expression and of the right to education that basically permitted states to impose the exclusive use of an official language in the administration, the judiciary and the school system.[42]

Cases contesting more limited aspects of the Belgian official language regime were again lodged in Strasbourg during the 1980s. In the case of *Clerfayt, Legros*

42 This judgment of 1968 is still considered as one of the '*grands arrêts*' of the Strasbourg Court, especially for its early formulation of the Court's non-discrimination test. For a recent analysis of the case in the light of later developments in human rights law and theory, see Ringelheim (2006: 278–93).

and others v Belgium, the applicants, who were local councillors in the six *communes à facilités* [local communities providing public services in the minority language],[43] contested the fact that they were not allowed to speak French in the local council as a result of the system of territorial unilingualism that allowed for the exceptional use of French only by the *citizens* but not also by the elected *officials* of the locality when performing their official duties. They argued that this violated their political rights as protected by Article 3 of Protocol No.1 to the Convention. The European Commission of Human Rights rejected their claim on the simple ground that Article 3 only applied to legislative organs and not to local councils,[44] and the case did not reach the Court. One of the applicants in this case, who had also been elected in the Flemish regional parliament on a French minority party list, managed to take another claim up to the level of the Court in *Mathieu-Mohin and Clerfayt v Belgium*.[45] This claim was similarly unsuccessful.[46]

After this episode, the ECHR system lost its attractiveness for litigants seeking to contest the Belgian language regime. However, a new 'European' battlefront was opened in the 1990s with the adoption and subsequent entry into force of the Charter of Regional and Minority Languages and the Framework Convention on National Minorities. In particular, the question of whether Belgium should sign and ratify the Framework Convention became the object of heated debates, the main divisive issue being whether French-speakers resident in the Flemish part of Belgium might claim the status of 'national minority' under the Framework Convention and the accompanying language rights accorded to minorities, thus leading possibly to an extension of the bilingual area around Brussels to the detriment of the unilingual Dutch-language region. The discussion was rather open-ended and inconclusive due to the fact that the authors of the Convention had avoided including a definition of minority, thereby leaving it to each ratifying state to adopt its own interpretation of that concept.[47] Despite this scope for definitional discretion, Belgium refrained from signing and ratifying the Convention due to the opposition of the Flemish parties in the government. Thereupon, a number of French-speaking politicians (headed, once again, by Georges Clerfayt, a repeat-player in European challenges of the Belgian regime), managed to take the debate to the European level by convincing the Parliamentary Assembly of the Council of Europe to prepare a report and debate the issue. In October 2001, the Parliamentary Assembly's Committee on Legal Affairs and Human

---

43 These are the six local communities close to Brussels that form part of the Dutch language area but in which, in derogation from the normal rules, residents may choose to use French in their dealings with local authorities. On those exceptions to the territoriality principle, see Swenden (2002/3).

44 ECommHR, decision of 17 May 1985, *Decisions and Reports* 42.

45 ECtHR, Application No. 9267/81, judgment of 2 March 1987, series A, No. 113.

46 See discussion by Ringelheim (2006: 298–305).

47 On this question of the lack of definition of the term *minority*, see Verstichel (2008).

Rights asked the Venice Commission for a legal opinion.[48] At its 8–9 March 2002 session, the Venice Commission adopted its opinion with the innocuously worded title 'Possible groups of persons to which the Framework Convention for the Protection of National Minorities could be applied in Belgium'.[49] One of the main issues was whether, under the Framework Convention, a particular language group (such as the French-speaking population in Belgium) could be a co-dominant group at the national level (and therefore not qualify as a minority) but, nevertheless, constitute a minority when considered within the context of a particular region of that country, namely Flanders. The Commission held that, in a federal state such as Belgium, the existence of a minority group must be assessed both at state and at sub-state levels, and it found that French-speakers in the Dutch-language region, and also Dutch-speakers in the French-language region, were to be considered as minorities in the sense of the Framework Convention. The Parliamentary Assembly's *rapporteur*, Nabholz Haidegger, followed the interpretation adopted by the Venice Commission's opinion, and this view was also enacted in the Assembly's Resolution on the question.[50] The resolution, which has no legal binding value, was rejected by the Flemish political parties. The initiative of the Council of Europe's parliamentary body may, in fact, be considered as counterproductive, since it hardened the resolve of the Flemish parties to veto Belgium's ratification of the Framework Convention; the Convention is still unratified today, although the political pressure on Belgium, and on the few other 'conscientious objectors' among European states, is mounting. It may be noted, in this context, that Switzerland – unlike Belgium with its similarly delicate and cumbersome cultural accommodation regime – did not refrain from entering into European obligations as regards the protection of minorities and regional languages. Indeed, it became a party to the Charter of Regional Languages (December 1997) and to the Framework Convention (February 1999) precisely at the time the new Constitution was adopted. Upon ratifying the Framework Convention, the Swiss government submitted the following declaration:

> Switzerland declares that in Switzerland national minorities in the sense of the Framework Convention are groups of individuals numerically inferior to the rest of the population of the country or of a canton, whose members are Swiss nationals.

---

48 The European Commission for Democracy through Law, better known as the 'Venice Commission', is a committee of independent experts that assists the Council of Europe bodies through providing legal expertise, in particular by identifying best practices and formulating advisory opinions in matters of constitutional law. It has mainly been active in relation to proposed constitutional and judicial reforms in the countries of Central and Eastern Europe.

49 CDL-AD (2002) 1. The opinion can be found on the Commission's website. Available at: www.venice.coe.int.

50 Parliamentary Assembly of the Council of Europe, Resolution 1301(2002) 1, *Protection of Minorities in Belgium*, 26 September 2002.

Thus, while it was careful to exclude the large foreign population from the benefit of the Convention,[51] Switzerland did accept to include local minorities ('within a canton'), which is precisely the question that – as we saw – makes Belgium hesitate to ratify the Convention.

Conclusion

During the past two decades, there has been an important evolution in the legal regulation of minority languages all across Europe, involving, in particular, greater legal recognition for regional and minority languages and new rights for their speakers that are now often entrenched in the constitution and, therefore, put beyond the reach of transient political majorities in the national parliament. This evolution took place along rather different lines in each country, depending on its constitutional framework, state structure and ideological attitude to cultural diversity. A common trend, at least in the Western part of the European continent, which was the main focus of this chapter, is that the expansion of language rights did not occur primarily through litigation but through political mobilization. In some countries (such as Spain, Italy and the UK), devolution of state powers to regions has empowered regional governments that are dedicated to the protection of minority interests, but one can also observe the successful emergence of minority language interests in the national political discourse, whereby minority languages are seen as part of the country's overall identity (see, in this respect, the recent constitutional amendment in France).

This domestically driven evolution has been affected, since 1990, by important Europe-wide legal developments. The elaboration of European minority protection instruments, primarily intended to prevent conflict in central and Eastern Europe, has had an unanticipated indirect effect in Western Europe by entrenching 'best practices'. Since around 2000, the impact of these European instruments has been strengthened by the active attitude taken by the non-judicial monitoring bodies established under the Framework Convention and the Charter on Languages. The non-judicial nature of this monitoring practice blends easily with the 'rights without litigation' approach that dominates domestic language legislation and has been arguably more effective, so far at least, than the 'hard law' impact of European Union law and the European Convention of Human Rights. This state of affairs may change in the years to come: Since the European Union has now recognized minority protection as one of its foundational values (in Article 2 of the Treaty on European Union, as amended by the Treaty of Lisbon), and as the European Court of Human Rights is actively exploring the minority protection potential of

51 Similarly, the Charter of Regional Languages was declared by Switzerland to apply only to Italian and Romansh, to the exclusion of both French and the immigrant languages.

the Convention rights, we may yet see a more direct form of Europeanization of language laws in the years to come.

References

Agirreazkuenaga Zigorraga, I. 2006. La carta Europea de lenguas regionales o minoritarias del Consejo de Europa como derecho interno, in *Estudios sobre el estatuto jurídico de las lenguas en España*, Pérez Fernández, J.M. (coord.). Barcelona: Atelier Editorial, 105.

Arzoz, X. 2009. Language Rights as Legal Norms. *European Public Law*, 15, 541–74.

Cardi, V. 2007. Regional or Minority Language Use before Judicial Authorities: Provisions and Facts. *Journal on Ethnopolitics and Minority Issues in Europe*, 6, 2.

Cichowski, R.A. 2007. *The European Court and Civil Society – Litigation. Mobilization and Governance*. Cambridge: Cambridge University Press.

Costa, J. 2003. Catalan Linguistic Policy: Liberal or Illiberal? *Nations and Nationalism*, 9(3), 413–32.

Daftary, F. 2008. Experimenting with Territorial Administrative Autonomy in Corsica: Exception or Pilot Region? *International Journal on Minority and Group Rights*, 15, 273–312.

De Schutter, O. 2008. The Framework Convention on the Protection of National Minorities and the Law of the European Union, in *The Framework Convention for the Protection of National Minorities: A Useful Pan-European Instrument?*, edited by A. Verstichel, B. De Witte and P. Lemmens. Antwerp: Intersentia, 231–72.

De Varennes, F. 1994. Language and Freedom of Expression in International Law. *Human Rights Quarterly*, 16, 163.

De Witte, B. 2002. Politics versus Law in the EU's Approach to Ethnic Minorities, in *Europe Unbound: Enlarging and Reshaping the Boundaries of the European Union*, edited by J. Zielonka. London: Routledge, 464.

De Witte, B. 2004. Language Law of the European Union: Protecting or Eroding Linguistic Diversity?, in *Culture and European Law*, edited by R. Craufurd Smith. Oxford: Oxford University Press, 205–41.

De Witte, B. and Horváth, E. 2008. The Many Faces of Minority Policy in the European Union, in *Synergies in Minority Protection – European and International Law Perspectives*, edited by K. Henrard and R. Dunbar. Cambridge: Cambridge University Press, 365–84.

Dunbar, R. 2002/3. Language Legislation and Language Rights in the United Kingdom. *European Yearbook of Minority Issues*. The Hague: Martinus Nijhoff Publishers, 95–126.

Dunbar, R. 2005. The Gaelic Language (Scotland) Act 2005. *Edinburgh Law Review*, 9, 466–79.

Dunbar, R. 2008. The Council of Europe's European Charter for Regional or Minority Languages, in *Synergies in Minority Protection – European and International Law Perspectives*, edited by K. Henrard and R. Dunbar. Cambridge: Cambridge University Press, 155–86.

Eide, A. 2008. The Council of Europe's Framework Convention for the Protection of National Minorities, in *Synergies in Minority Protection – European and International Law Perspectives*, edited by K. Henrard and R. Dunbar. Cambridge: Cambridge University Press, 119–54.

Favoreu, L. 1991. La décision Statut de la Corse du 9 mai 1991. *Revue française de droit constitutionnel*, 2, 305.

Fraisseix, P. 2001. La France, les langues régionales et la Charte européenne des langues régionales et minoritaires. *Revue française de droit administratif*, 17, 59–86.

Gilbert, G. 2002. The Burgeoning Minority Rights Jurisprudence of the European Court of Human Rights. *Human Rights Quarterly*, 24, 736–80.

Henrard, K. 2000. *Devising an Adequate System of Minority Protection: Individual Human Rights, Minority Rights and the Right to Self-Determination*. New York: Springer.

Henrard, K. 2008. A Patchwork of 'Successful' and 'Missed' Synergies in the Jurisprudence of the ECHR, in *Synergies in Minority Protection – European and International Law Perspectives*, edited by K. Henrard and R. Dunbar. Cambridge: Cambridge University Press, 314–64.

Hogan-Brun, G., Mar-Molinero, C. and Stevenson, P. (eds) 2009. *Discourses on Language and Integration: Critical Perspectives on Language Testing Regimes in Europe*. Amsterdam: John Benjamins.

Lavialle, C. 2008. Du nominalisme juridique. Le nouvel article 75-1 de la Constitution du 4 octobre 1958. *Revue française de droit administratif*, 24, 1110–15.

López Basaguren, A.L. 2007. Las lenguas oficiales entre constitución y Comunidades Autónomas: Desarrollo o transformación del modelo constitucional? *Revista Española de Derecho Constitucional*, 27, 83–112.

Mancini, S. and de Witte, B. 2008. Language Rights as Cultural Rights: A European Perspective, in *Cultural Human Rights*, edited by F. Francioni and M. Scheinin. The Hague: Martinus Nijhoff Publishers, 247–84.

Medda-Windischer, R. 2009. *Old and New Minorities: Reconciling Diversity and Cohesion*. Baden Baden: Nomos.

Mélin-Soucramanien, F. 1999. La République contre Babel – A propos de la décision du Conseil constitutionnel no. 99-412 DC du 15 juin 1999. *Revue du droit public*, 115, 985–1000.

Milian i Massana, A. 1994. *Derechos linguisticos y derecho fundamental a la educación*. Madrid: Civitas.

Milian i Massana, A. 2002. Comentarios en torno de la Ley del Parlamento de Cataluña 1/1998, de 7 de enero, de Política Lingüística. *Revista de Administración Pública*, 157, 337.

Palermo, F. 2008. Domestic Enforcement and Direct Effect of the Framework Convention for the Protection of National Minorities, in *The Framework Convention for the Protection of National Minorities: A Useful Pan-European Instrument?*, edited by A. Verstichel, A. Alen, B. de Witte and P. Lemmens. Antwerp: Intersentia, 187–214.

Pentassuglia, G. 2001. The EU and the Protection of Minorities: The Case of Eastern Europe. *European Journal of International Law*, 12, 3–38.

Pérez Fernández, J. M. (coord.) 2006. *Estudios sobre el estatuto jurídico de las lenguas en España*. Barcelona: Atelier Editorial.

Piergigli, V. 2001. *Lingue minoritarie e identità culturali*. Milano: Giuffrè.

Poggeschi, G. 2002. *Le nazioni linguistiche della Spagna autonomica*. Padova: CEDAM.

Ringelheim, J. 2006. *Diversité culturelle et droits de l'homme: La protection des minorités par la Convention européenne des droits de l'homme*. Brussels: Bruylant.

Ringelheim, J. 2010. Minority Rights in a Time of Multiculturalism – The Evolving Scope of the Framework Convention on the Protection of National Minorities. *Human Rights Law Review*, 10 (1), 99–128.

Rubio Marín, R. 2003. Language Rights: Exploring the Competing Rationales, in *Language Rights and Political Theory*, edited by W. Kymlicka and A. Patten. Oxford: Oxford University Press, 52.

Sasse, G. 2004. Minority Rights and EU Enlargement: Normative Overstretch or Effective Conditionality?, in *Minority Protection and the Enlarged European Union: The Way Forward*, edited by G.N. Toggenburg. Budapest: LGI, Open Society Institute, 61.

Swenden, W. 2002/3. Personality versus Territoriality: Belgium and the Framework Convention for the Protection of National Minorities. *European Yearbook of Minority Issues*, 2, 331–56.

Toggenburg, G.N. (ed.) 2004. *Minority Protection and the Enlarged European Union: The Way Forward*. Budapest: LGI, Open Society Institute.

Toggenburg, G.N. 2008. Regional Autonomies Providing Minority Rights and the Law of European Integration: Experiences from South Tyrol, in *Tolerance through Law: Self-Governance and Group Rights in South Tyrol*, edited by J. Woelk, F. Palermo and J. Marko. Leiden: Brill, 177–200.

Verstichel, A. 2008. Personal Scope of Application: An Open, Inclusive and Dynamic Approach – The FCNM as a Living Instrument, in *The Framework Convention for the Protection of National Minorities: A Useful Pan-European Instrument?* edited by A. Verstichel, A. Alen, B. de Witte, and P. Lemmens. Antwerp: Intersentia, 127–57.

Viola, A. 2002. Ecoles Diwan: L'impossible intégration. *Revue du droit public*, 5, 1351–62.

Wintemute, R. 2004. Filling the Article 14 "Gap": Government Ratification and Judicial Control of Protocol No.12 ECHR. *European Human Rights Law Review*, 5, 484–99.

Chapter 10

The Model Character of Swiss Language Law

Dagmar Richter

Outline of a Model Function

This chapter does not propose the simple transfer of Swiss Language Law into any other legal system. Its aim is rather to exemplify the fundamental principles and constitutional concepts that are forming the "Swiss Model" of a multilingual federal state.[1] It will be shown that any linguistic situation, no matter how specific it may be, can be governed by a basic set of general rules. Some of these rules may already now be helpful for a more systematic approach to the language law of the European Union, while the Swiss language system as such will become an important model, once the number of EU citizens realizing their freedoms of movement and establishment (Articles 45 and 49 of the Treaty on the Functioning of the European Union) assumes considerable proportions.

Facts and Figures

If we look at the linguistic map of Switzerland,[2] four territories can be discerned, though they are far from homogeneity: There is the large German-speaking territory in the Northern and Eastern part of Switzerland, the French-speaking "Romandie" in the West, the Italian-speaking territory in the Southern *peninsulae* and some little Rheto-Romanic (or Romansh) islands in the Canton of Grison. It is apparent even from the first sight of the map that the linguistic communities, which constitute the Swiss people, are varying considerably in size and that the Rheto-Romanic group is close to extinction. On the other hand, the small Italian parts being pressed into the corners of Switzerland may have a good chance to overcome, because they adjoin Italy. The most problematic region is where the linguistic border divides the German-speaking from the French-speaking territories or, more precisely, where the so-called "*Röstigraben*" ["roasted potato rift"][3]

1 The author has examined this issue comprehensively in Richter (2005).
2 See Lüdi and Werlen (2005: 12).
3 See Büchi (2001).

runs through the Cantons of Berne, Fribourg and Valais. If any linguistic conflict arises in Switzerland, it is to appear there, particularly in the Canton of Fribourg, where the French-speaking population is alarmed by the fact that the linguistic border is moving steadily to the West, thereby diminishing the French-speaking territory.

The optical impression is reflected by the statistical data, which are being taken on grounds of the *Volkszählungsgesetz* (Federal Census Act):[4] Switzerland is subdivided into 26 cantons, of which 17 have declared themselves to be German-speaking either by explicit constitutional provisions or have to be regarded as such by virtue of customary law; four cantons are formally declared to be French-speaking and one canton (Ticino) is declared to be Italian-speaking. Only four cantons are multilingual in the official sphere: Berne, Fribourg and Wallis have recognized German and French as official languages, whilst Grison is the only canton that has recognized three official languages – German, Italian and Rheto-Romanic (Romansh).[5]

According to the comprehensive census in 2000, German is spoken by 72.5 per cent of the nationals, French by 21 per cent, Italian by 4.3 per cent, Rheto-Romanic by 0.6 per cent and other (non-national) languages by 1.6 per cent.[6] If we look at the inhabitants of Switzerland – without regard to nationality – German is spoken by 63.7 per cent, French by 20.4 per cent, Italian by 6.5 per cent, Rheto-Romanic by 0.5 per cent and other languages by 9 per cent.[7] We may derive from this a couple of conclusions:

1. The language groups are very different in size;
2. German (including the Alemannic varieties of German) has a clearly dominant position;
3. Rheto-Romanic is very close to extinction;
4. The Italian-speaking community is apparently backed by immigrants from Italy (if one compares the data for nationals with those for inhabitants);
5. The percentage of non-Swiss languages being imported by immigrants or migrant workers is growing considerably. Taken together the non-Swiss languages (e.g., Serbo-Croatian, Turkish, and so on) have already gained the third position.

4 From 2010 on the census will be regulated by the Bundesgesetz über die Eidgenössische Volkszählung (Act on the Federal Census) of 22 July 2007, SR (Systematic Collection of the Swiss Law) 431.112, whilst the census of 2000 was based on the precedent Act of 1998. An English translation of the Census Act is published by the Federal Authorities of the Swiss Federation at: http://www.admin.ch/ch/e/rs/c431_112.html [accessed: 9 February 2010].

5 For the cantonal figures, see Lüdi and Werlen (2005: 23).

6 See Lüdi and Werlen (2005: 9).

7 See Lüdi and Werlen (2005: 7).

Constitutional Principles in the Field of Language Law

Switzerland is a federal state that consists of the Federation and the constituent states (cantons), the latter being subdivided into districts (regional entities) and local communities. All state power is separated between the Federation and the cantons in a way that regularly entrusts the cantons with competence, whereas the Federation may act only if the Constitution explicitly attributes a specific competence to the latter (Article 3 of the Federal Constitution of the Swiss Confederation of 18 April 1999).

According to Article 4 of the Constitution, Switzerland has four national languages (*Landessprachen*), which are German, French, Italian and Rheto-Romanic (Romansh). However, only German, French and Italian are full-fledged official languages of the Federation, whereas Rheto-Romanic has a special status with respect to its use as an official language (Constitution, Article 70(1)).[8] Although the Federation is competent to regulate the employment of official languages by federal institutions, its power is limited by the rule that, for example, a federal court is not supposed to switch to German or any other language, if the respective case originates from a French-speaking canton (see infra, *The Functioning of the Territorial Principle – with Particular Regard to the Situation of Linguistic Minorities*). Rules like this shall prevent the linguistic systems from the spillover effects that are likely to appear if a case is being referred to higher instances, in particular to federal instances.

The Principle of Territoriality

There is one core article in the Constitution that reflects the decisive position of the Swiss cantons. Article 70(2) of the Constitution reads:

> The Cantons shall decide on their official languages. In order to preserve harmony between linguistic communities, the Cantons shall respect the traditional territorial distribution of languages and take account of indigenous linguistic minorities.

It follows from this norm as well as from a long-standing legal tradition[9] that in the federal system of Switzerland the constituent states (cantons) are competent to determine the status of official languages in their respective territories. This rule is named the *territorial principle* or the *principle of territoriality*. According to this principle, any of the four Swiss language groups may play a different role in one of the cantons as compared with the whole country; hence, the notion of a

8 See Appendix.

9 Kägi-Diener (2008), margin note 20, pleads for unwritten constitutional law of the cantons being the original source of the principle of territoriality.

linguistic "majority" or "minority" always has a *relative* character.[10] According to the *territorial principle*, the relevance of each language in a specific area is determined by certain factual and normative criteria, which have always been a subject of dispute and controversy.[11] If two or more languages must be recognized as official languages according to these criteria, coordination of the use of these languages will become necessary and, consequently, a rather complex linguistic regime will follow. For example, the official language of the Canton of Zurich is German, the official language of the Canton of Génève is French, the official languages of the Canton of Berne are German and French and the official languages of the Swiss Federation are German, French, Italian and, with a special (minor) status, Rheto-Romanic.

The effects of such a system are to be sensed intensely by any single person living in Switzerland: for example, if you are an Alemannic native-speaker living in a community, district or canton, the official language of which is French only, you will have a problem if you do not speak any French. Public authorities, including courts, public schools, and so on would not communicate with you in German, even if the public servant, with whom you communicate in a given case, may have a very good command of German. Of course, there could be some exceptions being granted "behind the curtain" or illegally tolerated.[12] However, one should be prepared to pay for translation services even as a citizen of Switzerland unless he or she has learnt the language that is recognized as the official language of the relevant community or district. As the Federal Court of Switzerland, which is the supreme court of the land, has held in earlier decisions, any person who migrates from one Swiss region to another has to "assimilate" to the language that is declared official in the new place of residence.[13] Of course, such obligation has always been related to the *official* use of languages and never pertained to the private use of languages. Although contemporary jurisprudence has long since started to replace the problematic notion of "assimilation"[14] by the notion of "linguistic integration", the basic idea of any region having a linguistic "imprinting", which is protected by the law, is still alive.

---

10 See Richter (2005: 157–9, 1119 et seq.).

11 For more details, see infra, "*The Recognition of Languages*".

12 See, e.g., Schweizerisches Bundesgericht (Swiss Federal Court), Case 2A.201/2001, Judgment of 24 July 2001 – *Swisscom* (at 3b.bb.), where the Court had to clarify that "English is not among the official languages of the Federation".

13 BGE (Entscheidungen des Schweizerischen Bundesgerichts/ Reports of the Swiss Federal Court) vol. 91 I: 487 et seq. – *Association de l'École française*.

14 Cf. Article 5 (2) of the Framework Convention for the Protection of National Minorities of 1 February 1995 (European Treaty Series No. 157): "Without prejudice to measures taken in pursuance of their general integration policy, the Parties shall refrain from policies or practices aimed at assimilation of persons belonging to national minorities against their will and shall protect these persons from any action aimed at such assimilation".

The Principle of Linguistic Freedom

It is apparent that the application of the territorial principle may prevent individuals from using their own language when communicating with cantonal authorities and courts or when attending classes at school and so may frustrate a legitimate individual interest. For this reason, Swiss constitutional law explicitly grants the individual *linguistic freedom* (Article 18 of the Constitution).[15] If this or any other individual right collides with the territorial principle, both of them must be brought into balance considering all the circumstances of the case. The outcome of this weighing of interests, which is the individual's interest to use freely any language on the one hand and the state's interest to preserve "the traditional territorial distribution of languages" (Article 70(2) of the Constitution) on the other hand, depends on the context where the respective language is being used. Some fictive cases may clarify the functioning of the concept in law and in practice:

> Example No. 1: Urs Breitenmoser, who only speaks Alemannic-German lives in the French-speaking canton of Jura. When he applied for a building permit in German, his application was sent back to him with the advice to file a new application in the proper language, which is French. Though Breitenmoser may claim his linguistic freedom, his individual right with respect to the territorial distribution of languages will recede into the second line. In this case, the individual interest in using the German language, which is protected by the linguistic freedom, collides with the territorial principle authorizing the canton to defend the linguistic regime of the relevant area, which is a French-speaking one. As there is no good reason for arguing that the applicant must be exempted from the official language regime or that his individual freedom prevails for any other reasons, he has to adapt himself to that regime – if need be with the aid of a translator.

> Example No. 2: Madame Dutroux, a French-speaking lady, ran a person over when driving too fast through the city of Bellinzona. She was put to trial before a criminal court in Bellinzona, where Italian is the only official language. The criminal court in this case is obliged to use Italian as the official language of the court. However, Dutroux has a strong individual right, which is the human right to be informed promptly and in detail in a language which she understands of the nature and cause of the accusation against her and also to have the free assistance of an interpreter if she cannot understand or speak the language used in court.[16] These rights supersede the territorial principle in the case of conflict.[17]

15 See Appendix.

16 See Article 6(3) lit. a and e of the European Convention on Human Rights and, accordingly, Article 14(3) lit. a and e of the International Covenant on Civil and Political Rights.

17 In some earlier decisions, the Federal Court had come to the opposite conclusion. See, e.g., *Schweizerisches Bundesgericht, Europäische Grundrechte-Zeitschrift* (1995: 611 et seq.).

Example No. 3: A global assurance company named "Zürich Versicherungen" opens a branch office in Scuol, where Rheto-Romanic is the official language. The local authority orders the company to translate its name into "Turitg segiradas" and to use this name *only* whenever addressing the public, for example, by inscriptions at the building. This case is debatable: On the one hand, the Rheto-Romanic (Romansh) language is an endangered language, which may justify strict measures. On the other hand, one must consider that the use of languages for commercial inscriptions or banners relates to private or social communication, where no "official" language is at stake. However, there may be a certain impact on the use of languages in the public sphere, which in the long run could also touch upon the vitality of the official language. In a case like this, the Swiss Federal Court has held that the public interest in the preservation of the Rheto-Romanic language prevails over the commercial interest of the private enterprise.[18]

Example No. 4: The Kälin family moves from Luzern to a small village in Grison, where Romansh is the only official language. The 8-year-old son of the family, who only speaks German, has to attend classes at the local public[19] school in Romansh. However, every school is obliged to respect the individual's right to education and, therefore, must not practice any rigid form of territoriality. Although children can be obliged to adapt even to a small minority language at school, the school authorities must provide for additional lessons in Rheto-Romanic in order to integrate every child into the class. As the Federal Court has pointed out in other cases, the territorial principle must generally be practiced much more considerately at schools than in any other area.[20]

There are many more examples showing that the individual's legitimate interest, which is the right to employ his or her native language freely, is to be weighed against conflicting interests and principles, such as the public interest in defending the linguistic "imprinting" of a region according to the principle of territoriality. Generally, there exists a rule that can be characterized by the short formula "the more private, the less regulation": The more private the context of the communication is, the less regulation or restriction will be justified. On the one hand, the state has no legitimate interest at all to regulate the use of languages in private bedrooms and, on the other hand, the state's interest clearly prevails if the use of languages in courts and public administration is at stake.

18 Judgment of 12 October 1992 (1 P.554/1991/bme; unpublished). For a similar case see, e.g., BGE (note 13) 116 Ia 345 – *Bar Amici*.

19 Some of the Swiss cantons even prevent children from escaping from the official language by attending a private school. For a famous case see BGE (note 13) 91 I 480 – *Association de l'École française*.

20 Cf. BGE (note 13) 106 Ia 299: 305–6 – *Brunner*.

We may conclude from this that the *antagonism* of "territoriality versus individual linguistic freedom" calls for the weighing of interests in each individual case. With this method, any territorial language order can be adapted to the requirements of the rule of law, which is one of the core ideas of the Swiss model suitable to be transferred to any other legal order.

The Principle of Minority Protection

According to Article 70(2) of the Constitution, the cantons, when deciding on their official languages, shall take into account the "indigenous linguistic minorities". This means that traditional minorities, which are to be distinguished from "new" minorities or migrants, must never be oppressed.[21] On the contrary, they can be exempted from the rules of territoriality by virtue of Article 70(2) of the Constitution, even if their size is not considerable in terms of the territorial principle.

Understanding the "Mechanism" of Territoriality

The merits as well as the deficiencies of the Swiss language system may be exemplified by two selected issues: the "mechanism of territoriality" and the "recognition of languages".

The Functioning of the Territorial Principle with Particular Regard to the Situation of Linguistic Minorities

The first example relates to the multilingual cantons. It is typical for the Swiss system that the number of official languages increases from the bottom to the top, that is to say, from the local to the cantonal level, but never vice versa. In other words, any language that is an official language in any single village is supposed to be an official language of the respective district and also of the canton. According to the territorial principle, a canton cannot declare itself to be monolingual if it contains an officially bilingual district. It can be derived from constant practice that there exists a *consistency rule* that guarantees the population a consistent linguistic regime comprising all instances of courts or authorities from the local instance up to the federal level: For example., if Italian is the official language of a specific regional court, the same language can be (and should be) employed in all further instances including the Swiss Federal Court. Accordingly, there are judgments of the Swiss Federal Court in German *or* French *or* Italian *or* (very rarely) Rheto-Romanic. One may speak of the *starting language principle* that, due to the territorial principle, prevents the parties from switching to any other official language during the course of procedure.

---

21 See infra, "*The Functioning of the Territorial Principle – with Particular Regard to the Situation of Linguistic Minorities*" (with further references).

However, contemporary Swiss federal law tends to relatively pragmatic norms in this respect[22] or even denies the validity of the starting language principle as, for example, the Canton of Bern does with regard to the cantonal authorities.[23]

If in exceptional cases, a certain language is recognized as an official language on the local level although it is not an official language of the district or canton, the principle of territoriality will have given way to the protection of minorities. This is why the territorial principle on the one hand and the principle of minority protection[24] on the other hand can be distinguished from each other quite clearly. For example, the community of Jaun in the Canton of Fribourg is German-speaking, although in the district where it is situated, French is the only official language. This appears to be irregular. However, in this case, the territorial principle has given way to the protection of a "historic minority" living in a single village, the language of which is too small to be recognized as a second official language of the whole canton. Whereas this constitutes an exceptional case – the protection of indigenous minorities as a special justification for deviating from the territorial principle – the principle of territoriality must be applied generally in a way that would not endanger *linguistic peace*[25] nor oppress minorities,[26] two constitutional exigencies limiting the principle of territoriality, nor ignore the limits being set by the general principle of proportionality.

The Recognition of Languages

The second example relates to the recognition of official languages in the individual districts of a multilingual canton. Usually, the bilingual cantons

22 Article 54 of the *Bundesgerichtsgesetz* (Code of Procedure for the Swiss Federal Court) of 17 June 2005, SR (note 4) 173.110, reads: "(1) The procedure shall be conducted by using one of the official languages (German, French, Italian, Rumantsch Grischun) which regularly is the language of the contested decision. If the parties are employing any other official language, the procedure may be conducted by using this language. (2) In the case of contentious procedures the language of the parties shall be taken into consideration, provided that it is an official language". (Unofficial translation by the author).

23 Article 6(4) of the Constitution of the Canton of Bern of 6 June 1993 (BSG [*Berner Systematische Gesetzessammlung*/ Systematic Collection of the Laws of the Canton of Berne] 101.1) reads: "Within the authorities responsible for the Canton as a whole, anyone may use the official language of their choice." An English version of this Constitution is published by the Federal Authorities of the Swiss Federation. Available at: http://www.admin.ch/ch/e/rs/c101.html [accessed: 9 February 2010].

24 Article 70(2), line 2 of the Federal Constitution of the Swiss Confederation of 18 April 1999 explicitly mentions "indigenous linguistic minorities".

25 See, e.g., BGE (note 13) 100 Ia 466; 122 I 236: 240. Cf. Article 70(2) Const.: "In order to preserve *harmony between linguistic communities*, the Cantons shall respect the traditional territorial distribution of languages and take account of indigenous linguistic minorities". (Emphasis by the author).

26 See, e.g., BGE (note 13) 106 Ia 302.

have constitutional provisions recognizing certain languages as cantonal and official languages. However, they are not very eager to determine the linguistic character of the single districts, neither in the Constitution nor in statutory law. As linguistic borders often have a *traditional or historic character*, the need for an explicit determination occurs only if the linguistic composition of the inhabitants of a specific region starts to change or where the linguistic question for any other reason has become a matter of dispute. This is why, for example, the Canton of Berne has stipulated in Article 6(1–2) of its Constitution[27] explicitly:

1. German and French are the Bernese cantonal and official languages;
2. The official languages are:
   a. French in the Bernese Jura;
   b. German and French in the district of Biel-Bienne;
   c. German in the other districts.

Determining the linguistic regime of the various local entities and districts has also been a difficult topic in the Canton of Fribourg. For example, if the German-speaking minority in a traditionally French-speaking district of the canton increases from 10 to 30 per cent, the question will be, whether German must be recognized as a second official language. While the members of the Alemannic minority would love to have that, the members of the French-speaking majority would clearly or even aggressively refuse any movement towards bilingualism because bilingualism is feared to be the prelude to a linguistic switchover that sooner or later would put the former majority into the minority's position. As my studies have shown,[28] such conflicts are more likely to arise in the traditionally French-speaking regions because those areas serve as a preserve for the *Francophonie*, which with respect to the federal level has to defend its position against the German-speaking majority. The Alemannic population, because of its position as the strongest linguistic community in the Swiss Confederation, seems to be more tolerant towards bilingualism in favour of a French-speaking minority in a specific canton than vice versa. This is what I would call the "charm of relativism".

It is very difficult to change the linguistic denomination of a district from monolingual to bilingual if the democratic majority is to decide, because this majority is quite likely to coincide with the linguistic majority. Why should the traditional linguistic majority accept a change to bilingualism, which may foster the further increase of the minority until the latter finally becomes the new majority? And even if the majority is tolerant, why should it agree to the additional costs the introduction of bilingualism would incur, even if those expenses might pay in the future? Generally, the majority has no interest at all in depriving itself of power.

27 See note 23.

28 See Richter (2005: 1124–5).

Therefore, it is necessary to establish by law certain objective criteria that induce the necessity of change with regard to the linguistic denomination of a town, a district or the canton. At least, this is the method being chosen by the Canton of Fribourg. Since 1980, the Swiss Federal Court has initiated a new approach to the issue of linguistic change by interpreting the territorial principle in a more sophisticated way. According to the Federal Court's jurisprudence, not only the linguistic majority but also linguistic minorities must be represented within the official language order, wherever a minority language is relevant or *considerable* in certain terms.[29] Concerning size or quantity a minority *may* be considerable, if it has reached 30–33 per cent of the living population in the reference area. However, this is not enough. On a pure statistical basis, recognition of a minority language as a second official language is obligatory only if the percentage of its speakers comes close to 50 per cent, whereas in the range of 30–50 per cent, additional criteria are playing a decisive role. Those quality criteria or normative criteria may be:[30]

- the permanence of the minority in the respective area;
- the overall size of the community concerned – the smaller a community is, the more per cents will be needed in order to establish a second official language;
- a capital town should be more open to bilingualism than any other community without such function;
- the contiguity of the linguistic border should be considered to be a relevant factor, as the creation of linguistic islands must be avoided;
- and, last but not least, it is discussed whether any linguistic change must be based on the consent of all groups. As a result, however, social consensus would become a blocking criterion encouraging the formerly dominant group to obstruct any attempt to achieve a linguistic change.

The sensitivity of the issue is documented in the unpublished judgment of the Swiss Federal Court in the case of *Cressier* (1997).[31] Cressier then was "an only French" community within the bilingual "Lake District" (*district du Lac*) in the Canton of Fribourg. As the proportion of the German-speaking minority in Cressier had actually amounted to 40 per cent, a couple of German-speaking applicants petitioned to have their German mother tongue recognized as a second language. Despite this rather high percentage and despite the fact that

29 See particularly BGE (note 13) 106 Ia 299 and unpublished judgment of the Swiss Federal Court of 22 January 1997 (2P.211/1996).

30 See, e.g., Voyame (1992 : 2813 et seq.). As Kägi-Diener (2008), margin note 25, points out, the Canton of Grison in its Language Act of 2006 has introduced a new rule, according to which a two-thirds majority will be needed if a community wishes to switch from a bilingual to a merely German-speaking regime.

31 Judgment of 22 January 1997 (note 29).

Cressier was situated in a bilingual district, the applicants failed: As the Federal Court explained in its judgment, the denial of bilingualism is not yet arbitrary, if the proportion of the minority, though it has surmounted the crucial limit of 35 per cent at the last census of 1990, had not yet surmounted the limit at the earlier census of 1980. Therefore, the community was held to be still in a "*state of linguistic mutation*" so that the recognition of a second official language would have been premature. However, the Federal Court spoke of a "*borderline case*", in which the territorial principle must not be applied too rigidly. We may derive from this judgment that the Swiss system seeks to retard the process of linguistic mutation in order to gradually accustom people to the change and so to preserve linguistic peace. With this intention, the judgment actually fits into the legal purpose of the territorial principle, which is not to guarantee a monolingual regime to the regional majority but to preserve *traditional*-speaking areas in order to preserve linguistic peace.

Struggling for the Language Act

Despite all laws and experience Switzerland has accumulated in the course of time, it is still occupied with major conflicts among the various linguistic communities. Some of those were even said to have the capacity of splitting the country. This applies particularly to the top question of whether English or rather any other of the national languages should rank as the first foreign language in school education. The decision of some of the German-speaking cantons to prefer English as the first foreign language instead of French was widely understood as an unfriendly act against the French-speaking countrymen, to which the French-speaking cantons responded with profound irritation. Some of them even initiated amendments to their Constitutions in order to make sure that the first foreign language to be taught at school must be a national language only.[32]

The controversy on "L 2" (language No. 2, regarding the first foreign language to be taught) even prevented the achievement of a statutory Language Act for many years. After some unsuccessful attempts were made in the 1990s, the new Swiss Federal Constitution of 1999, which has reshaped the constitutional fundamentals of the federal language law,[33] initiated a new start. However, in 2004, the Federal Government (*Bundesrat*) cancelled the project – allegedly for financial reasons, whereas it was clear that there were a couple of obstacles such as the debate on the role of English in the cantonal schools, the alleged attempts

32 E.g., Article 64(3) of the Constitution of the Canton of Freiburg/Fribourg of 16 May 2004 (*Systematische Gesetzessammlung des Kantons Freiburg*/Systematic Collection of the Laws of the Canton of Fribourg 10.1.) reads: "The first foreign language to be taught [at school] is another official language". (Unofficial translation by the author).

33 See Appendix to this chapter.

of the Federation to intervene in the cantonal sphere and the relationship between the standard forms of languages and its non-standard or "dialect" versions. Not until the autumn of 2007 was a compromise formula set up, modelled after the so-called "Concord on the Harmonizing of Schools", which the cantons had agreed upon on 14 June 2007. The core idea of this concord was that the cantons shall coordinate their curricula and teaching methods but not through the selection of specific languages but though agreements concerning certain aims and standards with respect to competence in foreign languages that should have been acquired at the end of school education. After the Federal Parliament (*Nationalrat*) had given up its plan to explicitly oblige the cantons to introduce a national language in the capacity of "L 2", the latter agreed to Article 15(3) of the new Language Act, which entered into force on 1 January 2010:[34]

> They [the cantons] promote, within their competences, the teaching of foreign languages in a way which guarantees that the school children by the end of their obligatory school days have some competence at least in one second language of the land and also in another foreign language.

It is quite apparent that this compromise lacks any clear determination. Whereas the concord stipulates that there should be an "equivalent standard" of command in two foreign languages at the end of the obligatory period of school (Article 4), Article 15(3) of the Language Act – due to the dispute on federal competence in this field – leaves open how "some competence" is to be envisaged.

Concluding Remarks

Towards a Modern Understanding of Territoriality

The core idea of this chapter has been to show that a modern and sophisticated version of the principle of territoriality can serve as a model structure for the solution of language problems all over the world, if it is applied with respect to the fruitful antagonism of "territoriality versus linguistic freedom". However, we must not forget that any application of the territorial principle, in the field of language law or any other law, is nothing but a variant of the ancient principle of *cuius regio eius religio* [whose the reign, his the religion].[35] This will say that the Swiss cantons, in

34 *Bundesgesetz über die Landessprachen und die Verständigung zwischen den Sprachgemeinschaften – Sprachengesetz* (Language Act), of 5 October 2007, SR (note 4) 441.1. (Unofficial translation by the author).

35 The creation of this formula has been attributed to *Joachim Stephani* (1544–1621), Institutiones iuris canonici, Frankfurt 1604. It was meant to describe the core mechanism of preserving peace among the religious communities (confessional parties) in the context of the Peace of Augsburg of 1555 and other relevant documents of the time.

principle, are prescribing the use of a specific official language to the population in the single territories or entities similar to the way a specific religious confession had been prescribed to the people in a specific territory in earlier times. Linguistic territoriality, however, came into existence only in the course of the nineteenth century when religious territoriality had faded away.[36] Both linguistic and religious forms of territoriality remain concepts, which are geared to the traditional territorial state in regard to the nation state. There is no realistic chance for abandoning any form of territoriality in favour of individual rights, as territoriality corresponds with the need for an efficient allocation of resources: The more languages there are, the more resources will be needed to cope with them. Accordingly, there exists a "natural" trend towards limiting the number of languages in the public sphere at least in practice, which can be observed even in the multi-linguistic state of Switzerland.[37] Nevertheless, the basic idea of the territorial system still works – in a contemporary mode: Linguistic territoriality nowadays may serve only as the fundamental or basic structure, whereas the individual case must be examined with due regard to individual and minority rights.

European Perspectives

This is not the place to present the language regime of the European Union. However, two major tasks of the EU shall be pointed out in order to illustrate the utility of the Swiss model: First, the Union has to cope with the use of languages within its organs and institutions, and, second, it has to communicate with the Member States and the citizens. Accordingly, the competence of the EU to act in the field of language law is rather limited while the status of the relevant languages is determined by primary law: According to Article 55 of the Treaty on European Union (TEU),[38] 23 languages are declared to be authentic treaty languages. The same languages are recognized as official languages of the Union (Article 1 of Regulation No. 1 determining the languages to be used by the European Economic Community).[39] Although the EU, like Switzerland, proclaims the equality of languages in principle,[40] the differentiation between the external and the internal use of languages as reflected by Regulation No. 1 has considerably compromised

36 For further details, see Richter (2005: 159 et seq.).

37 As Georg Kreis mentions, public authorities on road traffic affairs officially decided to offer the oral test for the driving license in the three mostly spoken national languages only, which from the beginning of 2008 has excluded the fourth national language (Rheto-Romanic) from any consideration. See Kreis (2008: 351–2).

38 Official Journal C 83/13 (30 March 2010).

39 Official Journal L 17, 6.10.1958: 385 (with later amendments). The regulation is based on Article 342 (ex Art. 290) of the Treaty on the Functioning of the European Union.

40 It is debatable whether this can be derived indirectly from Article 55(1) TEU, according to which the texts of the Treaty on European Union shall be "equally authentic" in each of the languages. Denying ECJ, Case C-361/01 P, § 87 – *Kik* (2003). Some authors

formal equality. On the one hand, the EU communicates in any of the *official languages* with individual persons in the Member States (Article 24(4) of the Treaty on the Functioning of the European Union (TFEU),[41] Articles 2 and 3, Regulation No. 1) and also speaks to the public by an Official Journal, which is published in all official languages (Article 5 of Regulation No. 1). On the other hand, the rules governing the languages of the institutions of the EU (*working languages*) continue to be determined by the Council, acting unanimously by means of regulations (Article 342 TFEU), which empowers the organs to regulate much more than the details when it comes to the issue of working languages (Article 6, Regulation No. 1). Therefore, the language practices of the individual organs and institutions vary significantly.[42] It is only the European Parliament that, for democratic reasons, practices formal equality with regard to all official languages of the Union.[43]

An individual's right to officially communicate with the EU in one's own language can be discerned in the existing EU language law; it is also guaranteed as a basic right by Article 41(4) of the Charter of Fundamental Rights of the European Union.[44] Although this seemingly conforms to the freedom of language known from Swiss Constitutional Law, it actually is but a single aspect of the comprehensive freedom of language, that is to say, a mere right to communicate with the European public authorities. This is certainly no accident, for if the EU would guarantee a comprehensive freedom of language, retroactive effects on the language order of multilingual Member States would be feared to follow from it.[45]

As concerns the status of languages, EU law notoriously lacks any conceptual approach, particularly in the field of "working languages". Despite the fact that the use of languages usually is addressed in the rules of procedure of the respective organs,[46] it is common practice rather than doctrine that decides whether a certain language must be or must not be considered at all. Yet there

---

speak of the "principle of the equality of all official languages in external relations". See, e.g., Wichard (2007), margin notes 4 and 9.

41 Official Journal C 83/47 (30 March 2010).

42 A precise survey with references to all relevant rules of procedure is given in German by Priebe (2009), margin notes 9–11 and by Wichard (2007), margin note 15. See also Creech (2005) and de Elera (2005).

43 Article 138 of the Rules of Procedure of the European Parliament, 16th edition, July 2004.

44 Although this, regularly, is one of the official languages at one's own choice, Regulation No. 1 reserves to the Member States the right to regulate the use of languages, if it has more than one official language (Arts 2 and 8 of the Regulation).

45 Cf. Article 8 of the Regulation No. 1 addressing this issue: "If a Member State has more than one official language, the language to be used shall, at the request of such State, be governed by the general rules of its law".

46 See, e.g., Articles 29 to 31 of the Rules of Procedure of the ECJ of 19 June 1991 (consolidated version available at: http://curia.europa.eu/jcms/upload/docs/application/pdf/2010-04/rp.en.pdf [accessed: 7 May 2010].

is no such thing as the principle of territoriality governing the use of official languages throughout Europe in order to preserve the traditional language areas in the individual Member States.

However, things are likely to change. As is well known, the freedoms of movement and establishment (Articles 45 and 49, TFEU) have not yet been used to a very large extent by citizens of the EU. The barrier of language prevents people from any intense use of the market freedoms and hampers mobility to a great extent. That is why the EU started to address the issue some years ago, resulting in the Council Resolution of 21 November 2008 on a *European strategy for multilingualism*.[47] But the more successful this strategy is, the more mobility and migration will result from it, and the more the composition of certain language areas, particularly those of border regions, will be affected. If, for example, a considerable numbers of Poles moved across the German border (or Germans moved across the French border, and so on), and, in the course of time, constituted local majorities in certain regions of the neighbouring state, the language frontier would be put under pressure, as happened in Switzerland during the nineteenth and twentieth centuries when a great number of German-speaking citizens migrated into the French-speaking regions, enjoying the freedoms of movement and establishment that had been introduced by the first Federal Constitution of 1848.

Of course, it must always be the responsibility of the Member States of the EU to determine their official languages, to organize linguistic diversity and to regulate the coexistence of language groups in order to preserve linguistic peace (see Article 165, TFEU). However, regulation in this field by the states concerned provokes the danger of infringements upon the market freedoms, discrimination against citizens of other EU Member States and one-sided protectionism. For this reason, an objective management of such scenarios sooner or later will become crucial for the cohesion of the European Union. The more integrated Europe becomes, the greater will be the need for a minimum set of guiding principles that will bind any Member State when it limits market freedom by its national law for linguistic reasons. Elementary principles of the kind may be the principle of territoriality, the freedom of language and also the duty of the states to protect traditional minorities and to preserve linguistic peace with particular respect to its European dimension. The Swiss model can provide the expertise necessary to answer questions, such as whether a person may use his or her mother tongue or rather must "assimilate", that is, adapt to the official language of the region; what languages must or may not be considered as official languages; whether a linguistic change has already taken place or is still in progress; whether a linguistic minority must be exempted from the rule of territoriality and so forth. In conclusion, the language law of the European Union still is in an embryonic and rudimentary state, but there it will not remain.

47 Council Resolution 2008/C 320/01. See also the preceding Communication from the Commission "A New Framework Strategy for Multilingualism", COM/2005/0596 final (22 November 2005).

References

Büchi, C. 2001. "Röstigraben", Das Verhältnis zwischen deutscher und französischer Schweiz. 2nd Edition. Zurich: NZZ Libro.

Creech, R.L. 2005. *Law and Language in the European Union – The Paradox of a Babel "United in Diversity"*. Groningen: Europa Law Publishing.

De Elera, Á. 2005. What Place for Linguistic Diversity, Language, Equality and Rights in the Language Arrangements of the European Union? *Maastricht Journal of European and Comparative Law*, 12, 271 et seq.

Kägi-Diener, R. 2008. Kommentar zu Art. 70 (Sprachen), in *Die schweizerische Bundesverfassung*: Kommentar. B. Ehrenzeller, P. Mastronardi, R.J. Schweizer and K.A.Vallender (Hrsg). 2nd Edition. Zürich: Dike–Schulthess, 1258–78.

Kreis, G. 2008. Prinzipien und Praxis der Multikulturalität in der heutigen Schweiz, in *Sprachenvielfalt und Kulturfrieden*, edited by G. Lüdi, K. Seelmann, and B. Sitter-Liver. Fribourg: Academic Press, 339 et seq. (with English abstract).

Lüdi, G. and Werlen, I. 2005. *Eidgenössische Volkszählung 2000: Sprachenlandschaft in der Schweiz*. Swiss Federal Statistical Office. [Online]. Available at: http://www.bfs.admin.ch/bfs/portal/de/index/news/publikationen.Document.52216.pdf. [accessed 9 February 2010].

Priebe, R. 2009. Art. 290 EGV, in *EU-Kommentar*. 2nd Edition, edited by J. Schwarze. Baden-Baden: Nomos.

Richter, D. 2005. *Sprachenordnung und Minderheitenschutz im schweizerischen Bundesstaat.* New York: Springer.

Voyame, J. 1992. Avis de droit délivré au Conseil d'Etat du canton de Fribourg le 30 septembre 1991 au sujet du nouvel article constitutionnel sur les langues officielles et au sujet de son application dans la législature et la pratique. *Bulletin officiel des séances du Grand Conseil de canton de Fribourg*, 2813 et seq.

Wichard, J.C. 2007. Art. 290 EGV, in *EUV/EGV (Kommentar) Das Verfassungsrecht der Europäischen Union mit Europäischer Grundrechtecharta.* 3rd Edition, edited by C. Calliess and M. Ruffert. München: Verlag C.H. Beck.

Appendix

Federal Constitution of the Swiss Confederation of 18 April 1999:[48]

Art. 4 [National languages]
The National Languages are German, French, Italian, and Romansh.
Art. 18 [Freedom to use any language]
The freedom to use any language is guaranteed.

Art. 69 [Culture]
1. Cultural matters shall be a cantonal responsibility.
2. The Confederation may support cultural activities of national interest as well as art and music, in particular in the field of education.
3. In the fulfilment of its duties, it shall take account of the cultural and linguistic diversity of the country.

Art. 70 [Languages]

1. The official languages of the Confederation shall be German, French and Italian. Romansh shall also be an official language of the Confederation when communicating with persons who speak Romansh.
2. The Cantons shall decide on their official languages. In order to preserve harmony between linguistic communities, the Cantons shall respect the traditional territorial distribution of languages and take account of indigenous linguistic minorities.
3. The Confederation and the Cantons shall encourage understanding and exchange between the linguistic communities.
4. The Confederation shall support the plurilingual Cantons in the fulfilment of their special duties.
5. The Confederation shall support measures by the Cantons of Graubünden and Ticino to preserve and promote the Romansh and the Italian languages.

---

48 An English version of the Constitution is published officially at: http://www.admin.ch/ch/e/rs/c101.html.

Chapter 11

Language and Languages in European Ideology, Political Documents and Real Life

J. Normann Jørgensen

Introduction

During the past decade, a critical understanding of the concept of "languages" has developed in sociolinguistics. This perspective sees "individual languages" as based on linguistic normativity rather than real-life language use. In particular, we cannot expect people to use "pure" language (in the sense that they do not "mix" features associated with different languages), and it is, therefore, no given thing that we should expect authorities to do so. This has important consequences for the way we think about "rights" related to language. In this chapter, I present a late modern sociolinguistic perspective on language that goes beyond the general understanding of language. I argue on the basis of observable language use phenomena in an increasingly urban Europe. In the conclusion, I raise some problems this has for society, including the understanding of language rights.

Languages as Sociocultural Constructions

The view of human language that can categorize "different languages" considers language as a range of phenomena that can be separated and counted. This view has been the object of increasing scepticism in sociolinguistics during the past decade or so. "Languages" have traditionally been understood as neatly separated packages consisting of different features. This is reflected in the terminology used to describe individual language users. Without much consideration, words such as "monolingual", "bilingual", and "multilingual" are used to characterize individuals with respect to their relationship to "languages". This terminology is based on the assumption that "languages" can be counted: one, two, three and so on. Sometimes even the term "zerolingual" (for example, editorial, *Jyllandsposten*, Danish right-wing newspaper, 26 October 2006) is used in the public debate to denigrate the linguistic skills of individuals or even whole groups of people. The slightly less denigrating term "semilingual" (coined by Hansegård 1968, but abandoned by sociolinguistics long ago) is still routinely cited as a powerful explanation of especially minority failure in the educational systems of Europe.

Sociolinguists suggest that "languages" in this sense are sociocultural constructions, or indeed, ideological constructions, rather than representations of real-life language use. They are abstract ideas about certain linguistic features belonging together as if in a package and certain other features being excluded from the package. However, this does not fit with the way language is used in the real world:

> Languages do not exist as real entities in the world and neither do they emerge from or represent real environments; they are, by contrast, the inventions of social, cultural and political movements (Makoni and Pennycook 2006: 2).

The emergence of this concept of "languages" is closely related to European ideologies as they have developed at least since the 1700s, particularly National Romanticism, and indirectly to the linguistic standardization processes that began in the 1500s with what later became the "national languages" of the European nation states:

> If we understand, organize, and draw on those resources as belonging to whole, bounded systems we call 'languages', it is because that notion makes sense in the context of the ways language has been bound up in ideologies of nation and state since the nineteenth century (Heller 2007: 1).

This ideological notion of "languages" has been exported by Europeans to the rest of the world, both through colonization and through emigration. In today's Europe, it is taken for granted that the "individual languages" are closely related to "cultures", and furthermore these "languages" and "cultures" are taken to be "national" – indeed to be "of national importance" – and the "maintenance" of the languages is emphasized by nation state governments and national elites.

The linguistic aspect of the ideological concept of "separate languages" is a multitude of separate sets of linguistic features. The features belonging to each set are seen as particularly closely related, for instance, as a set of words in the vocabulary of "a language". This vocabulary excludes words belonging to other sets of features (with the possible exception of loan words from "other languages"). The idea of "learning a language" means that speakers acquire a range of these features (both words and grammar). However, human beings do not learn (or use) "languages" in this sense. Human beings primarily learn and use linguistic features, and secondarily they may also learn how these features are socioculturally ascribed to sets of features called languages.

Linguistic features appear in the shape of units or rules. Units are words, sounds, expressions and so on. Rules are not rules in the legal sense, or even the normative sense, of the word. Rules are regularities of how units are combined into larger units that are given meanings. A consequence of this is that there is no such thing as inherently correct language. Correctness is social convention about the characteristics of specific linguistic features. Correctness has nothing to do with the linguistic characteristics of features; correctness is ascribed to the features by (some) speakers. Speakers ascribe many other values to features, that is, some features are "vulgar" or "ugly", whereas others are "posh" or "poetic". Speakers also ascribe values to sets of features, and these values may easily develop into stereotypes, such as the (Hollywood-propelled) stereotype of German being rough and rude or French being elegant.

Linguistic Normativity

Individual linguistic features are, in other words, taken to be representatives of sets of features. Speakers refer to these socioculturally constructed sets of features as "languages" (or "dialects", "codes" and so on). Educational systems similarly refer to the teaching of language as "teaching of languages".

It is a trivial observation that this does not represent the reality of language use. Nevertheless, language behavioural norms that are firmly enforced by school systems, media gatekeepers, and other powerful forces in the European societies emphasize linguistic purity, or so-called "monolingual" behaviour at all times (individuals may be so-called "multilinguals", but their behaviour at any given time should be "monolingual"). There are several, at least four, strands of ideas about proper linguistic behaviour with respect to "different languages".

> *The monolingualism norm*: Persons with access to more than one language should be sure to master one of them before getting involved with the other.

This norm has been expressed in different ways, but basically it assumes that there is a certain measure of available mental capacity that should be filled by one language only. This thought has also been expressed by linguists, although quite some years ago (Jespersen 1941, Skutnabb-Kangas 1981), but it has been abandoned (cf., for instance, Martin-Jones and Romaine 1986). The arguments raised in favour of the monolingualism norm are rarely linguistic; they are more often ideological, alternating between referring to morality or referring to aesthetics.

> *The double or multiple monolingualism norm*: Persons who command two languages will at any given time use one and only one language, and they use each of their languages in a way that does not in principle differ from the way monolinguals use the same language.

According to this norm, people may know and speak two or more different languages, but they (are expected to) speak each of them like those people who only know that particular language. At all times, people who "know more than one language" are expected to disguise as monolinguals. By and large, educational systems are built on this view of language behaviour. Students are expected to aim at learning languages as closely to "native" speakers as possible, and they are praised when they achieve this.

> *The integrated bi- or multilingualism norm*: Persons who command two languages will employ their full linguistic competence in two different languages at any given time adjusted to the needs and the possibilities of the conversation, including the linguistic skills of the interlocutors.

The integrated bilingualism norm acknowledges the functionality of code-switching. Code-switches are resources above and beyond monolingual behaviour (double or not). With this norm, "knowing" two languages adds up to more than the sum of one language and another language. People may achieve their communicative goals by intentionally employing features ascribed to different languages side by side. A rich literature that analyzes and describes what it means to "know more than one language" has been around for quite some time, stressing this point (prominent examples are Romaine 1995, Grosjean 1982 and, particularly with respect to code-switching, Auer 1998, Milroy and Muysken 1995, Heller 1988). It is no new insight that "mixing languages" is nothing that should be avoided or rooted out by educational systems.

> *The polylingualism norm*: Language users employ whatever linguistic features are at their disposal to achieve their communicative aims as best they can, regardless of how well they know the involved languages; this entails that the language users may know – and use – the fact that some of the features are perceived by some speakers as not belonging together.

The difference between multilingualism and polylingualism lies in the view of language. Multilingualism is a concept that refers to the knowledge of more than "two different languages", that is, sets of features that are supposed to be separate. In this view, it makes some sense to count "how many languages" an individual knows (the problem of defining when a person "knows" a language notwithstanding). Multilingual behaviour according to this norm may thus involve features from more than one of these sets in the same linguistic production. Polylingualism refers to the view that speakers use whatever features they have access to, sometimes even in spite of these features being generally considered to belong to "a language" to which the speaker may not have access or may not "know" (Rampton 2005, Jørgensen 2010). This is the view of late modern sociolinguistics. In this view, it makes no sense to try to count "how many languages" are involved in much of the interaction going on, for instance, among young people in the European cities.

Observable Language Use

There is nothing in the nature of language as a human phenomenon in itself that forces us to think of linguistic features as necessarily bundled together in sets of features that we can call "languages" or "dialects". In addition, the linguistic behaviour that we can observe in the urban areas of Europe in the 2000s does not in any way respect the monolingualism norms. In fact, European late modern urban youth behave linguistically in ways that cannot even be described by the traditional "multilingualism" concept. The young speakers do indeed use whatever features are at their disposal to achieve their interactional goals. This has been documented in a range of ways, mainly with respect to oral interaction, but also in written production influenced by new technology, such as sms, cmc, and graffiti (Rampton 2005, 2006 about London, Keim 2007 about Mannheim, Dirim and Auer 2004 about Hamburg, Jaspers 2007 about Antwerp, Quist 2000 about Copenhagen, Christensen 2004 about Århus, Jørgensen 2010 about Køge). Example 1 illustrates the extensive use of features that are traditionally associated with different "languages".

Example 1: Facebook-conversation among three Danish girls (English in *italics*, standard Danish in recte, youth Danish underlined, **other language in bold**):

Maimuna 13:45: har købt *the equipment*, skal bare finde tid til at lave en spektakulær én kun tje dig, morok, den skal være speciel med ekstra *spice* :P, *sorry* tar mig sammen denne weekend! **insAllah**.

Translation: have bought *the equipment*, must just find the time to make a spectacular one just for you, **morok**, it must be special with extra *spice* :P, *sorry* pull myself together this (weekend)! **insAllah**.

Ayhan 15:20: **gracias muchas gracias**!! jeg wenter shpæændt **gardash** ;-)) *love youuu …*

Translation: **gracias muchas gracias**!! I wait excitedly **gardash** ;-)) *love youuu …*

İlknur 23:37: Ohhh Maimuna, Du havde også lovet mig en skitse … Og du sagde, at det ville været efter eksamener, men??? *Still waiting like* Ayhan, *and a promise is a promise* :D :D :D

Translation: Ohhh (Maimuna), you had also promised me a sketch … And you said that it would be after exams, but??? *Still waiting like* Ayhan, *and a promise is a promise* :D :D :D

In the exchange in Example 1, the three girls discuss a promise that Maimuna, who is a bit of an artist, has made to Ayhan and İlknur. She has promised to provide drawings for both of the other girls. In her contribution, Maimuna uses several words that are English (that is, which are conventionally associated with the sociocultural construction labelled English), and there are a number of words which are Danish. Some of these are standard Danish, but some of them appear in forms that are not standard Danish. For instance, the spelling "tje" corresponds to a pronunciation (of the word usually spelled "til") that has developed among young Copenhagen speakers in recent years (cf. Maegaard 2007). In addition, Maimuna uses the word "morok" which historically is an old Armenian word "moruk" ("old man or woman"), which has been borrowed into Turkish meaning, and which is here further borrowed by Maimuna, who does not speak Turkish, to address a close friend, roughly as in "you old geezer". She closes her line with the Arabic "insAllah".

In her answer, Ayhan first uses words associated with Spanish and then continues with words spelled in a way that reflects young Copenhagen speech plus the word "gardash", an adapted version of the Turkish word "kardeş", which means "sibling". Among young urban speakers in Denmark, it means "friend". The last line, İlknur's contribution, is partly Danish, partly English, both in vocabulary and in grammar.

It makes little sense to classify this exchange as belonging to one or the other language. It makes no more sense to try to count the number of "languages" involved. There is a gradual shift in association and meaning from Armenian "moruk" to young Copenhagen "morok", and there are several overlaps, for instance, between standard Danish and young Copenhagen Danish, such as the words "skal være" ("must be") and "gardash" can not very easily be classified anywhere.

Similar linguistic phenomena can be observed in graffiti all over Europe. Figure 11.1 presents an example from Berlin. "LE KAPITAL C'EST FUN, LE COMMUNISME C'EST NUF." The graffito appeared at the foot of the Marx-Engels sculpture memorial by Alexanderplatz at least in 2007–09. The base language of the graffito statement is standard French with standard orthography (that is, most of the features used are traditionally associated with standard French). In addition to French, several other sets of features seem to be involved. The word form "Kapital" points to the title of Karl Marx's main work *Das Kapital*, in its German version. The word "fun" is associated with English. When this word is turned around we get the form "nuf". Using words backwards (turning around the syllables in words of more than one syllable, or turning around the consonants in one-syllable words) is a phenomenon that is characteristic of French urban youth language, especially the language of minority youths. The phenomenon is known as *verlanization* (for instance, Doran 2004, or at http://languedeculture.forumpro.fr/bigornes-verlans-jurons-dialectes-neologisme-archaisme-f23/verlans-t7.htm). The producer of this graffito has employed a range of different linguistic features, which are traditionally ascribed to at least three different sets of features that are

Figure 11.1 Graffito, Berlin, August 2007

so-called "national languages". Of these three, one is further represented by at least two distinctly different subsets. The languages and varieties used join nicely together in a jocular interplay between values and connotations. The German word *Kapital* is – outside German – to a certain extent synonymous with Karl Marx's famous work. It is not very often considered to be "fun"; on the contrary, describing it as "fun" reflects a rather unconventional or at least uncommon point

Figure 11.2 Graffiti, Tartu, December 2006

of view, and in the continuation, it appears to be meant ironically. The contrast between das Kapital and communism is pointed out and illuminated by the use of the verlanized word form "nuf". The linguistic character of the graffito is further complex because a process, a regularity, associated with French (minority youth language) is applied on a unit, a word, which is generally taken to be English.

A similar type of interplay between different sets of features appears in Figure 11.2, which shows a graffito from a run-down house in an otherwise "nice" part of Tartu, Estonia. The graffito was photographed in 2006. As in Figure 11.1, we see how regularities that are generally associated with one language may be applied to units that are associated with another language. The statement "BIIG TUSSU LAAV" contains English, Estonian and English spelt according to Estonian orthographical principles. The word form "biig" represents an emphatic presentation of the word "big" that is associated with English. This emphasis is not incompatible with the word being considered English – an American, a South African, or anybody considered a "native" speaker of English could write the same. The word form "tussu" is associated with Estonian, although not everyday public standard Estonian. Among Estonians the word can be used with a meaning corresponding to the word "cunt", or it can be used in a less provocative sense. The word form "laav" represents the word "love" (English), but treated orthographically as if it were an Estonian word. This is what the word would have looked like in Estonian. The continuation follows the same principles with "FUCK

HEMORROIDID" which means "fuck (the) hemorroids". In these graffiti, we see an interplay between English and Estonian both with respect to vocabulary and orthography. The two languages are both represented by taboo words to the graffiti, and both are represented by orthographic regularities. However, at least in the case of the word form "laav" we cannot categorize the unit as either English or Estonian. It is neither, but of a third category, namely linguistic features resulting from polylingual behaviour.

Polylingualism and European Societies

Late modern urban European youth presents a particularly obvious, but by no means unique, pattern of language use. Other groups in society are also capable of using features that are generally believed "not to belong together". To mention just one example: Latin words and phrases are used as markers of intellectualism in at least several North European societies and also by speakers who know very little Latin. Speakers thus continue language-behavioural patterns that were also commonplace among medieval and early renaissance European rulers (see, for instance, Schendl 2004) and, indeed, European everyday urban life (see, for instance, Lüdi 1989). The insistence on the interweaving of "nation", "culture" and "language" is thus historically bound to a few hundred years of European history and not in any way based in the nature of language or humankind. The whole construct contributes to the maintenance of the imagined communities (Anderson 1991) that function as ideological motivations for the nation states of Europe. "The national language" of most European nation states are inventions (like a range of comparatively newly invented nationally constitutive traditions such as the Scandinavian Viking helmets or the Scottish tartans; see Hobsbawm and Ranger 1983).

There is no doubt that the concept of "national languages" is very strong. It is a political fact. The European educational systems would break down overnight if they were forced to teach language the way people really use language. (This is not only true for language choice patterns: Another important linguistic phenomenon is swearing, which has rarely, if ever, been taught in schools, but which is nevertheless frequent among real-life language users, and which develops and changes just like other patterns of language use.) The concept of national languages also has political implications. Some nations (Denmark is an example) prescribe language testing of applicants for citizenship, and interestingly enough, such testing can be carried out by amateurs whose only skill is that they "know" the language (for instance, police employees without the slightest trace of training in language assessment; see Fogtmann 2007). It seems to be considered self-evident that if you "know" a language, then you can also judge whether other people "know" it. This amounts to a sweeping categorization of large groups of people with respect to specific "languages" (and it is, by the way, an example of very concrete political effects of the nationalist or even national romantic view of language).

The concept of "languages" as separate and bounded packages also pervades everyday life. The way we speak about language, language learning, and language behaviour is heavily influenced by the concept. If we want to describe language and go beyond this concept, we are sometimes forced into cumbersome expressions, of which I have used a few here (such as "a word, which is generally taken to be English" and not "an English word"). In other cases, I have just taken it for granted that the reader would understand my point. For instance, I have said about Maimuna that "she does not speak Turkish". It should now be clear that by this I mean that she "does not (know or) use (very many) features which are generally associated with Turkish (and particularly not grammatical ones)". The traditional way of understanding what "languages" are, is not on its way out. But it gives us problems, precisely because it is unclear how it relates to the behaviour of real people in the real world. One thing is socially constructed norms; another is individual behaviour.

It follows from our observations that language is both individual and social. Language is individual in the sense that – as far as we know – no two people share precisely the same features because they have met and now remember exactly the same words and meanings, the same pronunciations, associate the same meaning with everything and so on. For all we know about language, it is individual. On the other hand, language is also social – in the sense that every feature we do "know" or "possess", we share with somebody else. We cannot imagine a linguistic feature that is unique to one person (with the possible exception of an innovation that has still not been used by the innovator in interaction with others); the very basis of language is that it enables us to share experience, images and so on.

Language and Rights

Just as speakers ascribe values to the socioculturally constructed sets of features, they assign relationships between individual persons and sets of features. Speakers categorize each other socially with respect to language. Social categorizations of speakers involve stereotypes about their relationship to specific codes (that is, ideologically determined sets of features). In some cases, this relationship is (comparatively stable and) described with the term "native speaker". In the case of *a-native* speaker, this relationship involves other social categories and is more readily negotiable. The "native speaker" of "a language" can claim several rights or specific relations to the involved "language". A native has "access" to that language, has "ownership" of the language, can claim "legitimacy" in the use of the language, can claim "rightful control" over the development of the language, can claim that the language "belongs" to her or him, and she or he can claim to be "entitled" to the language. All of these relational words denote a relationship between individuals and "a language" without much doubt or criticism. A native speaker is also taken to "know" and "command" the language in question. As shown by Fogtmann (2007), this may, in some cases, include the ability to rate and evaluate the quality of non-native speakers' use of the "language".

In varying degrees, *non-native* speakers can claim some of the same rights and specific relations such as "access", "ownership", or "legitimacy", depending on the acceptance by their interlocutors of their "having learnt" the language. When a speaker has "learnt" or "acquired" a language, this speaker can also claim to "know" it and "command" it.

A-native speakers can claim "access" and more to the "languages" ("registers", "codes", and so on) to the extent that their interlocutors accept their membership of the categories to whom the "language" (or "register", or "code" or "jargon") is stereotypically ascribed. A colonel will typically be accepted as one who can claim rights to military language, but a nun will usually not be. Being in my 50s, I cannot claim any rights to youth language; at least such claims are highly unlikely to be taken seriously by others, particularly not by young speakers.

Our relations to the socioculturally constructed phenomena called "languages" are thus social categorizations, not naturally given relations, and certainly not a consequence of the nature of language.

Within Europe it would, nevertheless, be theoretically possible to accept a degree of self-determination with respect to language use between individuals and authorities. It is theoretically possible to express rights in terms such as "every individual has the right to express herself or himself in language which she or he knows (commands, understands and so on)" and "every individual has the right to be addressed in language which she or he understands", instead of "*a* language which he or she understands". This is, of course, not a viable solution under the current ideological self-understanding of European nation states. In the long term, however, language policies are poorly substantiated when they build on an understanding of language that is outdated by decades, if not centuries.

Even less useful is the idea of the "rights" of individuals to express themselves in ways that fewer and fewer people (if any) use in their real-life interaction, especially if the multiple monolingualism norms are upheld. There are only a few North Frisian speakers left. If the local authorities provided services in North Frisian and only accepted dealing with individuals who spoke North Frisian without switching into German, the service would not be worth much, and it would certainly not meet the linguistic needs of a lot of people, nor would it represent very much of a reality. The collusion of "language" and "culture" and "nation" is not only in function with respect to nation states; it is also used on behalf of Frisians, Kurds, Sorbs, and so forth.

The national romanticist notion of "language" and "culture" and "people" has also been so efficiently exported to the rest of the world that it is the cause of much strife, even war, in other parts of the world (Schieffelin, Woolard and Kroskrity 1998). Europe has very little to be proud of in this respect, even if one accepts the concept of languages as separate sets of features. On the contrary, Europe could probably learn from others, for example, India. As long as the so-called "language rights" are tied to the concept of "nation" (meaning nation-state or "cultural" nation) and therefore afforded to only "national" minorities, they are difficult to understand as "rights". They are probably better described as privileges assumed and granted by haves, and the "rights" seem serve to maintain marginalization of have-nots.

European Documents on Language and Rights – Some Problems

European documents about linguistic rights have dealt with *groups* of speakers rather than individual speakers, since the Neuilly Treaty of 1919. Article 57 of this treaty covers "des minorités de race, religion ou de langue" and obliges Bulgaria to protect such minorities. This was in line with the treaties, especially involving the new nations in the West and South, after World War I. After World War II, the Universal Declaration of Human rights focussed much more intensively on individual rights. Nevertheless, the development of linguistic rights in Europe has continued to focus on groups. One example is the Council of Europe 1992 European Charter, which deals with "Regional and Minority languages", again understood as tied to groups. Another one is the 1995 Framework Convention, which deals with National minorities. Another problem lies precisely in this concept. Documents such as the CSCE Vienna 1989 document on the education of "national minorities" and the EU Council of Ministers 1977 Directive 77/486 about minority language mother tongue teaching share an explicit and problematic definition of minorities that excludes groups that are considered to be "migrants" (even when the educatees in question have grown up in a given European country as children of people who have grown up in the same country, they are called "third generation immigrants" and are, therefore, excluded from the language "rights" granted to "national minorities").

As we have seen, language is both individual and social. The theoretical rights are, nevertheless, generally expressed through the understanding of languages as neatly separated packages of features belonging to definable groups of speakers (who may even be geographically located). All of these refer to *collective* language rights, although not all collectives are granted these rights. What do we do with individual linguistic rights? We know that every human being has language. Each individual possesses a number of resources that is unique. No two persons share exactly the same set of features. On the other hand, every single feature that an individual possesses, somebody else also possesses.

Consequently, language rights with respect to the relationship between authorities and individuals could involve expressions in terms such as: "Every human being has the right to use language she or he knows (has access to, owns, commands, has learnt, likes and so on)". "Every human being has the right to be addressed in language she or he has the comprehension potential to decode". We need not add that every individual – in the European understanding – would have the right to interact in society at large through language of his or her own choice. We could imagine formulations like the following being incorporated into the thinking about linguistic human rights:

> In private, as well as in business, people have the right to communicate through language of their choice. In their relationship with public institutions, people have the right to expect that the communication be held in language they understand.

The long-term goal of European linguistic policies could be to really democratize language use to allow for all the real-life variations that will be present in society and to educate fully and constantly both in these and in language as used by authorities.

References

Anderson, B. 1991. *Imagined Communities: Reflections on the Origin and Spread of Nationalism*. London: Verso.

Auer, P. (ed.) 1998. *Code-Switching in Conversation: Language, Interaction and Identity*. London: Routledge.

Christensen, M.V. 2004. Arabiske ord i dansk hos unge i multietniske områder i Århus, in Taler De dansk? Aktuel forskning i dansk som fremmedsprog. Københavnerstudier i tosprogethed bind 37. Københavns Universitet, 33–52.

Dirim, İ. and Auer, P. 2004. Türkisch sprechen nicht nur die Türken. *Über die Unschärfebeziehung zwischen Sprache und Ethnie in Deutschland*. Berlin: De Gruyter.

Doran, M. 2004. Negotiating Between Bourge and Racaille: Verlan as Youth Identity Practice in Suburban Paris, in *Negotiations of Identities in Multilingual Contexts*, edited by A. Pavlenko and A. Blackledge. Clevedon: Multilingual Matters, 93–124.

Fogtmann, C. 2007. Samtaler med politiet. Interaktionsanalytiske studier af sprogtestning i danske naturalisationssamtaler. Københavns Universitet.

Grosjean, F. 1982. *Life with Two Languages: An Introduction to Bilingualism*. Cambridge, MA: Harvard University Press.

Hansegård, N.E. 1968. *Tvåspråkighet eller halvspråkighet?* Stockholm: Aldus.

Heller, M. (ed.) 1988. *Codeswitching: Anthropological and Sociolinguistic Perspectives*. Berlin: Mouton de Gruyter.

Heller, M. 2007. Bilingualism as Ideology and Practice, in *Bilingualism: A Social Approach*, edited by M. Heller. London: Palgrave Macmillan, 1–22.

Hobsbawm, E. and Ranger, T. (eds) 1983. *The Invention of Tradition*. Cambridge: Cambridge University Press.

Jaspers, J. 2007. In the Name of Science?: On Identifying an Ethnolect in an Antwerp Secondary School. Working Papers in Urban Language and Literacies 42. London: King's College.

Jespersen, O. 1941. *Sproget. Barnet, kvinden, slægten*. København: Gyldendal.
Jørgensen, J.N. 2010. *Languaging: Nine Years of Poly-lingual Development of Young Turkish-Danish Grade School Students, Vol. 1–2*. Copenhagen Studies in Bilingualism, the Koge Series, Vol. K15–K16. Copenhagen: University of Copenhagen.
Keim, I. 2007. Die "türkischen Powergirls". *Lebenswelt und kommunikativer Stil einer Migrantinnengruppe in Mannheim*. Tübingen: Gunter Narr.
Lüdi, G. 1989. Ein historisches Beispiel für Polyglossie: Stadtsprachen in Fribourg,Freiburg i. Ue. im XIV./XV: Jahrhundert, in *Historische Sprachkonflikte. Plurilingua VIII*, Nelde, P.H. (hrsg.). Bonn: Dümmler, 37–56.
Maegaard, M. 2007. *Udtalevariation og – forandring i københavnsk* – en etnografisk undersøgelse af sprogbrug, social kategorier og social praksis blandt unge på en københavnsk folkeskole. Danske talesprog, bind 8. København: C.A. Reitzels Forlag.
Martin-Jones, M. and Romaine, S. 1986. Semilingualism: A Half-Baked Theory of Communicative Competence. *Applied Linguistics*, 7, 26–8.
Makoni, S. and Pennycook, A. 2006. Disinventing and Reconstituting Languages, in *Disinventing and Reconstituting Languages*, edited by S. Makoni and A. Pennycook. Clevedon: Multilingual Matters, 1–41.
Milroy, L. and Muysken, P. (eds.) 1995. *One Speaker, Two Languages: Cross-Disciplinary Perspectives on Code-Switching*. Cambridge: Cambridge University Press.
Quist, P. 2000. Ny københavnsk 'multietnolekt'. Om sprogbrug blandt unge i sprogligt og kulturelt heterogene miljøer. Danske talesprog bind 1. København: C.A. Reitzel, 143–211.
Rampton, B. 2005. *Crossing: Language and Ethnicity Among Adolescents*. 2nd Edition. Manchester: St. Jerome.
Rampton, B. 2006. *Language in Late Modernity: Interaction in an Urban School*. Cambridge: Cambridge University Press.
Romaine, S. [1989] 1995. *Bilingualism*. 2nd Edition. Oxford: Blackwell.
Schendl, H. 2004. English Historical Code-switching in a European Perspective, in *Languaging and Language Practices, Copenhagen Studies in Bilingualism*, Vol. 36, edited by C.B. Dabelsteen and J.N. Jørgensen. Copenhagen: University of Copenhagen, 188–202.
Schieffelin, B.B., Woolard, K.A. and Kroskrity, P.V. 1998. *Language Ideologies: Practice and Theory*. Oxford: Oxford University Press.
Skutnabb-Kangas, T. 1981. *Tvåspråkighet*. Lund: Liber.

Index